THE NEW FIELD BOOK OF

Freshwater Life

THE NEW FIELD BOOK

ELSIE B. KLOTS

OF Freshwater Life

OVER 700 ILLUSTRATIONS
Drawings by SuZan Noguchi Swain

G. P. Putnam's Sons, New York

Contents

    The color plates appear as a group after page 32

Foreword

THE substance of this book has been brewing for many years. The text that is now distilled has ingredients from a variety of sources; some have been dipped from the fresh waters of ponds and lakes or gathered from beneath stones in swift streams; others have been weighed and sifted from the storehouses of man's knowledge. Great teachers have been its inspiration: over forty years ago Professors James G. Needham and George C. Embody of Cornell University led me up streams, through sphagnum bogs and waist-deep into lakes. Companions in collecting have added immeasurably to it: on thousands of miles of travel their dedication to *learning in the field* has sustained my enthusiasm and added to the fact and opinion upon which I now draw. Countless publications have provided background for it: carried in the side pockets of ancient touring cars, in the dash of modern sports cars, or stored in the saddlebags of trail horses, they have been dropped into mountain streams and desert water tanks, retrieved, dried and perused again and again until their contents have become so much a part of my thinking that their origin has been forgotten.

The rapidly increasing literature in limnology and the many new keys to identification, published by many authors, have been used over and again and borrowed from extensively. I acknowledge my indebtedness to each volume listed in the bibliography and also to many works not included there because they might be of little interest to the users of this book. Four books in particular have proven to be stalwart crutches: Ward and Whipple's *Fresh Water Biology; Fresh-Water Invertebrates of the United States* by Robert W. Pennak; *Aquatic Insects of California*, edited by Robert L. Usinger; and *Aquatic Plants of the United States* by Walter C. Muenscher.

7

To Mrs. SuZan Noguchi Swain I am more indebted than I can say. Her drawings are an integral and essential part of this work and make this her book as well as mine.

We both wish to thank the many staff members of the American Museum of Natural History who helped us. We are indebted to Dr. Charles Bogert and Dr. Richard G. Zweifel of the Dept. of Herpetology, to Mr. William E. Olds, Jr., of the Dept. of Living Invertebrates, and to Miss Farida Wiley of the Dept. of Education for their help with the illustrations; to Dr. Alice Gray of the Dept. of Insects and Spiders for her help in obtaining insect material; and most especially to Dr. Jerome G. Rozen of the Dept. of Insects and Spiders for the many courtesies he extended to us. We also express our gratitude to the Ronald Press for their permission to adapt drawings from *Fresh-Water Invertebrates of the United States* by Robert W. Pennak; to John Wiley & Sons, Inc., for their permission to adapt drawings from Ward and Whipple's *Fresh Water Biology*; to G. P. Putnam's Sons for the fish drawings from the *Field Book of Fresh-Water Fishes* by Ray Schrenkeisen; and to the photographers whose pictures add distinction to these pages.

Last of all I wish to pay tribute to Dr. Ann Haven Morgan, author of the *Field Book of Ponds and Streams,* first published by G. P. Putnam's Sons in 1930. The publication of her book was awaited with a fervent anticipation which I still recall. Sharing it with students these many years has given me great enjoyment. It truly began "in ponds where frogs sat on lily-pads and by swift brooks from which mayflies flew forth at twilight." I hope this *New Field Book of Fresh-water Life,* though different in scope and approach, will meet with her approval.

ELSIE BROUGHTON KLOTS

Pelham, New York

Introduction

AN old saying once took my fancy: "To name a flower is to know it." I now realize that naming a plant or animal merely puts one on speaking terms with it; most of us, however, find that familiarity with the name is a first and essential step toward further acquaintance. Limitations on the size of a field book have obviously made it impossible to name more than a very small percentage of the aquatic plants and animals of North America; but I hope that in giving guides to the major families or ecological groups I will have enabled the reader to take the first step that will lead to many pleasant hours of exploration at the water's edge.

Many readers of the *Field Books* have written of their distaste in having to use dichotomous keys, so a paragraphing system familiar to every schoolchild has been employed. In most groups this system serves as a guide to families. I am fully cognizant of the vagueness of the family concept and have not hesitated to be inconsistent; at times I have gone no further than orders, but when identification to genus or even to species seemed feasible, I have attempted it within the limits of available space. In presenting material on the higher plants I have ignored taxonomic classifications and have grouped the plants ecologically. Keys to a few frequently collected groups have been tucked away in the Appendix.

Bear in mind that this book deals only with the aquatic members of a group. Bog, swamp, marsh, and brackish water species have not been included; neither have those living in caves or subterranean waters.

Distribution is given in general terms only. Where none is listed it may be assumed that the form is more or less

9

widely distributed. Professor Eugene Odum has written: "A manual of freshwater invertebrates written for the British Isles, for example, serves almost as well for the United States. At least down to the family and generic level, the lower plants and invertebrates of fresh water show a great deal of cosmopolitanism."

Anyone interested in plants and animals, even in a non-technical way, should understand the use and importance of scientific names. Every plant and animal is known by its genus and species name: the generic name, always capitalized, comes first; the specific name, not capitalized, follows. The name of the Spotted Salamander is *Ambystoma maculatum*; that of the Tiger Salamander is *Ambystoma tigrinum*, showing that the two are different species but have been placed in the same genus and therefore have some characteristics in common. Note that the name is italicized. So is the name of the genus or species when standing alone. The genus name may be abbreviated before the species (as *A. tigrinum*) after the first appearance of the genus name in a given work or paragraph.

Genera are grouped into families (those of animals ending in *-idae*; of plants, in *-acea*); families into orders; orders into classes; and classes into phyla. Thus the classification of the large Electric-light Bug, *Lethocerus americanus*, is:

Phylum—Arthropoda
  Class—Insecta
    Order—Hemiptera
      Family—Belostomatidae
        Genus—*Lethocerus*
          Species—*americanus*

There are also *sub-* groups and *super-* groups, such as subfamilies and superfamilies, etc.

Scientific names seem to be constantly changing. This is chiefly because the name commonly used is found to be incorrect (for reasons set down in an International Code of Nomenclature), or because further study has revealed relationships not hitherto understood or has shown that the group needed to be further divided and each division separately named. I have tried to use the most recently accepted names, but occasionally, in the interests of popular usage and understanding, the older name has seemed better for the purposes of this book and I have not hesitated to retain it. Space has not permitted documentation of the reasons for each choice, so I beg indulgence of the specialist who feels that the revision of his group has been treated with indifference.

Although one member of my family has collected aquatic insects with a long dip net from a helicopter in which a microscope and dissecting tray were mounted, I do not anticipate that the average collector will travel thus elaborately equipped. A microscope will be necessary for the examination of the algae, protozoa, rotifers and a few other groups; but these groups could not be omitted even from a book that supposedly is meant for use in the field. Suggestions on collecting equipment will be found in the Appendix.

THE NEW FIELD BOOK OF

Freshwater Life

to year and their population is often extremely interesting. Artificial ponds, unless they have been left to develop naturally, are seldom of much interest to the general limnological collector; the old-styled millpond is often washed clear of life by the stream that flows through it; the swimming pool is too heavily treated with chemicals; the farm pond is so managed as to discourage growth of rooted plants, or if used for fish culture offers the fish first pick; and the beaver pond is, as a rule, too short-lived.

Most ponds, when left undisturbed, develop in richness and variety, reach a peak of maturity, and then grow old. A young pond is clear-bottomed. Gradually it acquires clumps of stoneworts, hornworts and submerged pondweeds, and becomes populated by a few amphibians and then small insects, snails and crustaceans. These, on entering the pond by accident and finding no competition, develop in abundance. Slowly, floating plants and the emergent shoreline plants become established; and the first animal settlers are crowded out by increasing numbers of species, more and more of which, as the water becomes less well oxygenated, breathe atmospheric air. Eventually the pond decreases in area because of encroaching shoreline plants, and becomes shallower from the deposition of decomposing organic material; bit by bit it is converted to marsh, to swamp (if trees become implanted) and then to dry land.

Lakes. Regardless of size, lakes have some deep water where no rooted plants can grow. Many lakes, it is true, are large and have sufficient expanse to permit the sweeping wind to pile waves and debris against the shore; but size is not the criterion. I have seen miniature lakes in Manitoba scarcely larger than a suburban backyard whose shoreline was so precipitous that even a few inches out no plants could take root; and I have collected in the Neusiedler See of Austria where one could wade for miles in the shallow, weeded stretches, often out of sight of the shore.

Thus some lakes have areas so protected from the wind and margins so shallow that pondlike conditions exist along the shore; here pond organisms thrive, and fish come to feed and spawn. But the chief area of productivity in lakes is to be found in the open water where a floating population of countless millions of microscopic organisms may drift along together to form the great nutrient *plankton.*

Lakes are formed by glaciers, by landslides that have blocked up valleys, and by the dissolution of certain minerals in the soil with a subsequent drop in surface level. Or they may be craters of old volcanoes, lagoons formed at the seaside, or oxbows cut off from a river's course.

Deep, cold lakes tend to be low in nutrient material, low in plankton and green plants, and low, therefore, in primary producers (see Chapter 2). They are described as *oligotrophic.* They are often rocky-bottomed and usually clear. In such waters few species thrive other than cold water fishes such as salmon, trout, whitefishes and possibly a few bottom feeders, or occasionally an isolated relict. Other lakes, older geologically, have become rich in nutrients, plankton and shore plants. They are more productive and, in consequence, become depleted of oxygen by the summer's end. They are called *eutrophic* lakes. As the years go on, these lakes will become warmer and shallower. Their resident animal population will increase in number of species; among fishes, for example, minnows, perch, pike and catfishes will be found. Eventually eutrophic lakes become pondlike. Brown water and acid lakes are rich in undecomposed plant fragments and low in calcium. They are the *dystrophic* lakes which, in aging, form bogs. Salt lakes and desert alkaline lakes have their special characteristics and therefore a specialized flora and fauna.

Ditches and swales. These may be thought of as small stagnant ponds. Their waters are often temporary but may be of sufficient duration to allow a large population to reach maturity. Duckweeds and water cabbage may float on the surface, and rooted plants that continue to live after the water is gone are abundant, sometimes nearly choking all open water (as anyone who has seen the hyacinth-filled canals of the south well knows). Oxygen content may be low, temperature variation great, and mineral content high; thus a large amount of plankton and algae may flourish, often coloring the water bright green in the spring and summer. In some areas rich in mud, gaseous bubbles may rise and occasionally ignite.

Springs. A spring exhibits a remarkable constancy of temperature, chemical content and velocity. It will often contain a very small number of species, many of which are different from those in nearby waters, some of which may even be relics of another geological period, and a few of which often tolerate temperatures far above or below normal. Spring-dwelling fish, for example, may live at a temperature of 122° F; protists at 120° and blue-green algae at 176°; while certain species of planarians, living in cold, spring-fed mountain water, find optimum conditions when the temperature is only a few degrees above freezing. Springs do not contain plankton and have little vegetation except along the margin. Many of them serve as winter resorts for hibernating amphibians, crustaceans and insects.

Springs connected with subterranean waters and caves have a unique fauna with marked reductions, especially in eye structure and in pigmentation. Warm springs in the north may have species that otherwise occur only far to the south.

Rivers and streams. The lotic waters of rivers and streams differ greatly from the waters of ponds and lakes. They also vary greatly as they flow down from their often cooler source to the warmer, lower stretches. Lotic waters vary not only in temperature, but in type of substratum over which they flow, soils through which they pass, areas of sunshine and of shadow, and successions of riffles, falls, pools, and steady flow.

Lotic waters, especially in the smaller streams, are more closely associated with life on shore. Food falls in freely from overhanging vegetation and banks, much of it of great importance to fishes; at the same time, predators enter more easily. Oxygen content is high except after hard rains or where mud and silt are carried along; for not only is moving water better aerated but oxygen-consuming organic detritus and plankton are washed away. Few rooted plants can become established except in lowland regions and backwaters. Filamentous algae, such as *Cladophora,* and the mosses *Fontinalis* and *Hypnum,* may stream out from rocks and shore; bryozoans and diatoms encrust submerged objects; sponges attach themselves to the substratum, the same colony remaining in the same spot for years; and in the lower reaches, the river weeds hold their footing. These sessile forms provide shelter for other small organisms that would otherwise be washed away.

Snails and flatworms that move by sliding across the substratum maintain their place against the force of the current by viscosity. Caddis fly larvae of many species live in cases cemented to stones or weighted down by the sand or pebbles of which they are made; other caddis fly larvae spin nets or silken retreats, fastening them to rocks in the swiftest part of the stream, living in the protection of these structures and clinging to the rocks with strong, curved hooks. The larvae of stoneflies, mayflies, flies and beetles have a wide range of special devices or habits enabling them to live in swift waters (see Chapter 12). Three widely different types of adaptation of body form to the exigencies of fast waters are represented by the hard, disclike water pennies (Fig. 63) flattened to the surface of rocks and stones; the soft, plump, cylindrical blackfly larvae (Fig. 66) swaying downstream but held securely in place by the adhesive posterior end of the body; and the depressed, laterally excised blepharoceratid larvae (Fig. 66) fastened to rocks by a row of adhesive suckers.

Free-swimming lotic water species must have a strong positive *rheotaxis* (response to current) which keeps them heading upstream, in addition to a positive *thigmotaxis* (response to contact).

LIMITING FACTORS

There are certain factors determining the presence, survival and success of living organisms that are called *limiting factors*. They give personality to our fresh waters. They are all interrelated and each is deeply involved with other substances or other conditions.

Temperature. The temperature of any body of water varies both seasonally and diurnally. These changes are far less in water than in air because of the higher specific heat of water (it takes more calories of heat to raise the temperature of a given amount of water a certain number of degrees than it does the same amount of air), the higher latent heat of fusion, and the higher latent heat of evaporation. Furthermore, the greatest density of water occurs when its temperature reaches 4° C (about 39° F). Any given layer of water dropping in temperature becomes heavier and sinks, but when it drops below 4° C becomes lighter again and rises. This water is kept in circulation, and thus most lakes and deep ponds seldom freeze solidly.

The changing temperature, then, has two important effects: its effect upon circulation and stratification, and its effect upon living organisms.

Circulation and stratification. Temperature fluctuates more in lotic waters than in lentic, but tends to be relatively more uniform at different depths. In the quiet waters of deep ponds and lakes in the northern and temperate zones it builds up noticeable stratification. In the summer the top water is warmed by the sun, mixing but little if at all with the cooler water below. As this top water becomes warmer the difference in temperature between it and the lower layer increases so much that a definite region of demarcation between the two layers can be noted. This intermediate layer is called a *thermocline*; the topmost water is the *epilimnion*; and the lower layer, the *hypolimnion*. When the weather becomes cooler the epilimnion also becomes cooler until it and the hypolimnion are more or less the same temperature. They then intermingle, normal circulation is resumed, and oxygen from the upper level is carried down to the bottom layer. This is known as the *fall turnover*. When the surface water, with the coming of winter, drops below 4° C it becomes lighter and stays at the surface, creating a new period of stratification. In the spring when the temperature of the surface water again approaches 4° C on its upward trend it again becomes heavier, sinks and initiates the *spring turnover*.

There are thus two periods of stagnation coinciding with the two periods of stratification: summer and winter. In each of these periods the hypolimnion suffers a reduction in oxygen, a condition which may be serious in the summer but less so in the winter when metabolic rates are low and less oxygen required. Winter, however, offers an additional hazard to life in the water, for then a blanket of snow may cover the ice, cutting out all light, stopping photosynthesis and sometimes causing winter kill.

Effect on organisms. Most aquatic organisms have a very narrow tolerance to change in temperature and therefore either cannot live where marked changes occur or else must be able to adjust to them in some specialized manner. They may adjust by a temporarily reduced metabolism which results in a suspended state of animation. With the resumption of normal temperature they may become quickly reactivated. (Witness the swirling of gyrinid beetles beneath the ice on a warm winter's day.)

Some plants and animals adjust by developing a special hibernating or aestivating phase or form. Among plants, *Anacharis* and *Ceratophyllum* produce winter buds which break off and drop to the bottom; these winter buds are really terminal shoots in which the leaves are very close together and in which is stored a supply of food. *Sagittaria* has tuberous roots which become buried in the mud of the bottom. Young plants of *Lemna* are carried to the bottom by the fragmentation and decay of older plants to which they are attached. Among animals, various devices are common: winter eggs of cladocerans, rotifers and rhabdocoels; the gemmules of sponges; the statoblasts of bryozoans; and the cysts of many protists, copepods and annelids.

Others may adapt by moving to another region or into a different environment. Snails and many fishes move away from the shore into deeper water. Most insects take refuge in the bottom, usually burrowing in the substratum, the mayfly *Heptagenia* moving to deeper water before burrowing. Reptiles and amphibians also usually burrow, sometimes in mud, sometimes in trash or debris.

But many species described as *stenothermal,* have an extremely narrow tolerance to change and are bound to a constant temperature; thus many of the deep cold-water fishes are never found elsewhere than in deep cold waters, except occasionally during the spring and fall turnover; and many warm-water fishes live always in warm water. Others, like the majority of freshwater fishes and some amphibians, can withstand great change; they are the *eurythermal* species. They may survive temperatures well below freezing in winter and fairly high temperatures in summer.

Light. Penetration of water by light is restricted by the amount of suspended material in the water. Even pure water absorbs and disperses light to the extent that there would be total darkness at a depth of 2 to 3 miles and scarcely enough light for photosynthesis below 25 feet. Water absorbs light more rapidly at the red end of the spectrum (an object lying at a depth of 10 feet often looks bluish), and since chlorophyll needs the light rays at the red end, green plants necessarily must live near the surface. If this condition exists in pure water one readily understands why turbid waters shelter less life than do clear waters, and deep-water lakes fewer species than shallow ponds.

Light penetration is also restricted when the water is colored. The color may be due to colloids in solution or suspension, to molecular factors that cause bending or dispersal of the light rays, or to the "false color" that comes from the presence of large numbers of red, green, yellow or brownish protists. It may be due to partial decomposition of organic material, to extracts from the roots and other tissues of certain swamp plants, and to contamination by industrial chemicals.

Many bodies of water have an "apparent color" that comes from reflections from a white sand bottom, the blue sky overhead, or the green trees or rocky hillsides of the surrounding shoreline; this is, of course, not true color, and does not restrict light penetration or deter growth of green plants.

Comparative measurements of the transparency of water can be made by lowering a white plate into the water and noting the depth at which it disappears to sight. In making comparisons, however, the time of day must be considered since the angle at which the light rays enter will effect their penetration of the water.

Current. The speed of the current differs in different parts of any stream and at different times of the year. In general, the velocity is increased with an increase in volume, or an increase in the steepness, narrowness or shallowness of the stream bed; but it may be retarded by turbidity; or by friction along the shore, with the bottom, or at the surface. Large rivers flow faster than small ones, other factors being the same, with the greatest velocity in midstream, below the surface layer, but above median depth.

Current flows in one direction and is continuous. It sweeps away organic debris, plankton, and other small organisms, thus depriving of nourishment the strong-swimming or heavy-bodied animals that might withstand the current.

Carbon dioxide. Carbon dioxide in the water may occur in the form of free gas; as the acid, both dissociated HCO_3 and undissociated H_2CO_3; as carbonates, especially of calcium and magnesium; and as easily soluble bicarbonates. Alkaline waters have a high percentage of the bicarbonates.

Plants use carbon dioxide in *photosynthesis*, that great and universal process whereby organisms containing chlorophyll are able to use the energy of sunlight to unite carbon dioxide and water to form the sugar *glucose*, releasing oxygen. Both plants and animals then use the glucose, and often other compounds derived from it, as a source of energy. In doing this they use oxygen and release carbon dioxide in respiration.

The amount of carbon dioxide in the water is affected by many other factors also and its relationship with them is complicated.*

Oxygen. Oxygen enters the water by diffusion from the atmosphere and from the photosynthesis of green plants in the water. The quantity retained is dependent upon temperature and pressure, and also upon velocity, pollution and decomposition. Clean surface water in shallow areas averages an oxygen content of 5 to 10 cc. per liter. Cold water will hold more oxygen than warm water; swift water contains more than slowly moving or stagnant water; but water tainted with pollution or containing decaying organic matter will show an immediate drop in oxygen content, for the aerobic bacteria involved in the decomposition use it up rapidly.

Deep lakes suffer from lack of photosynthetic organisms and from seasonal stratification. They therefore have less

* The student who is interested in these carbon dioxide relationships would do well to read *Fundamentals of Limnology* by Franz Ruttner and other limnological texts mentioned in the Bibliography.

oxygen than shallow waters even though they are colder and suffer less oxygen depletion because of their lower plankton population. To cope with this situation the deep-water tendipedid midges and tubifex worms have an oxygen-carrying pigment in their blood.

The high oxygen ratio of lotic waters relieves animals living in such waters from the need of special respiratory devices; but sometimes the amount of oxygen is greatly reduced near the bottom and, since many lotic species are bottom-dwellers, such streams have a smaller population than one would expect.

Inorganic salts. In most fresh waters the minerals represent only a few parts per million. Many common and widespread elements are seldom present; iron, for example, is found in water only when a variety of conditions are satisfied and therefore rarely. Other elements are commonly present but may show cyclic changes, dropping in concentration when

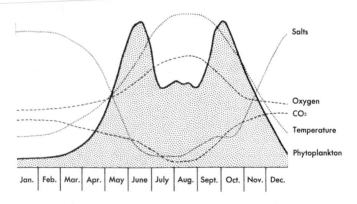

Fig. 1. Approximate seasonal relationship between temperature, oxygen, free carbon dioxide, mineral salts and growth of phytoplankton (partially after Dowdeswell).

the spring surge of organisms depletes the supply and rising after the subsequent death and decomposition of these organisms restores the minerals to the water.

Inorganic salts control osmosis (the passage of water through the cell membranes from a region of lesser density to one of greater density); they regulate the functioning of contractile vacuoles in protists, and of tracheal gills, blood gills and kidneys; and they help satisfy the nutritional requirements of all organisms. Proteins of plant and animal tissues require nitrates, sulphates and phosphates of many different metals; those of some organisms require some metals more than others. Planarians need more calcium than most organisms; sponges and diatoms need more silicon; crayfish need more copper, as well as extra calcium; and molluscs need extra calcium and sometimes extra magnesium. Floating plants, and some degenerated rooted plants, must get their minerals from the water since they do not have functioning roots to draw them from the soil.

Dr. Edward J. Popham has pointed out that the lower mineral content of fresh water compared with that of sea water may account for fewer species of plants and animals having colonized fresh waters from the sea than from the land. The scaly, impermeable covering of most fishes, the mucous coating of eels, the cuticle of arthropods, and the shells of molluscs have helped species in those groups to make the change. New reproductive devices and habits whereby sperm and egg cells are discharged simultaneously and fertilized immediately, or whereby sperm are introduced into the female body, have saved these sensitive cells from the harmful effect of fresh water. Other marine-descended species have provided a rich egg yoke for the developing young, or have become viviparous. Hard waters containing much calcium and magnesium have been colonized from the sea more often than have the softer waters.

Acidity. The pH concentration varies in different bodies of water and at different seasons. Pure water has a pH of 7; this represents a state of balance or of neutrality. A pH greater than 7 indicates alkalinity; less than 7, acidity. Normal optimum conditions lie between pH 4.7 and 8.5. Plants and animals vary in their preference and their degree of tolerance, however; some crustaceans will thrive in the acid waters of woodland pools, and certain tree hole mosquitoes will live only in rotting boles where the water has attained a pH well below the norm listed above. And yet Professor Dowdeswell has found that the dragonfly *Libellula pulchella*, collected in water with a pH of 7–8, could live in the laboratory at the very high acidity of pH 1, a truly remarkable range of tolerance.

The most widespread acid water environment is found in true bogs.

Isolation. Many bodies of water may seem to have all the characteristics contributory to optimum development of a large number of species, and yet be poorly populated. Their low population is often due to isolation, only those species having suitable modes of transportation being found there. Some crustaceans may populate one small pothole and be completely absent from a similar one nearby. On the other hand, many protists, mites and crustaceans are widely distributed; and many sponges are cosmopolitan, their tiny, silicious spicules having been wafted by the wind or caught upon drifting or flying animals. Fish are much less widespread and are often limited to certain drainage systems. The same is true of reptiles and amphibians.

Pollution. A small amount of organic pollution may increase the fertility of a body of water if it can be decomposed without seriously reducing the oxygen content. If the oxygen supply is too greatly cut down, anaerobic decomposition will be initiated and undesirable gases produced. (Inorganic pollution, such as that from chemicals, radioactive wastes, etc., is of serious portent. It is too complicated to be discussed here.)

Animals show a wide range of tolerance to organic pollution. Some are able to live in highly polluted waters, chiefly because of their tolerance to a reduced oxygen supply. Many of the protists, the rat-tailed maggots, the tendipedid midges and the tubifex worms live in such waters; some Spongilla flies live in sewage and some psychodids live in drains where they tolerate not only high temperatures but high concentrations of soap. The bivalves *Musculium* and *Sphaerium* are pollution-tolerant, as are the air-breathing snails, but the absence of other molluscs from an otherwise suitable place is often a warning of pollution. And certainly the absence of stonefly larvae from a clear, fast-moving stream is a sure indication of pollution.

When the oxygen content of water is suddenly reduced, fish will be seen rising to the surface to gulp air. Trout are extremely sensitive, for they can live only where the oxygen content is high; but buffalo fish, sticklebacks, the carp, the eel, and even the gars are quite tolerant of pollution. Stoneworts, duckweeds and water lilies can live in polluted waters and though their presence is not necessarily an indication of pollution it may be a warning.

Physical clues are often misleading if taken as indicators of pollution. Fluorescence, foam, or distinctive odors may be good evidence; but fluorescence may also be due to certain protozoans; the odors may be the characteristic ones of certain protists or blue-greens; and the foam (which in natural waters, as well as in dishwater or beer, results from the lowering of the surface tension) may be due to certain harmless inorganic salts or to species of *Potamogeton, Utricularia,* or water lilies.

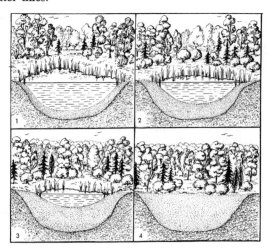

Fig. 2. Ecological succession. Four stages in the filling in of a lake, pond or bog.

CHAPTER 2

Terms You Will Find Useful

CLASSIFICATION OF ANIMALS BY FEEDING HABITS

Carnivores eat living animal material.

Detritus feeders eat dead plant and animal material in various stages of decomposition but usually when reduced to minute particles.

Herbivores eat living plant material.

Omnivores eat both plant and animal material, living or dead.

Parasites live upon other organisms, drawing nourishment from them.

Predators attack living animals, killing them.

Scavengers eat dead and decaying plant and animal material.

TERMS USED IN DIFFERENT TYPES OF
REPRODUCTION

Binary fission, reproduction by division into two similar cells.

Budding, reproduction by division into two very unequal cells or parts, the bud being much the smaller.

Fertilization, reproduction by the union of a male and female sex cell.

Gamete, a sex cell or germ cell capable of uniting with another to form a new individual.

Gametophyte, a stage in the life of a plant, from and including the spore to the zygote.

Hermaphrodite, an individual containing potentialities of both sexes.

Isogamete, a gamete not exhibiting sexual or other differences.

Parthenogenesis, reproduction by virgin females by means of unfertilized eggs.

Spore, a small, typically spherical, reproductive unit, usually resistant to dryness, heat or freezing.

Sporophyte, a stage in the life of a plant, from and including the zygote to the spore.

Zoospore, an asexual spore capable of swimming.

Zygote, the fertilized egg.

Classification of Organisms by the Part They Play in the Community

Producers	The photosynthetic and chemosynthetic organisms that manufacture food.	Chiefly bacteria and protists. Secondarily the higher plants.
Consumers	*Primary consumers* that feed directly upon green plant material. These are the herbivores; very few feed on higher aquatic plants.	Chief among these are the herbivorous insects (corixids, haliplids, caddis larvae, a few pyralid caterpillars), crustaceans and fish. Of secondary importance are the rotifers, protists, gastropods, worms, tadpoles and a few fishes.
	Secondary consumers that feed upon primary consumers or on other secondary consumers.	Carnivorous insects, most vertebrates, and parasites.
	Processors, the detritus feeders.	Rotifers, bryozoans, tubifex worms, midge larvae, some caddis larvae, some mayfly and stonefly nymphs, some molluscs, a few fishes.
	Scavengers, those that feed on dead or decaying plant or animal material.	Some ciliates; many worms, crustaceans; hydrophilid beetles; some molluscs; a few fishes and turtles.
Reducers	The organisms that change organic material back to inorganic, after which it may be used again.	Bacteria and some fungi.

Classification of Areas of Populations in Lentic Waters

Littoral[*]   Region of shallow water where light reaches the bottom.   Floating and rooted plants. Many groups of animals.

Limnetic   Area of open water too deep for rooted plants but with sufficient light penetration to permit photosynthesis. Many species migrate upward at night, downward during the day, but acting differently so as not to crowd one another. (Absent in shallow ponds.)   Diatoms, blue-green and green algae, flagellates, and many other protists (few in species but large in population). Copepods (*Diaptomus, Cyclops*), cladocerans (*Diaphanosoma, Lida, Bosmina*), rotifers (*Asplanchna, Notholca*). Most fishes.

Profundal   Area below photosynthetic light penetration. (Absent in ponds.)   Anaerobic bacteria, fungi. Blood worms, nematodes, tendipedid midges and the culicid *Chaoborus* (limnetic at night), a few molluscs, a few fishes.

[*] Psammolittoral is sometimes used for the area between sand grains along the shore; it includes protists, tardigrades, nematodes, copepods.

Classification of Littoral and Limnetic Organisms

Neuston   Organisms resting or swimming on surface.   Whirligig beetles, water striders, water measurers, an occasional spider, springtails; hydras and one hydrophilid beetle on underside of film; a few protists.

Nekton   Organisms swimming at will.   Beetles, bugs, fly and mosquito larvae. Fish, amphibians, reptiles.

Plankton   Organisms floating but submerged, depending primarily upon current for dispersal.   Protists; rotifers; heavier ostracods, cladocerans, copepods.

Periphyton   Organisms clinging to stones, plants or other projections from the bottom; or those lurking in the vegetation.   Protists, rotifers, some crustaceans, hydras, nematodes, oligochaetes, bryozoans, leeches, some molluscs, many insects (midges, aeschnid dragonflies, damselflies, stoneflies, caddis flies, *Ranatra,* moth larvae, chrysomelid beetle larvae). Many fishes, amphibians and reptiles.

Benthon   Organisms resting on bottom or burrowing.   Some dragonflies, mayflies, stoneflies, caddis flies, crayfish, isopods, turtles and amphibians *on* bottom. Some dragonflies, mayflies, midges, flies, molluscs and worms *in* bottom.

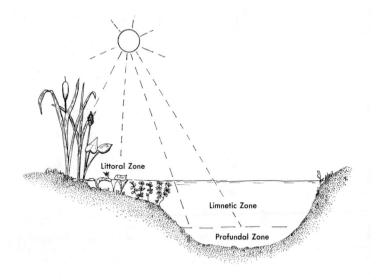

Fig. 3A. Diagram of areas of population in lentic water.

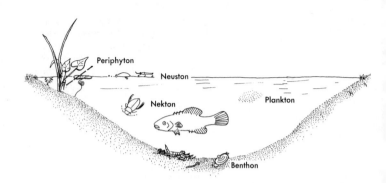

Fig. 3B. Diagram of types of littoral and limnetic organisms.

Plant zonation is clearly
seen at pond's edge.

A fast brook is home for many
insect larvae.

A bog pond becomes increasingly
smaller.

Lemna is on the surface, *Typha*
along the shore.

Toxorhynchites larvae live
in tree holes.

PLATE 1

A *Toxorhynchites* pupa rests
at the surface.

A *Sympetrum* alights
with wings outspread.

A male *Plathemis lydia* acquires
a white bloom.

An *Enallagma* alights
with wings folded.

Bittacomorpha clavipes, a
phantom cranefly.

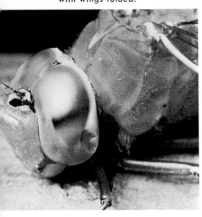

Aeschnine eyes meet in a long seam.

Gomphine eyes are widely
separated.

PLATE 2

Notonecta rests in characteristic position.

Peltocoris is a predator.

Tropisternus carries a bubble of air.

Ranatra lurks in the vegetation.

Benacus griseus dines on a dragonfly nymph.

PLATE 3

A *Gyrinid beetle* rests on a lily pad.

An aeschnid nymph climbs in the vegetation.

A gomphine nymph tries to burrow.

A libelluline nymph crawls, silt-covered.

A macromiine nymph is a sprawler.

The gills of *Argia* are very broad.   PLATE 4

The gills of *Ischnura* have tapering tips.

Nigronia, a fish fly larva, has lateral gills.

A caddis carries its case wherever it goes.

Tubifera tenax extends its respiratory tube.

Clemmys insculpta may travel far from water.

Eurycea longicauda is often at streamsides.

PLATE 5

Rana sylvatica wears a black mask.

Barred Tiger Salamander

Red Salamander

Red Spotted Newt

Spotted Salamander

Red Eft

Dusky Salamander

Two-lined Salamander

Narrow-striped
Dwarf Siren

Conger Eel

Mud Puppy

Hellbender

Plate 6. Salamanders

American Toad

Spadefoot Toad

Tailed Frog

Gray Tree Frog

Green Tree Frog

Green Frog

Pickerel Frog

Leopard Frog

Bull Frog

Plate 7. Frogs and Toads

Map Turtle

Softshell Turtle

Red-eared Turtle

Blanding's Turtle

Musk Turtle

Painted Turtle

Snapping Turtle

Plate 8. Turtles

CHAPTER 3

Some Microscopic Organisms

Figs. 4–12

A^N examination of the bright green scum on the surface of the pond, or of the slimy coating on the rocks of a stream bed, cannot be made in the field; it must be postponed until a microscope is available. This scum and this slippery film are made up of a great group of organisms most of which are invisible to the naked eye and make their presence known to us only when occurring in enormous aggregations. Even the handful of seemingly clear water we scoop from the lake may contain innumerable microscopic, living forms.

The smallest of these organisms, unless we wish to consider the viruses, are the bacteria. They play an essential role in synthesizing some compounds, in reducing others, and in serving as food for countless organisms larger than themselves but still invisible in our handful of water. But if, as it has been said, it takes more than 1,000,000,000,000 average-sized bacteria to weigh one gram and if the largest are no more than 60 microns long (1 micron = .001 millimeter), we are not likely to see them even with a compound microscope. We must take their presence for granted.

Grouping of Microscopic Organisms*

UNICELLULAR FORMS. Cells may be solitary or in colonies or filaments.

    Protista. P. 34. May be sessile, or motile and animal-like.

* Exclusive of worms.

MULTICELLULAR ORGANISMS. Usually motile, animal-like; never plantlike.

> **Rotifera.** Usually very active. Often with tapered foot. P. 54.
>
> **Gastrotricha.** Flattened, with caudal prolegs. Uncommon. P. 57.
>
> **Tardigrada.** Cylindrical, with four pairs clawed legs. Uncommon. P. 58.

ALGAE, PROTOZOA, FLAGELLATES AND FUNGI— THE PROTISTA*

The majority of these organisms are unicellular; a few are noncellular. Some are plantlike (the algae); some are animal-like (the protozoa); some resemble both plants and animals (the flagellates); and some are ghostly parasites (the fungi). They range in size from microscopic, solitary cells averaging 1–200 microns in length to colonies, filaments, and clusters of filaments 2 inches in diameter; a few, the stoneworts, are a foot or more long, resembling the higher plants in their manner of growth. *Chaos diffluens,* the amoeba known to every schoolchild, is 600 microns or more when actively elongated and thus large enough to be seen with the naked eye, and yet it is seldom observed in the field. Nevertheless, the effect of massed aggregations of protists may be considerable, in spite of their small size.

The algae comprise the great mass of producers in any aquatic society. Since they carry on 90 percent of its photosynthesis they provide food for many animals and are of considerable value as oxygenators. All have chlorophyll, although its presence may be masked by yellow, brown or red pigments. Some brightly colored species tint the water or

---

* The term Protista is used in so many different ways by various authors that I apply it in this inclusive manner without misgivings. This system simplifies the organization of this chapter, it retains the old names algae and protozoa, and it keeps the zooflagellates and phytoflagellates "under one roof."

produce the "pond scum" or "bloom" on quiet waters at certain seasons of the year; others coat the stones and vegetation with a slimy green or brown habit; some give a pungent or aromatic taste and odor to the water, and others an unequivocal foulness. Some species are epizoic: the green, filamentous *Basicladia,* for instance, grows on the backs of snapping turtles and alligators. In water high in carbon dioxide the filamentous forms predominate; in well-aerated water the colonial forms are more abundant.

The brown algae, Phaeophyta, and the red algae, Rhodophyta, are primarily marine. They will not be discussed here although a few live in quiet fresh waters and a few inhabit swift rocky stream beds. The brown *Heribaudiella,* for instance, encrusts the rocks of turbulent streams with olive-brown discs, and the red "seaweed" *Lemanea* forms brownish tufts on stream-washed stones.

The protozoa and flagellates are to be found in quiet ponds, in the scum on mud flats, in hot springs, on snowdrifts and glaciers, and in brine pools and salt water. Many are parasites living in or on other organisms. The functioning of the unicellular body is complex even though the mechanism that accomplishes it is invisible to us and even though it is contained within the confines of a single cell which has neither organs nor tissues. Some species contain chlorophyll and manufacture their own food; others obtain nourishment by engulfing small organisms or bits of organic nutriment from the water around them. Most forms discharge excess water by contractile vacuoles: a paramoecium is said to give off 700 times its own weight daily.

Reproduction. Protists usually reproduce by simple fission of the cell into two similar cells. Occasionally an exchange of nuclear material may occur between two cells just before they divide. A few species produce spores and isogametes.

Collecting. The scum on quiet waters may be scooped up with sieve or dip net; algae growing on submerged plant stems may be stripped off with the fingers and those on lily pads scraped off with scalpel or knife. Small and temporary pools must not be overlooked. Cliffs or rock ledges over which water flows, and rocks and substrata of swift waters should be scraped into a screen held beneath or downstream. Open-water plankton can be gathered with a plankton net or tow net.

Many of the colonial and filamentous algae can be seen at once but other protists will be best studied if left in covered jars for a day or two in a well-lighted window (but not in bright sunlight). Some will gather at the surface and others at the bottom or along the sides of the jar. Cultures may be kept for several weeks with the addition of minute quantities of malted milk or boiled hay infusion.

Green floating plants and bottom debris may be gathered and bottled without the use of special equipment.

Grouping of Phyla of Protista

ORGANISMS WITH CHLOROPHYLL

1. Chlorophyll not contained in special bodies. Cells without a nucleus.

   Cyanophyta. Usually blue-green.

2. Color contained in special bodies, chromatophores. Cells with a nucleus.*

   a. Without flagella.

   Chlorophyta. Usually grass green.

   Chrysophyta. Usually yellow, brown or yellow-green.

   b. With whiplike flagella.**

   Mastigophora.

ORGANISMS WITHOUT CHLOROPHYLL (See also worms in Chapter 9)

Mastigophora. Locomotion by flagella.

Sarcodina. Locomotion by pseudopodia.

Ciliophora. Locomotion by minute hairs or cilia.

Eumycophyta. Usually sessile and filamentous.

---

* Nuclei usually not visible without special staining.

** Very small gametes and zoospores of other groups are also flagellated.

Blue-green Algae—Phylum Cyanophyta*
Fig. 4; Pl. 9

Most Cyanophyta have a slightly bluish tint when viewed by transmitted light, but others may appear black, red-purple, yellow or green; for in addition to the usual green and yellow chlorophyll pigments they contain blue phycocyanin and red phycoerythrin. When present in large numbers they impart a reddish or bluish tinge to the water (see also the Mastigophora) and are often responsible for the familiar surface bloom (see also the Chlorophyta).

Each individual consists of a single, non-nucleated cell whose wall may be gelatinous, leathery or stony. These cells divide by simple fission but may remain attached to form filaments, clusters, or plates. The filaments may have, at intervals, enlarged, thick-walled cells called *spores*, or *heterocysts*, which have significance in the division of the filaments.

Some thrive best in polluted water even in manure-ridden, barnyard pools. Others live in hot springs at temperatures up to 176° F. Many prefer water of high oxygen content. Some, like *Anabaena*, are able to incorporate atmospheric nitrogen into the protein of their cells and are thus not dependent upon dissolved nitrogen; consequently they may grow profusely in the fall when water nutrients are low. *Anabaena* is also important as food for fish and crustaceans; it often grows on *Azolla* (Fig. 23) and other aquatic plants; and at times may be so abundant as to pile up in windrows along the shore. *Nostoc* forms the gelatinous "butter balls" occasionally seen rolling along in clear water, its filaments storing food for winter dormancy. *Rivularia* commonly forms gelatinous, brown clumps on stones in the stream bed and on such plants as *Chara, Myriophyllum* and *Typha.*

The members of one large group are spiraled; they wave and rotate in almost continual motion. Some of these are encased in a gelatinous sheath; others are not. Among the latter is the common and widespread *Oscillatoria* (Pl. 9)

* Called Myxophyta or Myxophyceae by some systematists; and grouped with the bacteria in a separate kingdom, the Monera, by others.

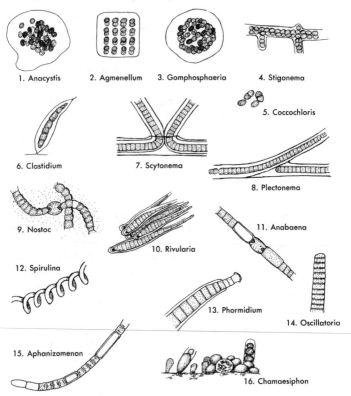

1. Anacystis
2. Agmenellum
3. Gomphosphaeria
4. Stigonema
5. Coccochloris
6. Clastidium
7. Scytonema
8. Plectonema
9. Nostoc
10. Rivularia
11. Anabaena
12. Spirulina
13. Phormidium
14. Oscillatoria
15. Aphanizomenon
16. Chamaesiphon

Fig. 4. Microscopic Blue-green Algae

which is not permanently spiraled but whose filaments twist and coil and uncoil and wave back and forth. It often forms purplish masses on rocks in pools, sometimes breaking loose to float free.

Grouping of Families of Blue-green Algae

UNICELLULAR, OR IN CLUSTERS, WITH CELLS SEPARATED BY SHEATHS

    Chroococcaceae. Cells divide equally into similar cells. (Fig. 4.1–3,5) Division may be in one, two or three planes.

Clastidiaceae. Cells divide unequally. Form a hair-tipped sheath attached to plants. (Fig. 4.6)

Chamaesiphonaceae. Cells divide unequally. Form cushions attached to submerged objects. (Fig. 4.16)

USUALLY FILAMENTOUS, WITH CELLS SEPARATED ONLY BY MEMBRANES

1. Filaments branched. Often on ledges over which water is dripping.

   Stigonematacea. Branching involves whole filament. (Fig. 4.4)

   Scytonemataceae. Branching involves sheath only. (Fig. 4.7,8)

2. Filaments not branched; tapered at end. Usually in flowing water.

   Rivulariaceae. Tip of filament often hairlike, but base thick. Filaments may radiate in a gelatinous mass. (Fig. 4.10)

3. Filaments neither branched nor tapered.

   Nostocaceae. Cells spherical or barrel-shaped, strung together like beads. With heterocysts. (Fig. 4.9,11, 15)

   Oscillatoriaceae. Cells cylindrical. Without heterocysts. Filaments usually single and often waving or rotating. (Fig. 4.12–14; Pl. 9)

Green Algae—Phylum Chlorophyta
Figs. 5, 24

Most of the green algae are a grass or yellow green, but some are yellowish or brownish and a few are even blue-green; so again, color is not a good distinguishing character. They may be solitary or they may live in pairs or in filaments; and one small group, the Characeae, are plantlike structures a foot long. Some unicellular forms, such as *Oophila*, live within amphibian eggs; some, such as *Chlorella* and *Eremosphaera*, within protozoans or hydras, coloring them green; others, in the gelatinous matrix of sponges. Some form platelike colonies, or open nets.

Green algae, especially the filamentous ones, are the chosen food of flatworms and many insects, and are commonly eaten by many other small creatures as well.

A grouping of the many families of this large and varied phylum is not practicable; mention is made of a few of the more common ones.

Desmidiaceae (Fig. 5.1–7,9). The desmids are one-celled but are usually found in pairs or in irregular or filamentous colonies. Each has a slight median constriction or a median light band; many are exquisitely patterned with geometric designs; some are shaped like stars or crescents and ornamented with spines. They are usually bright green and when present in profusion may tint the water. They reproduce, not by simple fission but by the fusion of two cells which escape from their cell walls. Desmids are more common in soft than in hard water.

Zygnemataceae (Fig. 5.10–12,21). The filamentous pond scums often form blankets of green on the surface of quiet waters in early spring, for many of them have flourished all winter long, providing a source of nutriment for insects and crustaceans wintering in the depths of the ponds. Their chloroplasts are large and conspicuous; those of *Spirogyra* are spirally coiled, and those of *Zygnema* are star-shaped and in pairs, each with a central starch-producing pyrenoid. *Spirogyra* reproduces sexually; two filaments come to lie side by side and send out conjugating tubes which unite, permitting the fusion of the living portions of the two cells and the formation of a thick-walled resting spore.

Other families (Fig. 5.8,13–20,22,23). A few genera of the many other families may be very common. *Ulothrix*, for example, often forms a hairy covering on rocks in cool streams, each filament attached by a basal holdfast. It reproduces by small, ciliated zoospores which break out from certain cells, swim about, and then settle down to form new filaments. It also reproduces by sex cells. *Oedogonium*, another common genus, can be distinguished by the rings at the apical end of each cell. *Hydrodictyon* forms a large, coarse net, each interspace of which is bounded by five or six cylindrical cells.

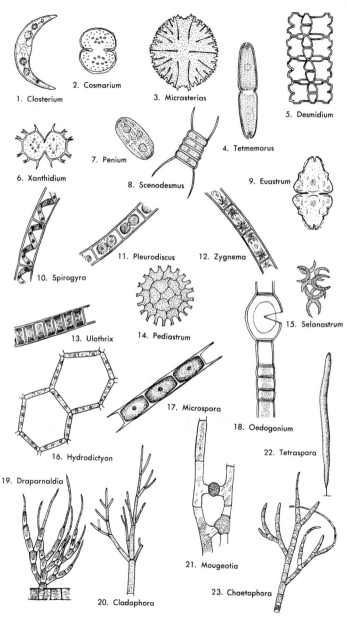

1. Closterium
2. Cosmarium
3. Micrasterias
4. Tetmemorus
5. Desmidium
6. Xanthidium
7. Penium
8. Scenodesmus
9. Euastrum
10. Spirogyra
11. Pleurodiscus
12. Zygnema
13. Ulothrix
14. Pediastrum
15. Selanastrum
16. Hydrodictyon
17. Microspora
18. Oedogonium
19. Draparnaldia
20. Cladophora
21. Mougeotia
22. Tetraspora
23. Chaetophora

Fig. 5. Microscopic Green Algae (5 after Ward and Whipple)

Characaceae (Fig. 24). These are the stoneworts which, because of their large size and whorled branches, have been placed in a separate phylum by some authors. Since they attain a height of a foot or more and grow attached to the substratum they may be mistaken for seed plants until a close examination reveals the apparent simplicity of their structure and their lack of roots.

Each *Chara* stem bears whorls of branches at the nodes. The inch-long internodes, as well as the branches, are made up of a single-celled core with an outer cellular layer. At certain times lovely fruiting bodies are borne along the branches. These may be pear-shaped, single-egged ovaries, or round, orange spermaries that contain thousands of sperm cells. *Chara* grows in water rich in calcium carbonate. Its slender stems and branches are so hard and brittle from lime deposition that they are spared depredation by animals that normally feed on aquatic green plants, and are eaten only by certain little haliplid beetles. Many minute algae live on the stems and it is they, and not the *Chara*, that serve as food for the many small, browsing creatures and for the wild fowl that are found so frequently in its proximity. Water containing a thriving population of *Chara* has a marshy or sulphurous odor.

Nitella, similar to *Chara* but more delicately formed and less harsh to the touch, lacks the outer layer of cells on the stem and is thus often transparent; its branches are several times forked. *Tolypella* is similar also, but has feathery, fertile branches.

Yellow Algae—Phylum Chrysophyta
Fig. 6

Most of the yellow, or golden, algae are single-celled but they often live in clusters. Although they contain chlorophyll their green color is masked by yellow and brown pigments and by stored oil droplets. Of the several families in this complex group the most interesting for the average collector is probably the one that includes the diatoms.

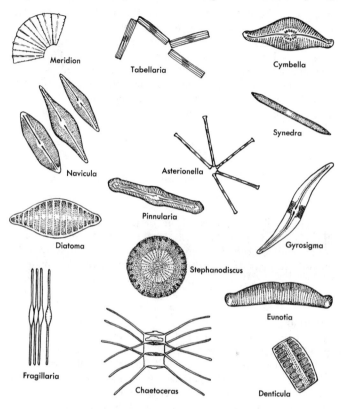

Fig. 6. Microscopic Diatoms

Bacillariophyceae (Fig. 6). The diatoms are one-celled, microscopic forms having a characteristically rigid cell wall made of silica and composed of two valves held together by a band or girdle. Each has a finely sculptured, bilateral or radial pattern, and a delicate gelatinous covering. They live as single pairs or in colonies or filaments. Reproduction is usually by fission.

Diatoms live in a wide variety of aquatic and marine environments although some have exacting requirements as to the quantity of calcium or magnesium in the water and the degree of acidity, salinity, or temperature. They may float, drift, or remain attached to the substratum or to plants and animals. At times, especially in the spring, they may cover a stream bed with a golden diatomaceous ooze that contains the silicious walls of many dead organisms as well as living ones. The diatomaceous earth of the uplifted ocean floor is widely used as a fine abrasive; and the oils stored by prehistoric forms have contributed to the petroleum deposits that man so greedily despoils. Diatoms are a significant item in the diet of a wide variety of aquatic animals.

Flagellates—Phylum Mastigophora*
Fig. 7

The flagellates represent one of the many links between the plant and animal worlds. Many of them have chlorophyll and manufacture their own food; some have starch granules or oil droplets; and still others absorb nutritive material through the cell membrane. Many also have the power of locomotion and the ability to feed upon plant and animal material, sometimes ingesting whole organisms through a mouthlike depression or gullet. A large number are colonial. They may form a flat plate of 4 to 16 cells as in the common pond and lake *Gonium,* or may continue to divide to form spherical or elliptical colonies of 16 or 32 cells, or even of many, many cells. The common pond species of *Volvox,* for instance, may form spherical colonies of as many as 10,000 individuals, and attain a diameter of 600 microns. The individual cells in some colonial species are of the same size; in others, of two different sizes.

Locomotion is by means of one or more long, whiplike protoplasmic threads, *flagella,* which perform undulating or spiral movements that propel or pull the organisms along. Many species become amoeboid under certain conditions.

Flagellates live in all waters from glaciers to hot springs. Many live in water of very low oxygen content, and a number are completely anaerobic, living in sewage or the mud and

* We are fully cognizant of the complexity of the classification of flagellated organisms but for the purpose of this book group them all as Mastigophora.

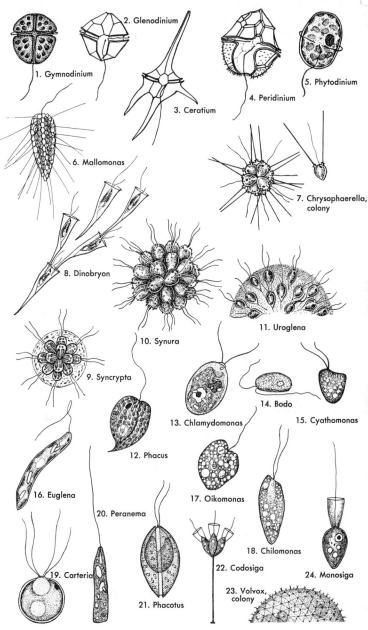

Fig. 7. Microscopic Flagellates

1. Gymnodinium
2. Glenodinium
3. Ceratium
4. Peridinium
5. Phytodinium
6. Mallomonas
7. Chrysosphaerella, colony
8. Dinobryon
9. Syncrypta
10. Synura
11. Uroglena
12. Phacus
13. Chlamydomonas
14. Bodo
15. Cyathomonas
16. Euglena
17. Oikomonas
18. Chilomonas
19. Carteria
20. Peranema
21. Phacotus
22. Codosiga
23. Volvox, colony
24. Monosiga

debris of stagnant water. Under such conditions they probably obtain their energy from processes similar to those in fermentation. Many Chrysomonadida give an offensive odor and taste to the water of reservoirs (*Synura,* for example, smells like overripe cucumbers). Others give a stickiness to running water. Many colonial green forms, on the other hand, live in highly oxygenated water. Many, especially the dinoflagellates, euglenoids and phytomonadids are an important component of open-water plankton. Others are common in the plankton blooms and the green scums of quiet waters. Dinoflagellates often color the water in which they live. *Gymnodinium* and *Gonylaux* may cause the "red tides" and also produce toxins poisonous to many animals, including man. The bright green *Euglena,* 150 microns, has a red eyespot and is often beautifully sculptured; it, too, sometimes contains red granules in such profusion that aggregations give a red tint to the scum of barnyard pools, especially in hot weather. *Euglena* is also a characteristic river form; so also is *Pleodorina.*

Grouping of Orders of Flagellates

USUALLY WITH ONE OR MORE CHROMATOPHORES.
Class Phytomastigophora
1. With 2 flagella, one of which encircles the cell.
    Dinoflagellida (Fig. 7.1–5). The cell is often covered with a thick exoskeleton that is sometimes grooved into separate plates. Common in plankton. *Ceratium, Peridinium* and *Gymnodinium* are limnetic.
2. With 1–4 flagella, but not as above. With yellow, brown or orange chromatophores.
    Chrysomonadida (Fig. 7.6–11). With 1–2 flagella, but without a gullet. Some are solitary and some colonial; many have a shell-like collar, or *lorica,* surrounding the protoplasmic body at one end. The collared forms are often stalked; if they are also colonial they then form a branching treelike structure.
    Cryptomonadida (Fig. 7.15,18). With a deep gullet.
3. With 1–4 flagella. With green chromatophores or with none.

Phytomonadida (Fig. 7.13,19,21,23). Without a gullet. Solitary or colonial; solitary forms often have an external, bivalve membrane.

Euglenida (Fig. 7.12,16,20). With a gullet. Usually with a red eyespot, which is really a cluster of granules in a light-sensitive area, showing positive reaction to weak or medium light but a negative reaction to bright light.

WITH NO CHROMATOPHORES. Class Zoomastigophora (Fig. 7.14,17,22)

The orders of this class are too numerous to be listed. The zooflagellates are colorless, but so also are many of the phytoflagellates. A few have pseudopodia and some have as many as 5 to 8 flagella. They may be collared, stalked or colonial. A few, such as *Trepomonas*, *Bodo*, and *Hexamita*, are sewage indicators.

Amoebalike Protozoa—Phylum Sarcodina
Fig. 8

The protists of this group move by the protrusion of temporary extensions called *pseudopodia* and by the accompanying streaming of the protoplasm. The forces that permit this phenomenon lie outside of the cell where they exert changes in the surface tension of the cell membrane. Everyone who has seen an amoeba under the microscope is familiar with this characteristic amoeboid movement. It not only makes locomotion possible but enables the organism to engulf bits of organic material or other living organisms from the surrounding water, and thereby enclose the food and water in a vacuole formed by the pinched-off cell membrane. Exchange of water, gases, food and wastes takes place between the vacuole and the surrounding protoplasm. Eventually the organism streams away leaving the contents of the vacuole behind.

Most species are colorless or grayish but a few are green from the presence of green algae within their cells. A few have shells. Species of *Pelomyxa* and *Euglypha* are sewage indicators. Some live in algae (Fig. 8.6,7) or feed on algae (Fig. 8.8).

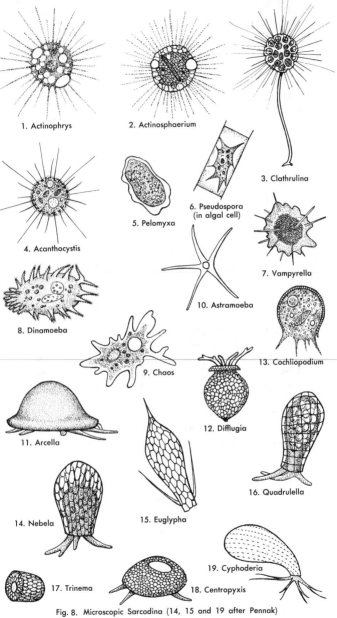

1. Actinophrys
2. Actinosphaerium
3. Clathrulina
4. Acanthocystis
5. Pelomyxa
6. Pseudospora (in algal cell)
7. Vampyrella
8. Dinamoeba
9. Chaos
10. Astramoeba
11. Arcella
12. Difflugia
13. Cochliopodium
14. Nebela
15. Euglypha
16. Quadrulella
17. Trinema
18. Centropyxis
19. Cyphoderia

Fig. 8. Microscopic Sarcodina (14, 15 and 19 after Pennak)

Grouping of Orders of Sarcodina

PSEUDOPODIA FLOWING
1. Pseudopodia fingerlike.
   Amoebida. Without a shell (Fig. 8.5,6,8–10)
   Testacida. With a shell, which may be membranous or contain mineral particles. (Fig. 8.11–19)
2. Pseudopodia filiform or pointed, often branched.
   Proteomyxida. (Fig. 8.7)
PSEUDOPODIA RADIATING, LONG, WITH STIFF CENTRAL AXIS
   Heliozoida. (Fig. 8.1–4)
PSEUDOPODIA KNOBBED, OR TENTACLELIKE.
   Usually parasitic
   Suctoria. Often on turtles (see Ciliates).

Ciliates—Phylum Ciliophora
Fig. 9; Pl. 9

The ciliates thrive where there is decaying organic material, on the edges of weedy ponds or in stagnant pools. Many are stalked and sessile. They are characterized by the presence of minute hairs, or *cilia*. These cilia may be restricted to one part of the body or may cover the entire body, in which case they are usually arranged in diagonal rows with their movements so coordinated that they beat with a wavelike rhythm. This waving is often accompanied by contractions and expansions of the body that enable it to shoot ahead at a rate of one-tenth of an inch a second, a greater speed than that attained by any other protists. In some ciliates the cilia around the mouth, or *oral groove,* are clumped to form triangular *membranelles*; in some the ventral cilia are clumped to form short, leglike *cirri*, used in locomotion.

Ciliates feed mostly on organic particles or bacteria, but some are carnivores and some scavengers. Many have an oblique lateral groove lined with cilia whose beating draws food material into the funnel-like gullet at the bottom of the groove. *Didinium, Coleps, Lacrymaria* and *Paramœcium* seek

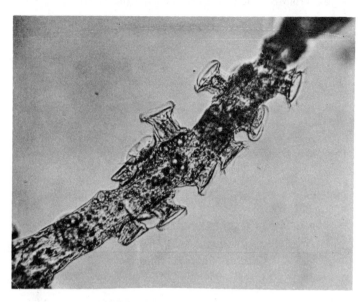

Trichodina, living as a commensal on *Hydra*.

A rotifer, swimming among filaments of *Oscillatoria*.

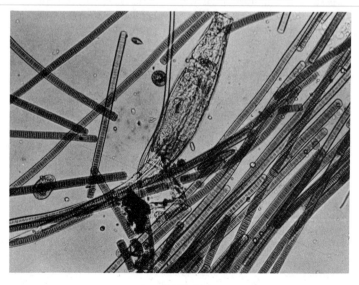

PLATE 9

out the bacteria and protists on which they feed, sometimes attacking individuals too large for immediate ingestion. A single didinium has been known to eat as many as 8 paramœcia a day. A few species are parasitic; and some common genera, *Trichodina* (Pl. 9), *Kerona*, *Euplotes* and *Stylonychia*, are usually seen living upon the body of hydras.

Reproduction is accomplished by simple fission or, as in *Paramœcium*, by *conjugation*, a type of sexual reproduction in which two individuals come to lie side by side, forming a bridgelike connection through which there is an exchange of nuclear material; they then separate, equipped with a new hereditary potential.

Several ciliates can be seen with the naked eye. *Spirostomum*, 900 microns long, is visible in shady pools where it may whiten the surface of the water if present in numbers. *Vorticella* and *Epistylis* are colonial forms that appear in streams as whitish blotches on submerged objects as well as on molluscs, turtles, insects and crustaceans. *Carchesium*, sometimes a sewage indicator, forms colonies an eighth of an inch in height.

Grouping of Orders of Ciliates

CILIA USUALLY COVERING MOST OF BODY; WITHOUT MEMBRANELLES
> **Holotrichida** (Fig. 9.1–5,16,17). Most species are free-living, although a few live as parasites in annelids, molluscs and crustaceans, or on the skin of fishes or the gills of tadpoles.

CILIA USUALLY NOT COVERING ENTIRE BODY; WITH MEMBRANELLES
> **Peritrichida** (Fig. 9.6–9; Pl. 9). Cilia in a ring around a bell-shaped orifice. Often on a long, contractile stalk. Membranelles form an undulating membrane that leads counterclockwise to the mouth.

> **Spirotrichida** (Fig. 9.10–15). Membranelles lead clockwise to the mouth. Cilia sometimes present over entire body.

CILIA PRESENT IN FREE-SWIMMING YOUNG ONLY; MATURE FORMS SESSILE, WITH TENTACLES
> **Suctoria** (Fig. 9.18–19). Most species are stalked, with

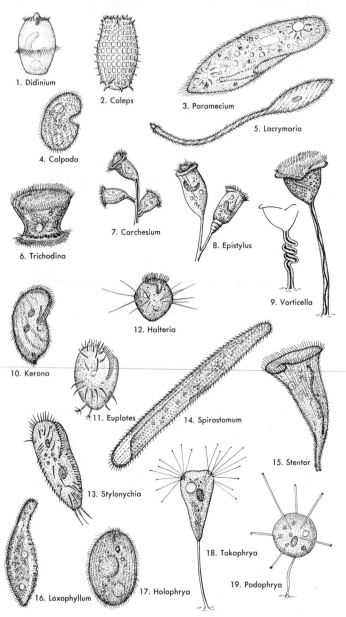

1. Didinium
2. Coleps
3. Paramecium
4. Colpoda
5. Lacrymaria
6. Trichodina
7. Carchesium
8. Epistylus
9. Vorticella
10. Kerona
11. Euplotes
12. Halteria
13. Stylonychia
14. Spirostomum
15. Stentor
16. Loxophyllum
17. Holophrya
18. Tokophrya
19. Podophrya

Fig. 9. Microscopic Ciliates

filiform, suctorial tentacles on which their prey become impaled. Many have a collar. Some grow on isopods, amphipods, turtles and the gills of fish.

Fungi—Phylum Eumycophyta

The fungi, unlike their relatives the algae, do not contain chlorophyll and therefore must live as parasites or saprophytes upon other organisms. They are of some importance in the decomposition of the chitinous exoskeletons of insects and crustaceans and of the lignin of wood. Fungi are made up of filaments, *hyphae*, that form a mesh, the *mycelium*. They reproduce by spores or by the fusion of sex cells.

Two of the four major classes have aquatic members: the Phycomycetes that have hyphae without cross walls, and the Ascomycetes, with septate hyphae. In addition, a fairly large number of the miscellaneous imperfect fungi, the Deuteromycetes, live in submerged, decaying vegetation, often in the vascular tissues of seed plants.

Phycomycetes. These algal-like fungi include the blights, mildews and bread moulds. Members of several orders live as parasites on algae and on other fungi. The water moulds of the order Saprolegniales are entirely aquatic, developing on the bodies of dead insects and other animals and as parasites on diatoms, fish and amphibia. The best known is *Saprolegnia* which can almost always be obtained by dropping a dead fly into stagnant water. Within a few days the white mycelium will be plainly visible over the insect's body. The hyphae are of two kinds: slender, tapering threads that penetrate the tissues of the host, and blunt ones that project into the water. The tips of the latter become separated from the rest of the filament by a cell wall, thus forming a *sporangium* within which develop the spores that are to escape into the water. Sexual reproduction also occurs. There are several other aquatic genera.

Ascomycetes. The sac fungi include the blue-green moulds, cup fungi, black fungi and yeasts. A few species grow on submerged, decaying vegetation and on submerged twigs.

ROTIFERS, GASTROTRICHS AND TARDIGRADES— MULTICELLULAR MICROORGANISMS

When examining protists under the microscope one often sees interesting little creatures of complex structure and behavior. These are multicellular organisms that are not at all related to the protists. Some of these will prove to be worms; others will belong to one of the three groups named above.

Each of these groups is placed here in a separate phylum though their true status in taxonomy has not yet been established.

Rotifers—Phylum Rotatoria
Fig. 10; Pl. 9

Wheel animalcules, or rotifers, are microscopic animals of great abundance and variety. They are the chief components of plankton. The majority are 100–500 microns in length although some are smaller and a few may be as long as 2.5 mm. Most species are colorless or lightly tinged with green, yellow, pink or blue, but they may sometimes appear to be green or brown because of the excretory granules in the protoplasm or because of the contents of the digestive tract. Many of the common species seem to have a pair of rapidly revolving wheels at the anterior end of the body, but the movement that so catches the eye is due to the synchronized beating of the *cilia* that make up the crown, or *corona*.

Rotifers have a distinct head end and sometimes a tapering foot. The foot may bear either two or more terminal toes, or an attachment disc, and may sometimes be ringed and retractile. The rotifers are seemingly occupants of glass houses, for through the external cuticle can be seen the nervous, excretory and reproductive systems as well as the *mastix*, the strange, grinding, bulbous structure that leads into the stomach and intestine.

Locomotion. The free-swimming forms move by the beating of the cilia of the corona, and sometimes by movements

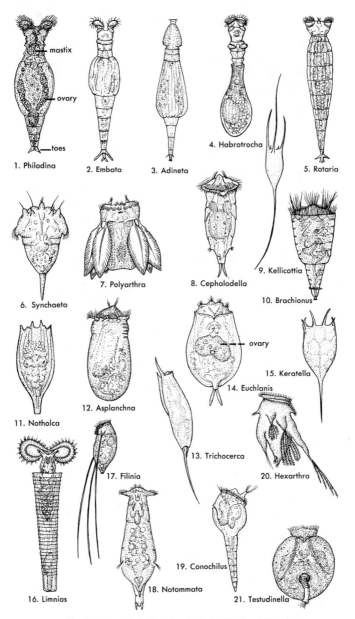

Fig. 10. Microscopic Rotifers (4 and 16 after Ward and Whipple)

1. Philodina — mastix, ovary, toes
2. Embata
3. Adineta
4. Habrotrocha
5. Rotaria
6. Synchaeta
7. Polyarthra
8. Cephalodella
9. Kellicottia
10. Brachionus
11. Notholca
12. Asplanchna
13. Trichocerca
14. Euchlanis — ovary
15. Keratella
16. Limnias
17. Filinia
18. Notommata
19. Conochilus
20. Hexarthra
21. Testudinella

of long filaments or appendages. Some rotifers progress by jerks and leaps. Others "creep" on the toes or even on the top of the head, the corona having been withdrawn to form a suction disc. Some species apparently never come to rest but spend their lives in the swimming, drifting plankton. A few are sessile, living in gelatinous tubes made of bits of debris.

Food. Most rotifers feed on minute organic particles; but a few are predatory on other organisms and a few feed on the fluid contents of filamentous algal cells.

Reproduction. Several types of eggs are produced, usually by parthenogenesis. Males are present for only a very short period of the year if at all, for in many species the male is completely unknown. Cycles of abundance are distinct but variable.

Collecting. Littoral species are collected from vegetation (their preference is often distinct and specific). They may be brought inside and left to stand in half-filled open jars. As the oxygen decreases, the rotifers tend to come to the surface, usually at the lighted side, and can then be removed with a pipette. Attached and sessile forms can be found by examining, with a binocular microscope, the vegetation that has been brought inside, or by culturing the washings from it. Limnetic or plankton forms can be caught in tow nets with a centrifugal tube at the lower end.

Grouping of Orders of Rotifers

WITH PAIRED OVARIES (Fig. 10.1)
> **Bdelloidea** (Fig. 10.1–5). These are the more elongate forms having the "rotating wheels." They swim freely or creep about the substratum on their heads. No males are known. Many live in sphagnum or moss, even in the moss on walls and bark, or in gutters, flower urns, etc., when moisture is present. Some withstand desiccation by forming cysts and have been reported by Dr. Pennak as able to live in that state for as long as 27 years.

WITH A SINGLE OVARY (Fig. 10.14) 90 percent of the known species.

Ploima (Fig. 10.6–15,18). Usually with a foot and 2 toes. (*Polyartha* has 12 lateral appendages instead.) Many are free-swimming plankton forms.

Flosculariaceae (Fig. 10.16,17,19–21). The foot, if present, is without toes. Some species are free-swimming but most are sessile. Some secrete a gelatinous case. *Conochilus* forms a spherical colony.

Collothecaceae. Usually sessile. Corona is large, with or without setae, cilia or lobes.

Gastrotrichs—Phylum Gastrotricha
Fig. 11

The multicellular gastrotrichs, often collected from aquatic vegetation and debris along with rotifers and protists, range in length from 70 to 600 microns. Though colorless they may appear light green or reddish brown because of the color of the contents of the digestive tract. They feed on bacteria, protists and detritus.

Fig. 11. A Gastrotrich, *Chaetonotus* × 50 (after Ward and Whipple).

Collecting. Gastrotrichs are found in puddles, bogs, marshes and in decaying vegetation along the shores of ponds. They frequently appear in old aquaria. The vegetation and detritus can be washed and then strained through bolting cloth; or a thin layer of top mud and debris can be set aside and allowed to settle. The filtrate of the former and the water from the surface of the sediment of the latter can be drawn off with a pipette and examined microscopically.

Water Bears—Phylum Tardigrada
Fig. 12

Often, when examining mosses and algae under the microscope, one sees a transparent, bearlike creature lumber across the field on four pairs of short fleshy legs each of which is armed with four claws. This is a tardigrade. Tardigrades range in length from 50 to 1,200 microns. Many species live in the capillary water between sand grains, exhibiting a remarkable ability to resist desiccation by shriveling into a ball. They feed on plant tissues, and occasionally on rotifers and nematodes, by piercing the tissues with long stylets and then sucking the liquid contents.

Fig. 12. A Tardigrade × 35.

CHAPTER 4

Liverworts and Mosses—
Phylum Bryophyta

Figs. 13, 14

THE liverworts and mosses are sometimes referred to as the amphibians of the plant world; even those that live on land must be wet, or at least moist, at some stage of their life. They are considerably more advanced in structure than the algae, for they are often several cell layers thick and usually have an outer protective layer, the *epidermis*. Like the higher plants, they have multicellular sex organs and produce sex cells that are protected by a cellular layer. But they do not have the conducting and stiffening tissues that are needed if a plant is to enjoy widespread terrestrial existence, and they do not have true roots. The majority live on land, usually in damp places, in shade or in bogs. A few live in arctic and arid regions by suspending activity under all conditions other than those of optimum temperature and moisture. A few are aquatic, living either along the banks or actually in the water.

Life cycle. Their life cycle is made up of two alternating stages: the *gametophyte* and the *sporophyte*. The former produces sex cells; the latter, spores. The green plant with which we are familiar is the gametophyte; it bears flask-shaped, egg-producing *archegonia*, and spherical or cylindrical *antheridia* within which ciliated sperm cells develop. Fertilization takes place within the archegonium. The sporophyte, the stage resulting from the union of the egg and sperm, remains enclosed within the archegonium in the

59

Fig. 13. Life cycle of a moss. a, a spore germinating, to form
b, the protonema; c, male gametophyte bearing antheridia that
produce male sex cells; d, female gametophyte; e, seta of sporophyte that grows from the fertilized egg; f, spore case without
calyptra.

liverworts, or hidden in the leafy bracts. In the mosses it
shoots up from the fertilized egg, usually forming a long,
capsule-bearing stalk, or *seta*. The spores that develop within
the capsule, or spore case, are released by the opening or
removal of a complex lid, the *calyptra*. Under proper conditions spores germinate, forming first a juvenile gametophyte, or *protonema*, and then the true gametophyte. In
the mosses the protenema is a small, branched filament of
elongated cells. In the liverworts it is even more greatly
reduced. Liverworts may also reproduce vegetatively by
budlike clusters of cells, *gemmules*. Aquatic byrophytes, for
the most part, reproduce by fragmentation.

Collecting. Bryophytes should be collected, if possible,
when the sporophyte is mature. They are best studied when
wet so should be brought in from the field in vials of water.
If it is necessary to dry them for storage they should be

spread out on paper, covered with a blotter and weighted down lightly until dry. For study purposes they will need to be resoftened by boiling or soaking in water or in a 10 percent solution of glycerine and water.

Liverworts—Class Hepaticae

The liverworts are terrestrial pioneers but some species still live in slow or stagnant waters, floating on the surface or lying flat on the ground or on rocks; a few live in lotic waters. They may consist of a flat, scalelike or ribbonlike *thallus*, 1 to 6 cells thick; or they may be stemmed, with two rows of leaves near the upper side of the stem. Each leaf is one cell layer thick and without a midrib. Occasionally a third row of leaves, called *underleaves*, is present on the under side of the stem. Stemmed species differ from the mosses in their flattened appearance.

Grouping of Families of Aquatic Liverworts

PLANTS SCALELIKE, RIBBONLIKE, OR IN ROSETTES
> Ricciaceae, crystalworts (Fig. 14.1,2). The thallus is opaque because of the presence of air cells. They float in shallow water, often mingled with duckweed, or rest on muddy shores. *Riccia fruitans* is a tiny, forked ribbon, 1–3 mm. wide. *Ricciocarpus natans* is a lobed, furrowed scale bearing many purplish or blackish hairs beneath; its lobes are 5–10 mm. wide, forming rosettes 2–3 cm. across; when submerged it is triangular. Common west to Texas and Minn.
>
> Riccardiaceae. Thallus translucent. *Riccardia* resembles *Riccia* but is more complexly branched, ½–2 mm. wide. *Dumortiera* of the southeast is unbranched, 1 cm. wide. *Riella*, southwestern, has a membranous "leaf" along one side of a stemlike cord.

PLANT WITH STEMS AND LEAVES
> 1. Leaves flat or curved, not folded, not lobed.
> Harpanthacea (Fig. 14.5). With small underleaves. The one aquatic species, *Chiloscyphus rivularis*, grows on stones in cold streams.

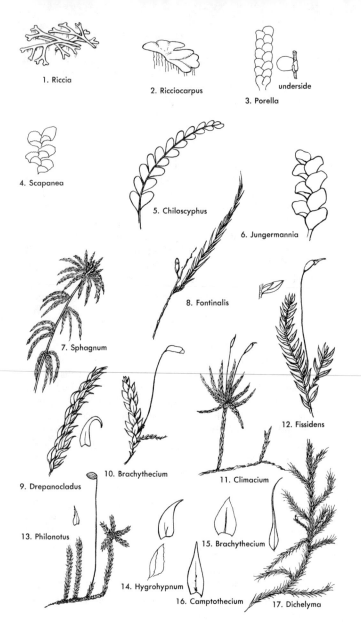

1. Riccia

2. Ricciocarpus

3. Porella
underside

4. Scapanea

5. Chiloscyphus

6. Jungermannia

7. Sphagnum

8. Fontinalis

9. Drepanocladus

10. Brachythecium

11. Climacium

12. Fissidens

13. Philonotus

14. Hygrohypnum

15. Brachythecium

16. Camptothecium

17. Dichelyma

Fig. 14. Liverworts and Mosses

Jungermanniaceae (Fig. 14.6). Underleaves absent or minute. Only one genus, *Jungermannia*, has aquatic species.

2. Leaves lobed (in two parts) and folded.

Scapaniaceae (Fig. 14.4). Under lobe roundish, larger than upper lobe. *Scapanea.*

Porelliaceae (Fig. 14.3). Under lobe tongue-shaped, smaller than upper lobe, concealed on under side of stem. *Porella.*

Mosses—Class Musci

The mosses bear their leaves evenly spaced around the stem or in two opposite rows. The leaves often have a midrib but their margins are never notched at the apex nor are they lobed. The cells that make up the leaves are dissimilar, differing in different parts of a single leaf. The sporophyte lasts several weeks or longer.

As a rule aquatic mosses are in shallow water only, but *Drepanocladus fluitans* and *Fontinalis antipyretica* have been found at depths of 18 to 20 meters where the water is very clear. In north temperate regions mosses are often common in running waters rich in calcium where by their ability to use carbon dioxide in a carbon fixation process they aid in the deposition of calcium to form calcareous tufa, or travertine.

Although *F. antipyretica* has long been used by Swedish peasants to pack around chimneys as a fire preventative (hence its specific name), it has probably not been so utilized in this country; but the Peat Moss, *Sphagnum*, has been of considerable economic importance here as it has in Europe. *Sphagnum* is a typical bog plant but it grows widely in wet places and even in water. The large soft plants bear alternate clusters of branches terminating in a dense head which may be over an inch across. It is an interesting plant for study in the laboratory where the microscope reveals a single layer of large, empty cells surrounded by slender green cells. In the field it offers a thick, cushiony carpet to the traveler in the bog, though it is a carpet that gives no support, letting the unwary sink through to the wet and muck beneath, a carpet which is itself deceptively filled with water. When dried, sphagnum plants are widely used for packing around fragile objects, and when wet, for packing around flowers and plants for long-distance shipment and for use in hanging baskets. In addition to their tremendous capacity for holding water they have an antiseptic quality which has made them valuable in making dressings for wounds during wartime shortages. Most important of all, of course, is the use to which they have been put when in the form of peat, lignite and brown coal. Compounded in the geological laboratory of time, they have served as fuel for countless generations of man. The collector who finds *Sphagnum* for the first time should gather a handful dripping with water, wring it out into a container and then measure or weigh the water gleaned. A comparison of its weight with that of the dried sphagnum will be of interest.

Grouping of Families of Aquatic Mosses

LEAVES WHITISH OR LIGHT GREEN
> **Sphagnaceae, peat moss.** (Fig. 14.7).

LEAVES NOT WHITISH
1. Leaves attached in two rows with edges directed toward stem.
   > **Fissidentacea** (Fig. 14.12). Leaf base so notched that it sits astride the stem and next leaf above (equitant). *Fissidens* is common on wet banks, rocks or floating in the water; stems 10–20 cm. long. East of Rockies.
2. Leaves attached all around the stem, or if in two rows not equitant.
   a. Spore capsule on very short stalk.
   > **Grimmiaceae.** Leaves dark green or blackish. *Scouleria* forms large blackish tufts on rocks in lotic waters. Northwest.
   > **Fontinaliaceae** (Fig. 14.8,17). Leaves are folded or keeled (rounded in *F. dalecarlica*). Blackish green to reddish or golden brown. All fountain mosses grow submerged or floating in running water or in

ponds of temperate and cold regions. Stems are long and dangling, often bare below if water is swift, and fastened at base by cushion of rhizomes. *Fontinalis*, with midrib lacking or not full length, has many widespread species; the cosmopolitan *F. antipyretica* has green, golden brown or coppery, ovate leaves; the lotic *F. dalecarlica* of the east and midwest has blackish stems and dark green to olive, glossy-tipped leaves. *Dichelyma* has midrib extending beyond middle of leaf, branches recurved at tip and leaves falcate (sickle-shaped); attached to sticks and branches usually near the surface where it can be submerged when water is high. *Brachelyma* is similar in extent of midrib but its leaf is not falcate; floating in streams and rivers.

b. Spore capsule on long seta at tip or from side of leafy branch or stem.

Bartramiaceae (Fig. 14.13). Spore capsule globose or ovate, tipped at right angles to stalk and furrowed when dry. Form deep tufts or cushions. Several genera, one of which, *Philonotis*, 1 cm., is common along margins or in water and occasionally under snowbanks; it has a 5-angled stem.

Aulacomniaceae. Capsule similar to above but more elongate. Often in pools though typically in bogs and woods. *Aulacomnium.*

Mniacea. Capsules not furrowed when dry. Plants robust with terminal leaves in a rosette. *Mnium.*

Pottiaceae. Leaves papillose. Rocky Mts. and westward. *Merceya.*

c. Spore capsule on a long seta growing from a short branch bearing modified leaves.

Hypnaceae (Fig. 14.9–11,14–16). A large aquatic family, common in swamps and sluggish streams, although *Hygrohypnum* grows on stones in waterfalls, south to Col. and W. Va. Many widely distributed genera, with glossy leaves.

Leskaceae. Leaves papillose. Several genera.

CHAPTER 5

The Higher Plants—
Phylum Tracheophyta

Figs. 15–30

THE SPORE-BEARING PLANTS

THE club mosses, quillworts, horsetails and ferns reproduce by means of spores and sex cells, and also by
creeping rootstocks. The conspicuous plant is the sporophyte,
not the gametophyte as it is in the bryophytes.

Club mosses and quillworts (Subphylum Lycopsida). Spores
develop in cases called *sporangia.* In the club mosses the
sporangia are borne on the upper surface of special leaves
that are grouped together to form a terminal conelike *strobi-
lus.* Some species have two kinds of spores: Large *megaspores* and small *microspores.* The only aquatic family of
this subphylum, the Isoetaceae, or quillworts (Fig. 28),
differ in bearing the sporangia in the swollen base of long
awl-like leaves or quills.

Horsetails (Subphylum Sphenopsida). Horsetails have two
types of erect branches growing from a creeping, underground stem. These branches are jointed, like miniature
stalks of bamboo, and bear a whorl of partially fused scales
at each node. The spore-bearing branches that come up in the
spring terminate in a cone covered with regularly aligned,
stalked sporangia. The slender vegetative branches that come
up in the summer have the whorls of green branchlets that
have given them the name horsetails.

Another vernacular name often used for these plants is "scouring rush." This derives from the harshness of the stems due to large deposits of silica in the cell walls. Campers still use horsetails for scouring their pots and pans.

Equisetum is circumpolar but extends as far south as Mexico. There are several species growing in sandy soils, along railroad embankments, in dry woods, meadows and marshes. *E. fluviatile* grows in ponds and sluggish streams, sometimes emergent, sometimes nearly or entirely submersed.

Ferns (Class Filicinae, Subphylum Pteropsida). Typically fern spores develop in sporangia borne on *fronds*, or leaves, of the green plant. Under suitable conditions of temperature and moisture a spore germinates, forming a small, green, flat *prothallus*. This inconspicuous sexual phase is the gametophyte, and bears on its under surface the sexual organs: the male *antheridia* and the female *archegonia*, each of which produce their respective sex cells. The egg remains in the archegonium after fertilization. Aquatic ferns have a greatly modified life cycle. *Marsilea*, for instance, has both macro- and microspores.

There are more than 8,000 species of ferns. Most of them are shade-loving, terrestrial plants. The beautiful Royal Fern, *Osmunda regalis*, often stands in the marshes and swales where it may grow profusely, reaching a height of six or more feet; and yet it is scarcely to be considered aquatic. Three fern families, however, are truly aquatic: the Marsileaceae (Fig. 24.6), the Salviniaceae (Fig. 24.5,8), and the Parkeriaceae which is represented in Florida and along the Gulf by two species of floating ferns of the genus *Ceratopteris*.

THE SEED PLANTS

The number of species of seed plants to be found growing in fresh waters is comparatively small considering the total number of terrestrial ones. The majority of these aquatic species belong to genera that are primarily on land. This is to be expected. After countless eons of adjustment the seed plants have become specialized for terrestrial life. The development of stiffening tissues, conducting tubes, stomata for respiration and transpiration, devices for bringing the sex cells together in fertilization, and the protection of the embyro within the resistant and nourishing seed would have been for naught were these plants to change their way of life again and live beneath the surface of the water. And yet, many species crowd the shoreline and many others consistently prefer the wet marshes, bogs or shallow, quiet waters; and several genera, and even a few small families, are wholly aquatic.

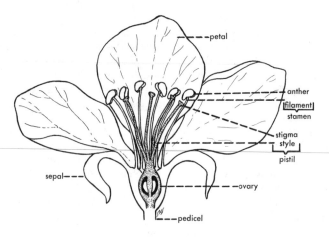

Fig. 15. Diagram of a flower, in section, to show structures. Since it has both male and female organs it is called a "perfect" flower.

The flowering plants (Class Angiospermae, Subphylum Pteropsida). Flowering plants reproduce typically by spores and sex cells. Vegetative reproduction is very common especially among the aquatics, many of which multiply by the formation of new shoots from underground rootstocks or by fragmentation. The conspicuous plant is the sporophyte. Both microspores and megaspores are formed within a reproductive organ, the *flower*. The microspores (called *pollen grains*) produce the males sex cells and the megaspores develop into female egg cells. The pollen grains are borne on the *anther* of the *stamen* and transported to the sticky top, or *stigma*, of the female *pistil*. There they pass down the *style* to the *ovary* where the fertilization of the egg takes place. Thus the gametophyte stage is not only very small but is usually of very short duration. If a flower produces both male and female sex cells it is called "perfect." If it bears only female cells it is a pistillate flower; if only male cells, a staminate flower.

CHARACTERISTICS OF AQUATIC PLANTS

Plants which have readapted to life in the water tend, in varying degrees, to have certain recognizable characteristics:

1. The submersed leaves are often ribbonlike or finely divided (Fig. 26). They thus offer less resistance to the force of the current but more surface area for absorption. A single plant may have submersed, floating and emergent leaves quite dissimilar. Submersed leaves are seldom bladed but if they are (as in some species of *Potamogeton*) the blades are sessile (without a petiole). Floating leaves tend to have a broad blade with margin entire (not toothed or lobed), and often a long petiole attached near the center of the leaf, either at the center of the blade or at the base of a deep incision. Thus the leaf is not easily overturned and may rise and fall with the changing water level.

When leaf shape varies within a single species and even on a single plant, the cause may be found in nutritional factors determined by the amount of light the plant receives. Submersed leaves of *Sagittaria* are often ribbonlike, whereas the floating leaves are dilated and blunt-tipped, and the emergent leaves broad and sagitate. Experiment has shown, however, that *Sagittaria* can be induced to put out ribbonlike aerial leaves if grown in dim light.

2. The epidermis is thin. It is usually covered with a cuticle. The cuticle of floating leaves is often hairy or waxy.

3. Conducting and stiffening tissues are greatly reduced. Aquatic plants obtain their minerals directly from the surrounding water, so conducting tissues from the root system are not needed to the extent that they are on land; and aquatic plants are supported by the buoyancy of the water.

4. Stomata are greatly reduced, nonfunctional or lacking. These minute openings, which in aerial leaves permit the exchange of carbon dioxide and oxygen and the transpiration of water, may be present on the upper surface of floating

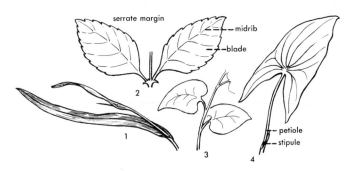

Fig. 16. Leaf terms. *1*, sheathing leaf; *2*, opposite leaves; *3*, alternate leaves; *4*, stipuled leaf.

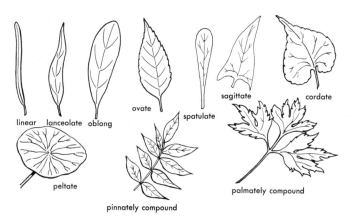

Fig. 17. Leaf shapes.

Fig. 18. Variations in leaf shape of *Sagittaria* (after Muenscher).

leaves. But they are not needed by submerged leaves that can carry on gaseous exchange through the cuticle, and if present would permit water to enter and "drown" the plant.

5. *Air-filled spaces are often present.* These may reach to the roots. Soluble carbon dioxide can easily pass through the cuticle. But there is less free oxygen in water than in the same volume of air, hence much of the oxygen used by submersed plants must be drawn from their own air spaces. It is this stored oxygen that many insects obtain when they puncture the tissues of aquatic plants, and it is in these air-filled spaces that some insects lay their eggs.

6. *Root hairs are absent.* Roots, too, are often dispensed with. These are needed by terrestrial plants in extracting water and mineral salts from the soil; they are not needed by aquatic plants.

7. *Sexual reproduction is usually of minor significance.* Propagation by creeping rootstocks or by fragmentation is more common. Flowers, when present, often grow on erect aerial shoots, or float on the surface. Sometimes the pistillate flower is floating or aerial but the staminate flower is submerged. The latter may then shoot to the surface on a long, coiled or elastic petiole; or break loose and float to the surface; or release smooth, buoyant pollen grains that float to the surface.

8. *Little or no secondary growth in stem thickness occurs.* The buoyancy of the water supports the stems.

ZONATION OF AQUATIC PLANTS

Water plants tend to grow in a definite pattern of zonation. This pattern is often quite regular.

1. Emergent water plants. These are rooted in the soil with their lower portions submersed. Some grow commonly in marshes or on the shore, though they may stand in as much as 6 to 7 feet of water. Most of their photosynthetic tissues are emergent. They are used for food and shelter by many water-loving animals, and as a means of entry and exit to and from the water.

2. Floating plants. These plants form a zone farther out in the water in depths ranging from a few inches to 8 or 9 feet. Most are rooted but a few are free-floating.

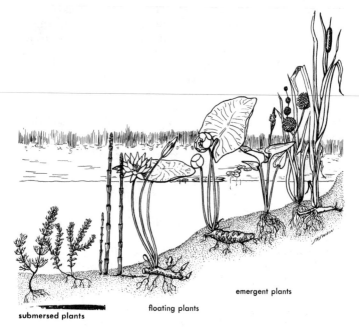

emergent plants

floating plants

submersed plants

Fig. 19. Diagram of Zonation at the Margin of a Pond.

3. *Submersed plants.* These often form large, dense masses, especially, in late summer. Enormous beds may sometimes be found considerable distances from the shore if the water is not too deep. These masses are of great importance to the life beneath the surface, since they provide shelter, food and materials for nest building. Their fragmentation may be the means of disseminating many sessile species of both plants and animals, and their decay restores organic material to the water and the substratum. The deposition of this organic material, however, decreases the depth of the water and may cause the choking of the stream or the filling-in of the pond or lake.

Grouping of Higher Plants

To facilitate identification some of the common seed plants and ferns are arranged according to their typical field habits and to easily observed characters, quite irrespective of their true relationships. However, many of those listed in Groups VI–XII may at times be emergent, and those of Groups II–VI may become stranded on land.

I. ROOTED ALONG THE SHORE, ERECT, OFTEN EMERGENT. Occasionally submersed or with floating leaves. Figs. 20–22.

II. FREE-FLOATING, REDUCED TO SIMPLE FRONDS. Fig. 23, in part.

III. FLOATING OR ROOTED, LEAVES IN ROSETTES, PETIOLES INFLATED. Figs. 23, 24, in part.

IV. FLOATING OR SUBMERSED, OFTEN ANCHORED BUT WITHOUT ROOTS, STEMS LEAFY. Fig. 24, in part.

V. ROOTED, LEAVES FLOATING, BROAD OR DISC-LIKE. Fig. 25.

VI. ROOTED, USUALLY SUBMERSED, LEAVES CLOVERLIKE, Fig. 24.6.

VII. ROOTED, USUALLY SUBMERSED, LEAVES DISSECTED, OFTEN IN WHORLS. Fig. 27.

VIII. ROOTED, USUALLY SUBMERSED, LEAVES SIMPLE, IN WHORLS. Fig 28, in part.

IX. ROOTED, USUALLY SUBMERSED, LEAVES

RIBBONLIKE or AWL-LIKE, FROM A BASAL ROSETTE. Fig. 28, in part.

X. ROOTED, USUALLY SUBMERSED, LEAVES SIMPLE AND OPPOSITE. Fig. 29.

XI. ROOTED, USUALLY SUBMERSED, LEAVES COMPOUND AND ALTERNATE. Fig. 30.

XII. ROOTED, USUALLY SUBMERSED, LEAVES SIMPLE AND ALTERNATE. Fig. 30.

I. Plants Rooted Along the Shore, Erect, Often Emergent

(Figs. 20–22)

These plants may occasionally be submersed or with floating leaves.

Cattails, *Typha* (Typhaceae). 4–8 ft. These plants (Fig. 20) spread by means of creeping rootstocks, often forming large stands several acres in extent, in marshes and shallow water. Their leaves are olive green, ribbonlike and quite stiff. The minute petalless flowers are thickly clustered on a long club-like spike the upper portion of which bears staminate flowers. These wither and drop after the pollen is shed, leaving the familiar inch-thick, brown club that bears the pistillate flowers. *T. latifolia* is widespread; *T. angustifolia*, with the two portions of the flowering spike separated, grows near the Atlantic Ocean. Other species.

Typha leaves are often crawling with aphids. They may also be mined by caterpillars of the moths *Arzama obliqua* and *Nonagria oblonga*, webbed by the caterpillar of the cattail moth *Lymnaecia phragmitella*, and punctured by the snout beetle *Colandra pertinax*. The stems may have *Arzama*, *Nonagria* and *Bellura* caterpillars and pupae living within long, water-filled burrows. In many places great stands of *Typha*, which provided a rich supply of food to birds and small mammals, have been replaced by the Eurasian *Phragmites* which, though beautiful to the eye as the great flowering panicles wave against the sky, are of little value to the animal population of the marsh.

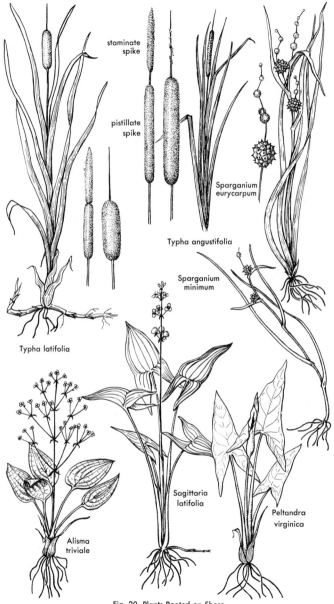

staminate spike

pistillate spike

Sparganium
eurycarpum

Typha angustifolia

Sparganium
minimum

Typha latifolia

Sagittaria
latifolia

Alisma
triviale

Peltandra
virginica

Fig. 20. Plants Rooted on Shore

Bur reeds, *Sparganium* (Sparganiaceae). 3–6 ft. The ribbon-like leaves and spherical flower clusters (Fig. 20) make this genus easy to recognize. The small spheres of staminate flowers are borne on the stem above the larger balls of pistillate flowers. The staminate flowers are fluffier and impermanent; the pistillate, which produce the closely packed wedge-shaped nutlets, are persistent. *Sparganium* often grows completely submerged. About 15 widespread species.

The noctuid caterpillar *Nonagria laeta* burrows in *Sparganium* stems.

Sweet Flag, *Acorus calamus* (Araceae). 1–3 ft. This aromatic relative of Jack-in-the-pulpit grows in shallow water of spring-fed marshes (Fig. 21). It may spread over great areas of dry land but in such places often does not flower. The grasslike leaves shoot up from a creeping rootstock. The tiny flowers grow on a yellowish-green spadix, or "jack," from the side of the leaflike tapering stem. The spadix is unsheathed; i.e., it has no spathe, or "pulpit."

Arrow-arum, *Peltandra* (Araceae). 1–2 ft. The arrow-arums (Fig. 20) grow on the margins of ponds and slow streams. The arrow-shaped leaves, each with a heavy central vein, grow from a basal cluster. The spathe has a wavy margin. The whitish spadix bears staminate flowers on its upper portion and pistillate ones below. *P. virginica* of the eastern states produces green fruit; the southeastern *P. luteospadix* has a whitish spathe and yellowish-orange spadix.

Golden Club, *Orontium aquaticum* (Araceae). 1–2 ft. This arum (Fig. 21) grows in ponds and tidal flats. The lanceolate leaves grow from a basal cluster; they are frequently floating, sometimes entirely submersed. The slender, golden spadix, which bears the tiny flowers, is unsheathed since the spathe is greatly reduced in size. The fruit is green. Atlantic coastal region, occasionally inland.

Wild Calla, *Calla palustris* (Araceae). 1 ft. The wild calla is restricted to cold, spring-fed ponds, brooks and bogs all across the north, south to Minn. and N. J. The broadly heart-

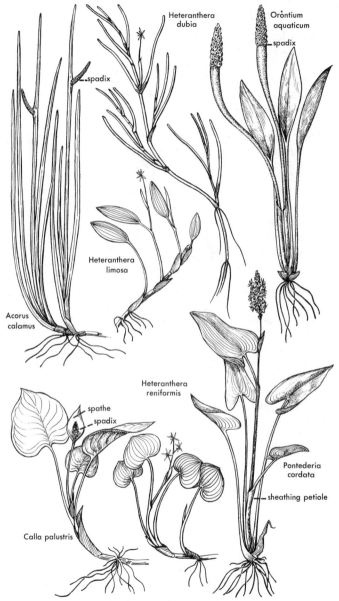

Heteranthera
dubia

Orontium
aquaticum

spadix

spadix

Heteranthera
limosa

Acorus
calamus

Heteranthera
reniformis

spathe
spadix

Pontederia
cordata

sheathing petiole

Calla palustris

Fig. 21. Plants Rooted on Shore or Emergent

shaped leaves, growing from a creeping rootstock, are often floating. The yellow spadix is shorter than that of the Golden Club and Sweet Flag; its upper flowers are staminate, its lower ones pistillate. The spathe is oval, 2–5 cm. long, and white on its upper surface. The fruit is red. Both insects and snails aid in its pollination.

Water Plantain, *Alisma* (Alismataceae). 1–3 ft. Water plantains grow in shallow water and muddy ditches but adapt easily to the shoreline. The leaf blades vary from oblong to lanceolate or even linear; they are sometimes floating. The small white or pinkish flowers are borne singly on a many-branched stem. *A. triviale* (formerly thought to be the European *plantago-aquatica*) is widespread. The northern *A. gramineum* has long-petioled, elliptical leaves and is more often submersed, preferring alkaline water. Other species and other genera.

Arrowheads, *Sagittaria* (Alismataceae). Up to 4 ft. The leaves of arrowheads (Fig. 20) vary in size and shape with the species, the depth of water in which the plant is growing, and the subsequent amount of light it receives. The plants adjust easily to changing water levels; when stranded on the bank the narrow ribbonlike leaves of the submerged stem drop off and wider, arrow-shaped ones develop. The 3-petaled flowers grow in three whorls, the lowermost of which is composed of pistillate flowers. Many species; the commonest and most widespread is *S. latifolia.*

Dragonflies and snails frequently visit the flowers and may effect pollination; the latter eat the petals. Caterpillars of the noctuid *Plusia verrisa* and many other species live in intimate association with these plants.

Pickerelweed, *Pontederia cordata* (Pontederiaceae). 3 ft. Pickerelweeds (Fig. 21; Pl. 1) are extremely common in shallow water and on soft, muddy shores. The leaves are cordate or sagittate, occasionally linear, with fleshy, sheathing petioles; they rise in clusters from the creeping rootstock. The 3-inch spikes of blue flowers surmount the single, small leaf of the flower stem. Pickerelweed may become a pest, choking small streams and shallow ponds. West to Minn. and Okla. *P. lanceolata* occurs in Fla. and Texas, rarely north to Del. *Arzama* caterpillars bore in its stems.

Mud Plantain, *Heteranthera* (Pontederiaceae). 3–6 in. Mud plantains (Fig. 21) have a small, usually solitary, flower that rises from the spathe on the side or base of a leaf petiole. The commonest species is the Stargrass, *H. dubia,* of quiet, calcareous waters. Its flower is yellow, and its leaves linear, often mostly submersed. Other species have blue or white flowers and either reniform or oblong leaf blades.

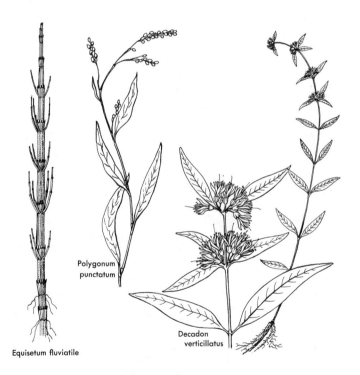

Polygonum
punctatum

Decadon
verticillatus

Equisetum fluviatile

Fig. 22. Plants Rooted on Shore or Emergent

Smartweeds, knotweeds, *Polygonum* (Polygonaceae). This genus, with jointed stem (Fig. 22), has its marsh, bog and pond species as well as those of seacoast and rocky, dry soils. They are sometimes erect and emergent; sometimes their topmost leaves are floating. When water levels fluctuate the plants may form tangled, floating mats. The bright, rose-colored, buckwheatlike flowers are often conspicuous.

Horsetails, *Equisetum* (Equisetaceae). For horsetails (Fig. 22) see page 66.

Other plants. Many other plants, such as the Water Willow, *Decadon* (Fig. 22), the Water Parsnip, *Sium suave,* and others too numerous to mention, may be found in the water along the shore, having crept out from their stand in wet woods and lowlands.

II. Plants Free-floating, Reduced to Simple Fronds
(Fig. 23, in part)

Duckweeds, *Lemna* (Lemnaceae), 2–12 mm. In midsummer *Lemna* (Pl. 1) often forms a green blanket on ponds and ditches and along the quiet edges of lakes and slow-moving rivers; or it may cover the mucky shore, lining the footprints where cows come down to drink. The plant body consists of a single frond or of a few small, flat fronds, each with one to five "veins" and each with a single, trailing root. Flowers are rare, for the normal method of reproduction is fission or budding. If flowers are present, they appear in a cluster of three in a pouch on the upper surface or edge of a frond. In the fall, tiny mats of green scales break away from the fronds and drop to the bottom where they overwinter. *L. minor,* the Lesser Duckweed, is the commonest species. *L. trisulca,* the Ivy-leaved Duckweed, has fronds 6–12 mm. long, often stalked, and often connected in zigzag chains that float just beneath the surface. Other species.

An ephydrid fly, *Lemnaphila scotlandae,* lays its eggs on the upper surface of the tiny fronds, its larvae boring into the thallus and its adults eating out parallel rows across its surface. A rhyncophorus beetle, *Tanysphyrus lemnae,* also

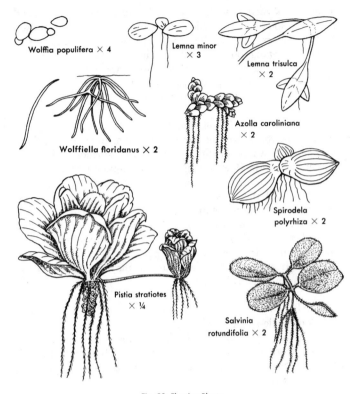

Wolffia populifera × 4

Lemna minor × 3

Lemna trisulca × 2

Wolffiella floridanus × 2

Azolla caroliniana × 2

Spirodela polyrhiza × 2

Pistia stratiotes × ¼

Salvinia rotundifolia × 2

Fig. 23. Floating Plants

lays its eggs on the upper surface, plugging in the holes with pellets of frass; the emerging larva then mines within the thallus. These two insects are probably obligatory parasites; but Dr. Minna B. Scotland has shown that there are many other species of insects that may lay their eggs in *Lemna* by chance, the emerging larvae then remaining there to feed. One little pyralid moth, *Neocataclysta,* makes its case out of the tiny fronds, as does the larva of a limnophilid caddis fly. Snails lay their eggs on them and hydras and planarians browse over their surface.

Greater duckweeds, *Spirodela* (Lemnaceae). 5–10 mm.

These duckweeds also form a blanket of green on pools and marshes, sometimes so thick as to prevent light penetration to the waters below. The fronds are not only larger than those of *Lemna* but are distinguished by being purple beneath; each has 4 to 15 "veins" and bears 2 or more roots. The common, widespread species of stagnant pools and streams is *S. polyrhiza*. Other species.

Water Meal, *Wolffia* (Lemnaceae). 1–2 mm. These, the smallest of the flowering plants, resemble green grains floating on the water or just beneath the surface. The tiny flowers are formed in a pouch on the upper surface of the fronds. The plants may become very abundant during June and July and then disappear. In the winter they thrive on the mud or damp vegetation at the pond bottom. *W. columbiana* has globular fronds; it is common in the eastern and central states. *W. punctata* and *W. papulifera* have ellipsoidal fronds, the former with upper surface flattened, the latter with upper surface low-conical; they are found in the southern and central states.

Wolffiella, *Wolffiella floridana* (Lemnaceae). 6–8 mm. The slender, sickle-shaped or linear green fronds of this species are stemless and rootless, usually clumped together in star-shaped masses. It is found in ponds, ditches and sluggish streams of the southeast, occasionally north to Mass., usually with *Lemna*.

Water Fern or Floating Moss, *Salvinia rotundifolia* (Salviniaceae). Leaves are ⅜ in. in diameter. This rapidly spreading, tropical fern has become established in ditches and ponds in a few scattered places. It occasionally turns up in old aquaria and artificial pools. The paired leaves are often folded along the midrib and may be heart-shaped at the base; they are blue-green with the upper surface covered with forked, water-resistant, white hairs. The brown, feathery, rootlike appendages hanging from the under surface are not true roots but represent a vestigial, third leaf. The spore capsules are borne in clusters of four at the leaf axils.

Mosquito fern, Water Velvet, *Azolla* (Salviniaceae). ½ in.

or less. Mosquito ferns are often found in association with the blue-green alga *Anabaena*. The tiny green fronds float on quiet waters forming a carpet of velvet, or they may be stranded on the mud along the shore. They occasionally grow in brackish water. The two-lobed leaves lie in overlapping rows resembling the leaves at the tip of an arbor-vitae stem. They are bright green when growing in the shade but autumnal red when exposed to the sun. This is a widespread southern fern which has moved northward and westward although it is killed by northern winters. *A. caroliniana* is the common species; one other is found rarely.

III. Plants Floating or Rooted, Leaves in Rosettes, Petioles Inflated

(Figs. 23, 24 in part)

Water Hyacinth, *Eichornia* (Pontederiacae). Leaves 3–10 cm. The lovely lavender flowers of this pickerelweed relative (Fig. 24) make a showy mass of color. The leaf rosettes have fibrous, branching roots that sometimes become anchored. The leaves when emergent are broadly ovate with short, bladderlike petioles. Introduced, probably from South or Central America, this plant has become a serious pest in Florida and along the Gulf. There it grows luxuriantly in ditches, ponds and slow streams, covering the water and hindering navigation. It has also become established in California but its spread northward will be inhibited because it is easily winter-killed. Great floating islands of the plant may move in and out with tidal waters. Its tangled roots may be inhabited by large numbers of aquatic animals. Conger eels, salamanders and water snakes are frequently collected by hauling in great masses of the water hyacinth and dumping them on the shore or pier. One little orchid, *Habeneria nepens,* grows in the decaying mats. *E. crassipes* is the common species. *E. paniculata*, also introduced from Brazil and now naturalized, grows rooted in the mud; its petioles are not inflated.

Water Chestnut, *Trapa natans* (Trapaceae). 2 ft. The long stems of Water Chestnut bearing plumelike leaves (Fig. 24)

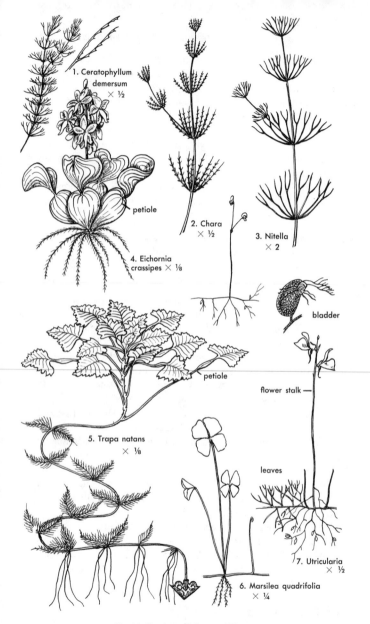

1. Ceratophyllum demersum × ½

2. Chara × ½

3. Nitella × 2

4. Eichornia crassipes × ⅛

petiole

5. Trapa natans × ⅛

petiole

bladder

flower stalk —

leaves

6. Marsilea quadrifolia × ¼

7. Utricularia × ½

Fig. 24. Floating or Submerged Plants

at each submersed node, are rooted in the mud. The floating leaves are coarsely serrate, with upper surface glossy and under surface hairy. The petioles are slightly inflated. The plant produces one-seeded, spiny nuts which, when mature, drop to the bottom; there the seeds remain viable all winter. The genus is the sole representative of a European and tropical Asian and African family. It grows in canals, backwaters, bays and rivers, in water from 3 to 15 feet deep; Mass. and N. Y. and the lower Potomac.

Water Lettuce, *Pistia stratiotes* (Araceae). Leaves 1–4 in. The fleshy, furrowed or plaited leaves, rising from a short vertical stem, form rosettes (Fig. 23); these rosettes are often connected to one another by rootstocks. The tiny flowers, like those of the other arums, are on a spadix surrounded by a whitish spathe. In the tropics the plant is common, often covering the surface of the water. It floats on the waters of ponds, sluggish streams and ditches in Fla. and along the Gulf. Many insects, including mosquitoes, lay their eggs and find shelter amidst the basal leaves.

IV. Plants, Floating or Submersed, Often Anchored But Without Roots, Stems Leafy
(Fig. 24, in part)

Hornwort, Coontail, *Ceratophyllum* (Ceratophyllaceae). Up to 2 ft. Masses of *Ceratophyllum* (Fig. 24) are usually found in shallow water of ponds and slow streams, often well out from shore, sometimes forming pure stands. It is the dominant plant of temporary and newly made ponds and lakes where the water is rich in organic material. The 3-forked, filamentous, rigid leaves grow in whorls from the floating branches which may become snarled in other vegetation or anchored in the mud. In the late summer the ends of the branches break off and fall to the bottom; in the spring they rise to the surface. *C. demersum* is widespread; its leaves are slightly serrate. *C. echinatum* is eastern; its leaves are entire. Waterfowl are attracted to this plant and *Arzama* caterpillars feed upon it.

Bladderwort, *Utricularia* (Lentibulariaceae). These are small, delicate plants (Fig. 24). They may have floating stems, submersed stems, or stems that creep along the bottom. The leaves are usually filiform or finely dissected, arranged alternately or in whorls. In most species the leaves have tiny bladders and these, when present, are a sure means of identification. These tiny bladders not only aid the stems in keeping afloat but serve as traps for the capture of small organisms from which the plant gains nourishment. The flowers, rising several inches above the surface, are blue, purple, yellow or white; though small and inconspicuous they often give a bright splotch of a color to an otherwise drab, muddy shore. There are more than a dozen species scattered throughout the eastern and southern states; in pools, ditches, slow streams, floating bogs or sandy shores.

See also *Chara* and *Nitella* (p. 42).

V. Plants Rooted, Leaves Floating, Broad or Disclike
(Fig. 25)

Water lilies, *Nymphaea* (Nymphaceae). White water lilies live in stagnant pools and ponds or in slow-moving streams. The disclike leaves, measuring from 2 inches to 2 feet in diameter, are deeply notched. The petiole rises from the base of the notch and the veins radiate from the petiole, branching near the leaf margin. During the summer, long, rubbery flower and leaf stems rise from the rootstock that lies in the muddy bottom, permitting the flowers and leaves to float on the surface. In the winter they withdraw to the bottom so that the fruits may mature beneath the surface. The common *N. odorata* of the eastern half of the country has white, exquisitely fragrant flowers opening usually from about seven in the morning until shortly after midday. The underside of the 5–9-inch leaves are purplish. *N. tuberosa*, of the eastern and central states and the far northwest, has odorless, white flowers that open from eight to three or longer; its leaves are all green. Many invertebrates are associated with these flowers (see *Nuphar*, below). There are a few other less common species.

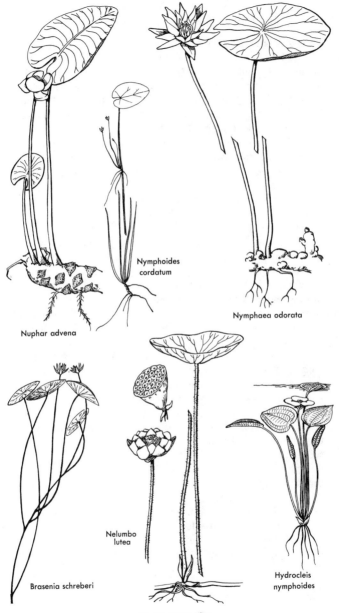

Nymphoides
cordatum

Nuphar advena

Nymphaea odorata

Brasenia schreberi

Nelumbo
lutea

Hydrocleis
nymphoides

Fig. 25. Water Lilies

Yellow Water Lily or Spatterdock, *Nuphar* (Nymphaceae). The leaves of the yellow flowered water lily are oval, 1–8 inches long, with the petiole rising from the base of the notch and the veins from the midrib. The flowers, smaller than those of Nymphaea, may be in bloom all summer. *N. sagittifolium* of sluggish streams and ponds of the southeast has the leaf blade less than half as wide as long; the several other species have it more than half as wide as long. *N. advena* is widespread from the Atlantic to the Miss. and may even be found in tidal flats. *N. polysepalum* grow west of the Rockies.

Caterpillars of *Paraponyx* live in cases cut from water-lily leaves; *Arzama diffusa,* the Brown-tail Diver caterpillar, and *A. vulnifica,* the Black-tail Diver of Florida, live in water-filled burrows in the petioles; the scatophagid fly *Hydromyza confluens* lives during its larval and pupal stages in the submersed petioles, the emerging adult having to leave through a trapdoor in the epidermis in order to float to the surface to take wing. It is related to the *Hydromyza* that lives in the water in the pitchers of the Pitcher Plant, *Sarracenia,* feeding on trapped insects. At almost any time during the summer pairs of the beetle, *Galerucella nymphaea,* are to be found *in copula* on its leaves and the *Donacia* water beetles feeding and mating upon it. The female *Donacia* oviposits upon the flower stem beneath the water level, or on the under surface of a leaf.

American Lotus, *Nelumbo lutea* (Nymphaceae). The enormous leaves of this lotus are sometimes 3 feet in diameter; they differ from those of the two preceding species but resemble those of *Brasenia,* in being peltate; they are sometimes emergent and saucerlike. The flowers, 4–10 inches in diameter, are yellow. Its seeds and tuberous rootstock were used by Indians for food. The large, top-shaped receptacles, with holes marking the location of the seeds, are popular in dried flower arrangements. It grows in scattered localities throughout the eastern states.

Water Shield, *Brasenia schreberi* (Nymphaceae). The peltate leaves of the water shield are from 1 to less than 4 inches in diameter; they are oval or elliptic rather than round and are sticky on the underside. The flowers are purple, each forming a 2-seeded nutlet that opens by a lid. Chiefly eastern, in ponds and sluggish water of high acidity, where the bottom is sandy or covered with decomposing vegetation. It often grows profusely with its long slender leaf stems intertwined. Occasionally found in far west.

VI. Plants Rooted, Mostly Submersed, Leaves Cloverlike
(Fig. 24.6)

Pepperwort, *Marsilea quadrifolia* (Marsileaceae, a fern family). This fern lives in shallow, quiet water, rooted in the mud and sending up long leaf stems to permit the four-lobed cloverlike leaves to float on or near the surface. Each leaflet is up to 1¾ cm. long. At night opposite pairs of leaflets often fold face to face. Purplish-brown, bean-shaped spore capsules are borne on short stalks rising from the rootstock or near the base of the petiole.

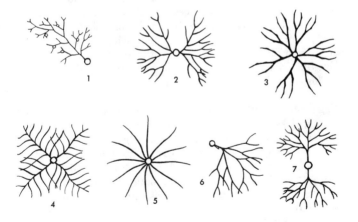

Fig. 26. Diagram of cross section of stems to show arrangement of dissected leaves about the stem (partially after Muenscher). *1, Utricularia; 2, Bidens; 3, Ceratophyllum; 4, Myriophyllum; 5, Chara; 6, Ranunculus; 7, Cabomba.*

VII. Plants Rooted, Mostly Submersed, Leaves Dissected, Often in Whorls

(Figs. 26, 27)

Water Milfoil, *Myriophyllum* (Haloragaceae). Sometimes up to 3 feet long. The leaves are finely dissected, at least on the lower part of the stem, although in *M. tenellum* they are reduced to small blunt scales; pinnately branched rather than forked, as in others of this grouping; and whorled or opposite on the stem. When the plant disintegrates in the fall a small round, cylindrical roll of unexpanded shoots persists, drops to the bottom and overwinters. Many insects feed upon the milfoil. *M. heterophyllum* is widespread; ten or more other species have a spotty distribution; *M. brasiliense*, the "parrot's feather" of aquarium dealers, is imported from Brazil but has become established around N. Y.

Fanwort, *Cabomba caroliniana* (Nymphaceae). Up to a foot or more in length. This plant slightly resembles hornwort but is actually related to the water lilies. This relationship can be appreciated when one sees the occasional small, peltate floating blades. The finely dissected, sometimes gelatinous leaves are petioled and opposite. The white flowers, 4/5 of an inch in diameter, are spotted with yellow. Grows in ponds and quiet backwaters in the east and south. Commonly sold as "fish grass" for use in aquaria.

Beggar-ticks, *Bidens* (Compositae). Up to 4 ft. The familiar beggar-ticks are often seen in low, damp places. *B. bidentoides* is common on tidal flats and shores of the northern Atlantic states, sometimes working up into fresh waters. *B. beckii*, the yellow-flowered Water Marigold (now in the genus *Megalodonta*) is a true aquatic, living submersed in ponds, lakes and sluggish streams. Its showy flowers rise above the surface. Many other species in swampy places.

Buttercups, crowfoots, *Ranunculus* (Ranunculaceae). Several of these have dissected leaves, but the leaves are alternate, with a basal stipule embracing the stem. The floating leaves

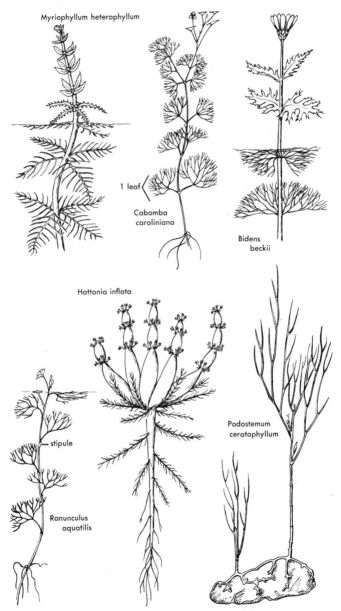

Myriophyllum heterophyllum

1 leaf

Cabomba
caroliniana

Bidens
beckii

Hottonia inflata

stipule

Ranunculus
aquatilis

Podostemum
ceratophyllum

Fig. 27. Rooted Plants with Submersed, Dissected Leaves

are undissected and usually palmately lobed. Flowers yellow
or white. Many species.

Featherfoil, Water Velvet, *Hottonia inflata* (Primulaceae).
Stems to 6 inches. Plants are easily recognized by their
feathery leaves which rise alternately from the very thick
stems, and by the whorl of white flowers borne on a cluster
of hollow or inflated stems. Found in pools and ditches west
to Mo. and Texas.

Riverweeds, *Podostemum* (Podostemaceae). Stems up to 30
inches. Distinct from others in this group in that it has rigid,
filiform leaves rising from nodes on the creeping rootstock.
It grows in fast water where it is anchored to stones or to
the hard substratum by rootlike processes or discs. Several
species, from Maine to Texas and southwest.

See also Groups IV and XI.

VIII. Plants Rooted, Mostly Submersed, Leaves Simple, in Whorls
(Fig. 28)

Mare's Tail, *Hippuris vulgaris* (Hippuridaceae). Leaves
1–10 cm. Like *Myriophyllum,* to which it is related, the
leaves of Mare's Tail are whorled but they are small and
simple. Widespread in rivers, streams, ditches and marshy
ponds in cool regions. In the St. Lawrence it sometimes grows
in swiftly flowing channels.

Waterweed, Frogbit, *Anacharis* (Hydrocharitaceae). Although normally rooted, the plants may break loose and form
large, floating mats. *A. canadensis,* with leaves averaging
2 mm. in width, is the common widespread species; often a
pest in waterways. *A. densa,* a large commercial species with
leaves 3–5 mm. wide, has become naturalized in many places.
A. occidentalis, with leaves averaging 1.3 mm. in width,
occasionally has leaves opposite, not whorled; it grows in
noncalcareous waters in the northeastern and central states.
Formerly known as *Elodea.*

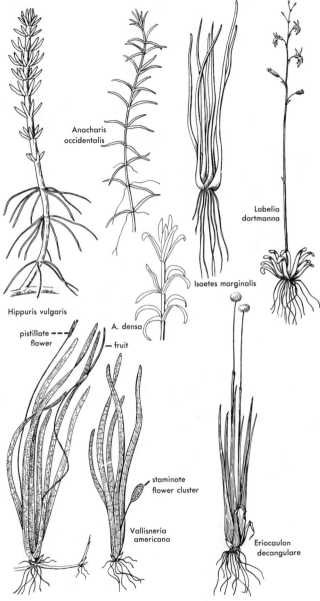

Anacharis
occidentalis

Lobelia
dortmanna

Isoetes marginalis

Hippuris vulgaris

pistillate - - -
flower

A. densa

— fruit

staminate
flower cluster

Vallisneria
americana

Eriocaulon
decangulare

Fig. 28. Rooted Plants with Submersed, Linear Leaves

IX. Plants Rooted, Mostly Submersed, Leaves Ribbonlike or Awl-like, from a Basal Rosette
(Fig. 28)

Quillworts, *Isoetes* (Isoetaceae). 1 ft. and over. The bright green, olive or reddish quill-like leaves are usually rigid, but occasionally are flaccid and floating. They emerge in a spiral from a short bulblike stem (*corm*). The plants may be completely submerged or, when waters are low, may form tufted, grassy meadows. In clear reservoirs they may grow 15 feet under water as well as along the gravelly shore. There are some 15 species of local distribution in our area but only *I. muricata* is common and widespread. Cattle and deer feed on the leaves, and muskrats and waterfowl on the fleshy corms.

Pipewort, button rods, *Eriocaulon* (Eriocaulaceae). The awl-shaped leaves rise in a rosette or bunch from a very short stem; they may be semitranslucent. The flowers form a depressed head on tall central stems. The few aquatic species grow in wet depressions in pine-barren ponds, swamps and tidal flats along the Atlantic coast and Great Lakes regions.

Plantain, *Littorella* (Plantaginaceae). The true plantain, *Plantago*, has one species, *P. maritima*, that grows in salt marshes and tidal pools but no truly aquatic species. *Littorella americana*, a close relative, grows in shallow ponds and lakes in a few places in the northeast, west to Minn. It differs from the two preceding members of this group in having the rosettes growing from nodes in a creeping rootstock rather than from a single bulblike stem. It differs from *Vallisneria*, below, in having awl-like rather than ribbonlike leaves. It might be confused with *Ranunculus flamula*.

Eel grass, wild celery, *Vallisneria* (Hydrocharitaceae). Up to 3 ft. or over. In addition to *Anacharis*, the Frogbit family includes several tropical and marine genera that occasionally get into fresh waters in Florida and the Gulf states. It also includes *Vallisneria*, commonly found in lakes and streams throughout the eastern half of the country. The clusters of ribbonlike leaves grow from nodes of a creeping rootstock; individual leaves sometimes reach a length of 3 or more feet with their upper part floating. Staminate flowers grow in a cluster within a spathe borne on a short stem at the base of the leaf cluster. When mature they will break loose and rise to float on the surface where they will gather about the solitary, floating pistillate flower. The pistillate flower is borne on a long stem which permits it to float until after pollination and then contracts, pulling the developing fruit down into the water. Although *Vallisneria* periodically grows so profusely that it chokes waterways it is nevertheless frequently planted since its fleshy stems and fruits provide excellent food for waterfowl. *Paraponyx* caterpillars and several species of caddis fly larvae may live in cases cut out from its leaves.

Water Lobelia, *Lobelia dortmanna* (Lobeliaceae). Occasionally found in acid ponds in northeastern and northwestern states as well as in the Great Lakes region. Its clustered, decurved, ribbonlike leaves grow in a single clump. The characteristically tubed flowers grow alternately on a foot-long stem that rises from the water.

See also: species of *Sparganium*, *Sagittaria*, *Ranunculus* and *Podostemum*.

X. Plants Rooted, Mostly Submersed, Leaves Simple and Opposite
(Fig. 29)

Waterworts, *Elatine* (Elatinaceae). Leaf less than 1 cm. long. The stems are usually partly buried in sand or mud of ponds and slow streams. Clusters of rootlets grow at the nodes. The leaves are ovate or spatulate; the flowers solitary, developing in the leaf axils.

Water starworts. *Callitriche* (Callitrichaceae). These low, slender, often tufted herbs have linear or spatulate leaves which are more crowded toward the tip of the stem. The stems are limp and are either supported by the water or lie prostrate on the mud. Some species live in quiet, calcareous waters, others in brackish or running water.

Naiads, *Najas* (Najadaceae). The naiads are sometimes called the bushy pondweeds because of their tufted stems. They resemble *Anacharis* in general appearance but have linear leaves that are widened at the base, coarsely or finely toothed, and with a conspicuous basal sheath. The flowers

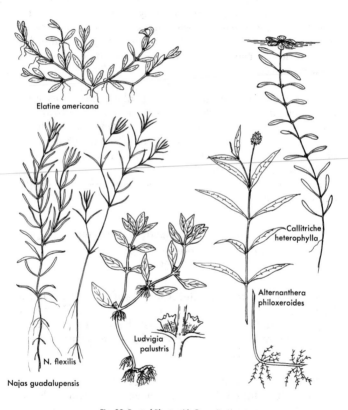

Fig. 29. Rooted Plants with Opposite Leaves

are inconspicuous, borne in the axil of the leaves. Eight or more species, varying considerably in size.

Alligator Weed, *Alternanthera* (Amaranthaceae). These creeping plants with net-veined leaves sometimes form floating mats. They are abundant locally in ponds, ditches and sluggish streams of the southeast where they may crowd out other plants and in dry seasons cover the banks.

False Loosestrife, *Ludwigia* (Onagraceae). Leaf more than 2 cm. long. *L. palustris,* also called Water Purslane, is widespread in ponds, streams and marshes where it may be rooted in the mud or may form floating mats. It also carpets wet shores. It is best recognized by the flower, in which the sepals, petals and stamens are borne at the top of the ovary to which the calyx tube is fused; the flowers are borne in leaf bracts. Three other species with alternately placed leaves are found in the southeast.

XI. Plants Rooted, Mostly Submersed, Leaves Alternate and Compound
(Fig. 30)

Water Cress, *Nasturtium officinale* (Crucifera). Stems 1–3 cm. long. The compound leaves each have 5 to 11 round or elliptical leaflets. The creeping stems often have slender roots hanging from the nodes, giving the plant a rooty appearance. Flowers are white, on slender pedicels and growing in a raceme; they produce long, slender, curved capsules. Plants often form tangled masses which break loose to form floating mats. This is the water cress of the market, introduced from Europe and now naturalized in cold, spring-fed brooks and ponds.

Lake Cress, *Armoracia aquatica* (Crucifera). The submersed leaves are deeply divided, the lowermost ones finely dissected; although occasional emergent ones will be barely serrate along the margins. This cress also roots freely at the nodes. The white flowers grow in racemes and form linear,

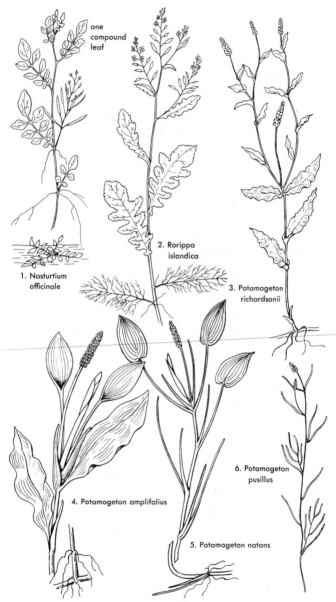

one
compound
leaf

1. Nasturtium
officinale

2. Rorippa
islandica

3. Potamogeton
richardsonii

4. Potamogeton amplifolius

5. Potamogeton natans

6. Potamogeton
pusillus

Fig. 30. Rooted Plants with Alternate Leaves

ovoid capsules. Found east of the Mississippi in soft, muddy bottom of backwaters, lakes and quiet streams.

Yellow Cress, *Rorippa* (Crucifera). Several species of cresses with yellow or greenish flowers may have compound leaves. Some are simple, some divided.

XII. Plants Rooted, Mostly Submersed, Leaves Alternate and Simple
(Fig. 30)

Pondweeds, *Potamogeton* (Potamogetonaceae). This is a large genus all of whose members are aquatic. It belongs to an aquatic family that includes the brackish and alkaline water *Ruppia,* the Widgeon Grass with slender, needlelike leaves (loved of waterfowl); *Zannichellia,* the Horned Pondweed, with needlelike leaves rising from stipuled nodes; and the common marine *Zostera.* The potamogetons themselves are everywhere abundant and of great variety. The 40 to 50 species range in leaf form from orbicular to hairlike. If one has doubt as to the identity of the plant in hand, and if it has alternately placed leaves, either sheathed or stipuled, and has jointed stems, the chances are good that it is a *Potamogeton.*

Caterpillars of *Paraponyx* live in cases made of its leaves and caterpillars of *Acentropis* may live in dense silken webs upon it; ephydrid fly larvae, *Hydrellia,* mine in its leaves; and birds, muskrats, beaver, deer and moose feed consistently on it.

CHAPTER 6

Sponges—Phylum Porifera
Fig. 31; Pl. 10

NO handsome bath sponges can be gathered from the shores or substrata of our ponds and streams; but small, freshwater sponges are to be found, sometimes covering an area of only a few square centimeters, sometimes spreading over a surface forty times that size. They differ from the marine forms in that they usually live but a single season, reaching their peak in July or August. As a rule they die and disintegrate long before winter, leaving small winter buds to survive the period of cold; but occasionally they are to be seen prosperous and green all winter, sometimes even thriving beneath the ice.

Like their marine relatives they live in colonies, forming hemispherical lobed cushions, small dactylate masses, or thin encrusting patches. When conditions are favorable, which means gently moving or clear water, low in calcium and containing plenty of microscopic organisms on which they may feed, sponges may cover every available surface: stones, logs, timber, etc. They may even encrust the insides of water pipes, sometimes to the point of retarding the flow of water. They are not common in very fast water and are seldom found in water over 6 feet deep, although they have been reported as deep as 100 feet. They are easily spread through a single drainage system and their spicules are transported by the wind as well as on the bodies of insects and wading birds.

Sponges do not require sunlight and thus are often on the undersides of submerged objects. Some, however, do grow

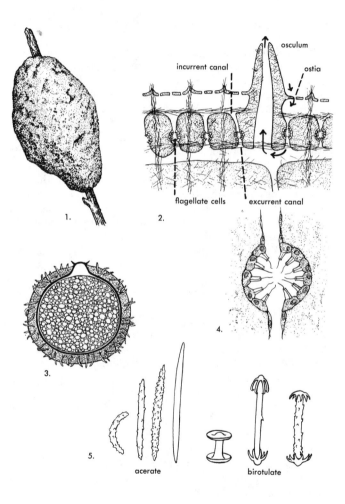

Fig. 31. Sponges. 1. *Spongilla* attached to a stick. 2. Diagram of portion of body wall. 3. Diagram of gemmule. 4. Enlargement of flagellated cells. 5. Types of spicules. (2–4 after Pennak.)

in sunlight, often becoming quite green from the presence of the alga *Chlorella* which at such times lives symbiotically within the tissues. These same sponge species when growing in dim light are pale yellowish, tan, flesh-colored, reddish or white.

Sponges have no organs. They are made up of loose, reticular tissues supported by siliceous spicules. The *dermal spicules* are scattered irregularly through the living tissues; while the *skeletal spicules* are bound in bundles. The outside of the sponge has two kinds of openings: many microscopic *ostia* in the outer membrane, and a few, larger *oscula* located typically at the ends of *lobes*, or chimneys. Water enters through the ostia into a subdermal cavity and then, by means of many *incurrent canals*, into a chamber lined with flagellate cells. It is then forced, by the waving of the flagella, through another series of canals, the *excurrent canals*, into the central cavity of the sponge, and then to the outside through an osculum. Although sponges vary in their degree of complexity the basic pattern of activity is the same.

Food. Water, sweeping into the ostia, carries microscopic organisms that serve as food for the sponge. These organisms are captured by the flagellate cells (which resemble mastigophorans) and are digested in the undifferentiated mesoglea beneath.

Respiration. The exchange of carbon dioxide and oxygen, and the discharge of waste materials, takes place primarily through the epidermis.

Reproduction. Reproduction may be sexual or asexual. During the summer an egg or a large number of sperm cells develop within special reproductive organs. The egg is retained within one of the internal cavities but the sperm are swept out through the osculum and are eventually drawn into the ostia of the same or other sponges, where fertilization takes place. The newly formed embryos swim out and settle down to form new colonies. Reproduction is also accomplished by the production of winter buds, called *statoblasts* or *gemmules*. These, ranging in size from 150 to 1,000 microns, are white, or brownish, spherical, spicule-covered clusters of cells that are scattered about through the body of the sponge and are freed upon its disintegration at the ap-

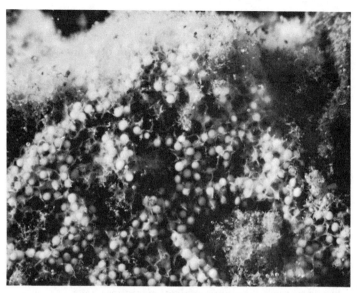

Gemmules of the sponge *Spongilla*.

Hydra stretching out from the underside of the surface film.

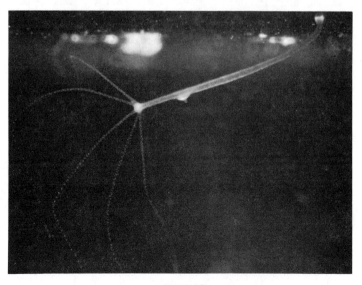

PLATE 10

proach of winter (Pl. 10). They are highly resistant to adverse conditions and they overwinter easily, sometimes remaining viable for three or more years.

A sponge is capable of a small amount of contractility but otherwise remains passively attached to the substratum, awaiting what comes its way in the water that gently flows through its body. Tiny insects and worms may live within its tissues, sometimes burrowing and sometimes merely taking advantage of the shelter it provides. Chief and most consistent of these are the larvae of the Spongilla flies (Fig. 49) that live only within the tissues of the sponge.

Collecting. The collector is seldom interested in taking an entire colony. But its general appearance and form should be noted, and a small piece should be removed for preservation in alcohol or formalin, or carefully dried. Identification requires the microscopic examination of the spicules of both the sponge body and the gemmules. They may be *acerate,* which means they are long and slender, cylindrical, and narrowed at each end; or *birotulate,* cylindrical, with a disc or *rotule* at each end. According to Dr. Minna Jewell the best way to separate the spicules from the surrounding tissue is to macerate a fragment of the sponge, leave it for 12 hours in nitric acid and then wash it in water. Since culturing sponges in an aquarium is not always practical, a trip into the field in the fall, possibly as late as November, will be necessary for gathering the gemmules. These may then be cultured on a glass slide immersed in clean natural water kept at room temperature and out of direct sunlight.

Grouping of Subfamilies of Sponges*

GEMMULE SPICULES ACERATE OR LACKING

Spongillinae. *Spongilla* has all spicules (skeletal, dermal and gemmule) acerate. There are several species of local distribution in addition to the worldwide *S. lacustris* and *S. fragilis.* The former has long, finger-like branches; it is often greenish, with a fishy or

---

* Identification can not be based on appearance because all sponges exhibit great variability. Even the spicule characters usually used are unreliable.

garlicky odor. The latter forms a thin-edged, encrusting circular patch, 1 or more inches thick. In standing or running water. Two other uncommon genera.

GEMMULE SPICULES BIROTULATE

Meyeninae. *Corvomeyenia* has dermal spicules birotulate; *Asteromeyenia* and *Dosilia* have them stellate. *Meyenia* and 6 other genera have the dermal spicules acerate or lacking, but *Meyenia* has the end discs of the birotulate spicules serrate or incised. It is widely distributed in Europe and North America, some species in rapidly flowing streams and some even in polluted waters. *Heteromeyenia,* another cosmopolitan genus, differs from *Meyenia* in having two kinds of gemmule birotulates, as does *Asteromeyenia.*

CHAPTER 7

Hydras and Jellyfish—
Phylum Coelenterata

Figs. 32, 33; Pl. 10

THERE are more than 9,000 species of coelenterates in
the sea but fewer than 20 in fresh waters, for only the
members of the class Hydrozoa have invaded inland waters
and some of them still prefer brackish and tidal pools.

The soft-bodied gelatinous coelenterates may be in the
form of a *polyp* or a *medusa*. A polyp is a cylindrical column,
usually attached at one end; whereas a medusa is umbrella-
like and free-swimming. One of our freshwater hydrozoans
has both polyps and medusae; another has polyps only; but
the hydras, our commonest freshwater representatives, consist of a single polyp.

Hydras

Hydras may be white, brick-red, bright pink, various
shades of brown, or colorless. If they are green it is because
of the green algal cells living symbiotically within their
bodies. They may hang from the surface film, dimpling its
upper surface; they may sit on vegetation, or drift passively
in open water. Their size and shape is difficult to describe
since a tiny semitransparent hydra may stretch until it looks
like a frayed strand of thread, or may contract into a small,
knobbed ball.

Each hydra polyp terminates in a sticky base, or *foot*, at
the proximal end, and in a circle of fingerlike *tentacles* at

the triggerlike action of a projecting bristle, a *cnidocil*, set off by contact or by stimulus from the presence of a small creature or object close by. They eject a penetrating, stinging *nematocyst* that paralyzes the tiny victim, or a coiling, threadlike one that fastens onto some part of its body. The tentacles then sweep the paralyzed or captured prey into the mouth. If food is abundant, hydras may eat until they bulge. They consume many small crustaceans and protozoa as well as young insects, small clams (casting out the shells), small tadpoles or even small fish. Thousands of them may line the hatching troughs in fish hatcheries to prey upon the small fry. In turn they are eaten by many carnivorous insects and are snapped up by young trout with seeming relish.

Locomotion. Hydras usually move by the slow gliding of the sticky foot across the substratum. In the confines of the aquarium a somersaulting type of motion is often seen. This somersaulting is made possible by the bending down of the tentacles and the fastening of their discharged nematocysts to the substratum; the subsequent release of the attached base enables the hydra to complete the somersault.

Reproduction. Hydras reproduce asexually by the formation of buds upon the sides of the body. The buds may break away as they are formed or they may remain attached for some time. Thus hydras are often found with several well-tentacled buds extending from their sides. Under certain conditions of temperature and carbon dioxide concentration (possibly caused by overcrowding), rounded ovaries and conical or pumpkin-shaped testes develop as protuberances on the side of the column. They may occur on a single individual although not usually at the same time. The sperm swim out from the testes when mature but the single egg remains in a cuplike depression of the outer wall of the ovary where it is fertilized and where it remains until the embryo is well developed. This sexual reproduction usually occurs in the autumn and early winter, although in *Chlorohydra* it is more common in the spring and early summer. Reproduction by fission is rare.

Collecting. Occasionally hydras are seen in their native habitat but as a rule it is not until jars of water and vegetation gathered along the edges of quiet waters have been brought in and allowed to stand, out of direct sunlight, that one is aware of their presence. Then they can be observed gathered on the side of greatest illumination, on the glass, reaching out from the vegetation or suspended from the surface film. They respond to temperature and certain chemicals as well as to light. When hungry, they react positively to the approach of the small creatures upon which they feed, exploring the area with contractions and expansions of their body and the waving of their tentacles. This makes them interesting little animals to keep in an aquarium; they can live for months if oxygen-producing plants are kept with them and plenty of small crustaceans for their delectation.

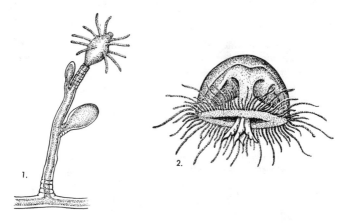

Fig. 33. 1. *Cordylophora lacustris*, upright branch. 2. *Craspedacusta sowerbyi*, medusa.

Other Coelenterates

The colonial *Cordylophora lacustris* grows attached to roots, sticks, stones, etc., by means of a network of threads. It does best in brackish water where its white, bushy colonies may reach a height of 2½ inches. In fresh water it is seldom over ½ inch high. Its one or more upright stems bear alternately arranged feeding polyps, *hydranths*; and, below them, bulbous bodies that produce small larvae, *planulae*, that break out and swim away to form new colonies. *Craspedacusta sowerbyi* is seldom more than 2 to 8 mm. high. It usually has from 2 to 4 polyps, occasionally up to 12, some of which produce bell-like, tentacle-fringed medusae which break off and swim away, sometimes in great profusion. These medusae are to be found from July to October in lakes, ponds, rivers, reservoirs and artificial waters such as old quarries.

Grouping of Families of Coelenterates

A SOLITARY POLYP WITH TENTACLES

> **Hydridae.** *Chlorohydra viridissima*, the Green Hydra, is usually less than 15 mm. long (exclusive of tentacles) but may stretch to twice that. The tentacles are shorter than the column and 4 to 12 in number. Common and widespread. *Hydra* is represented by about 10 species, none of which is green.

A COLONY OF POLYPS

> **Clavidae.** Polyps with tentacles. *Cordylophora*. Widespread but scattered.

> **Petasidae.** Polyps without tentacles. *Craspedacusta*. Widespread but seldom seen.

A FREE-SWIMMING BELL-SHAPED MEDUSA

> **Petasidae.** These are the medusae of *Craspedacusta*; 20 mm. in diameter.

CHAPTER 8

Moss Animalcules—
Phylum Bryozoa

Fig. 34; Pl. 11

THE fernlike overlays on lily pads, and the delicate, lace-
like strands stretching across insect bodies and other
submerged objects, do not look like animals. Neither do the
limy encrustations, "fluted rugs," or immense gelatinous balls
glimpsed in the dimly lighted waters of ponds and slow
streams. It is only when these branching, plantlike colonies
are examined under magnification that their animal characteristics become apparent. Although there are a large number
of these bryozoans in the ocean, only 14 or so live in our
fresh waters, but they are common and widespread, and
some are even cosmopolitan.

Bryozoans always form colonies. Each colony is made up
of units, called *zooids* (or polypides), which resemble the
polyps of coelenterates. Each zooid is crowned with a rim
of ciliated tentacles, the *lophophore*. In most freshwater species this can be retracted with the speed of a jack-in-the-box
into the basal, protective covering, the *ectocyst*. The ectocyst
may be thin and delicate, or thick, corneous or gelatinous.
The mouth lies in the center of the lophophore.

Food. The tentacles sweep up food particles consisting
of microscopic algae, protozoa and diatoms. Bryozoans are
of minor importance in the food chain, for though they are
eaten by many crustaceans, insects, snails and fish, they are
of little significance in the diet of these animals.

Reproduction. A single individual lives only a few weeks

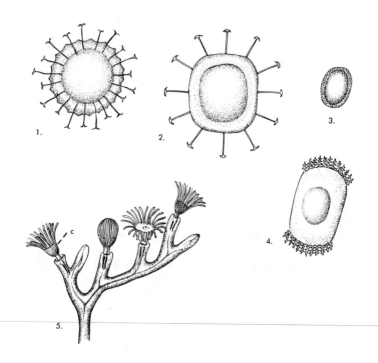

Fig. 34. Bryozoans. 1, *Cristatella mucedo*, statoblast, × 25; 2, *Pectinatella magnifica*, statoblast, × 20; 3, *Plumatella repens*, statoblast, × 20; 4, *Lophopodella carteri*, statoblast, × 25; 5, *Fredericella sultana*, colony, × 8, c, calyx, a membrane surrounding the base of the tentacles. (1,2 and 4 after Ward and Whipple.)

but the colony continues to grow throughout the summer. It develops by means of asexual buds that push outward or even backward into the mass, to grow upon the dead bodies of those which have gone before. Individual zooids may produce sex cells; these, after fertilization, develop into free-swimming larvae which settle down to form new colonies. Colonies may reproduce by fission. By the time a colony disintegrates in the fall, most species will have produced large numbers of circular or oval winter buds, the *statoblasts*.

These chitinous covered groups of cells are released from the body of the dead and ruptured zooids and may float on the surface or wash up along the margin of the pond in great numbers. Some remain attached to the dying colony. Statoblasts are sometimes armed with double-barbed hooks which anchor them to debris or vegetation or even to the feet of wading birds and mammals who transport them long distances. They resist desiccation and have been known to remain viable after passing through the digestive tract of reptiles and birds.

Bryozoans are never found in polluted water, or in strongly acid water, and rarely on sandy or pebbly beaches. They prefer dim light (except for *Cristatella*) and they prefer clear ponds, shallow lakes and slow streams. A few species of *Cristatella, Lophopus, Lophopodella* and *Pectinatella* may creep slowly over the surface of the substratum, a few inches a day.

Collecting. Statoblasts are needed for the identification of species and are also useful for propagating colonies in the laboratory, so their collection is of value. In late summer and fall they can be lifted with a net from the surface of the water or from the margin of the shore. Colonies, or pieces of colonies, may be picked with scalpel or forceps from the substratum, or with dredge or rake if the water is deep.

Grouping of Bryozoans

LOPHOPHORE NOT RETRACTILE

Urnatella. This uncommon genus is usually placed in a separate phylum. Each zooid is on a stalk made up of urn-shaped segments.

LOPHOPHORE RETRACTILE, CIRCULAR. MOUTH WITHOUT A LID

Paludicellidae. The common *Paludicella articulata* forms a pale yellow threadlike tracery on rocks, shells or insect bodies in standing water. The threads are made up of club-shaped units placed end to end. The rare *Pottsiella erecta* forms a colony consisting of stolons with erect zooids; it grows on upper surface of stones in rapid water. Instead of statoblasts, both form chitinous *hibernacula,* which are cemented to the bottom.

LOPHOPHORE RETRACTILE, OVAL, CIRCULAR OR HORSESHOE-SHAPED. MOUTH WITH A LID

1. Colony unbranched, ribbonlike, or ruglike; gelatinous. Statoblasts hooked.

   Cristatellidae. *Cristatella mergeda* forms a gelatinous, whitish colony. It often covers lily pads. Ohio, Pa. and R. I.

2. Colony branched, treelike. Statoblasts not hooked.

   Fredericellidae. With kidney-shaped or circular crown. *Fredericella sultana* (Fig. 34.5) forms tan or brownish, creeping colonies with erect antlerlike branches, on undersides of sticks and stones. Occasionally in deep water and occasionally in water pipes where it may obstruct the flow.

   Plumatellidae. With horseshoe-shaped crown. *Hyalinella* forms colonies of tubular, horizontal branches often so thickly grouped as to cover the substratum with a soft gelatinous layer. *Plumatella* colonies may be pale and transparent or brownish. The branches, measuring up to 5 cm. in length, are covered with a thin, firm, often horny layer. *P. repens* is found in all kinds of water on undersides of vegetation and submerged objects and in water pipes and reservoirs.

   Lophopodidae. *Lophopus,* with horseshoe-shaped crown, forms a sac-shaped, erect, lobed colony, less than 1 cm. across, on vegetation. Schuylkill and Illinois R. systems.

3. Colony soft, transparent, gelatinous, not treelike. Statoblasts hooked.

   Lophopodidae. *Lophopodella,* similar to *Lophopus* but larger; with oval statoblasts having 6 to 17 spiny hooks at each end (Fig. 34.4). Eastern central states. *Pectinatella* forms massive colonies (Pl. 11) which by autumn may be up to 40 cm. long and 15 wide. They are arranged in rosette shaped groups of 12 to 18 individuals in a gelatinous mass, growing on reservoir walls, twigs or other submerged objects; often covered with algae and resembling a large green grapefruit or small watermelon. The ball may break loose, clogging screens and machinery in water works. Statoblasts are circular with 11 to 22 hooked spines on the periphery. Widely distributed though not common west of the Mississippi.

CHAPTER 9

Worms—Several Phyla

Figs. 35–40; Pls. 11, 12

THE many small, insignificant, often microscopically small worms crawling over vegetation or debris are of tremendous importance in the economic life of any body of water. They feed on bits of organic material as scavengers, or upon small plants and animals, transforming those substances into animal tissue that can nourish larger invertebrates and even small vertebrates. A hand lens is needed for the most casual identification of nearly all species. A compound microscope and complicated techniques of preparation are required for exact identification.

Some of these wormlike creatures will prove, upon examination, to be insect larvae;* so it is necessary to appreciate at once that most insect larvae that might be confused with worms are not only segmented (like the annelids) but have a distinct head and fleshy prolegs. Some fly larvae, however, have neither head nor prolegs; with these the collector must become familiar.

Flatworms—Phylum Platyhelminthes
Figs. 36, 37; Pl. 11

The tapeworms (class Cestoda) and flukes (class Trematoda) are parasites, living in or on the bodies of other animals such as amphibians, fish, birds and the animals that prey upon them. Tapeworms in the encysted condition are

---

* See also multicellular microorganisms.

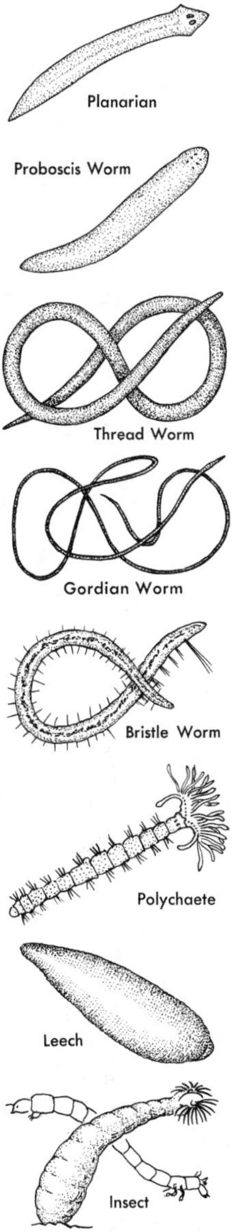

		Size	Shape	Distinguishing Characteristic
Planarian	Planarians	1–25 mm.	Depressed	Often with eyespots
Proboscis Worm	Proboscis worms	to 18 mm.	Slightly depressed	A long, protrusible proboscis
Thread Worm	Thread worms	to 3 mm.	Threadlike	Translucent. Motion whiplike
Gordian Worm	Gordian worms	4–40 in.	Hairlike	Yellow-brown. Motion whiplike
Bristle Worm	Bristle worms	1 mm.–12 in.	Cylindrical, segmented	Setae usually on each segment
Polychaete	Polychaetes	3–5 mm.	Cylindrical, segmented	With lateral projections and anterior tentacles
Leech	Leeches	5 mm.–18 in.	Depressed, segmented	With anterior and posterior suckers
Insect	Insect larvae	1 mm.–2 in.	Variable, segmented	Usually with legs or prolegs

Fig. 35. How to Recognize Worms

frequently collected from the tissues of freshwater fishes. *Diphyllobothrium latium* has become distributed in some of the large Canadian, Michigan and Minnesota lakes and in the Great Lakes, where it is picked up by plankton-feeding fishes from the copepods *Cyclops* and *Diaptomus* in which it lives for one period of its life. It is then passed on to cats, dogs, foxes, bears and other fish-eating animals including man. Flukes may be collected from the skin and gills of the mudpuppy *Necturus*, the mussel *Anodonta* and from many species of turtles, tadpoles and fishes.

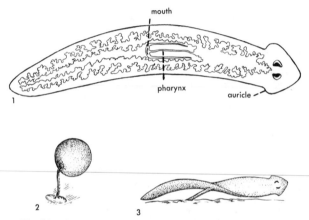

Fig. 36. A planarian. *1*, Diagram to show 3-branched digestive system; *2*, a cocoon; *3*, with pharynx extended.

Flatworms of the class Turbellaria, however, are not parasitic. They are widely distributed on land, in the sea and in fresh waters. These soft, flat, leechlike worms usually have a distinct head and a conspicuously pigmented gastrovascular cavity showing through the translucent tissues. This gastrovascular cavity combines the functions of digestion and circulation; it has a single opening leading into a muscular pharynx located near the middle of the body on the ventral side. Reproduction is sexual; most species are hermaphroditic.

Collecting. Aquatic species are to be found clinging to vegetation and to the undersides of stones and rubbish in shallow water, and occasionally in large aggregations in open water. They are probably most easily found by examining algae, the scrapings from lily pads and trailing vegetation in pools and ponds, or by turning over stones, submerged boards, etc., in fast water or along a wave-washed shore. The soft-bodied, clinging creatures can be lifted off with a pipette or gently scraped off with a knife blade or scalpel. Or one may gather vegetation and the upper layer of bottom debris, and place it all in a tray of water. A few worms will come to the surface in a few hours; others not for several weeks, after the oxygen is depleted. Following Dr. Libbie Hyman's technique of baiting for planarians with strips of liver or beef along the edges of small ponds and streams is often successful. From 15 to 30 minutes are required. Planarians may be collected even in midwinter.

Planarians can be kept in an aquarium of natural water if it is kept cool and dimly lighted and the water is changed frequently. They should be fed several times a week with bits of chopped liver, chopped earthworms, clams or hard-boiled egg yolk. Uneaten material must be removed in a few hours. The pigmented eyes give them a comical appearance, and the manner in which they explore the environment, reacting to the slightest stimulus of light, vibration, temperature and taste, provide the onlooker with a fertile field of investigation.

Grouping of Orders of Free-living Flatworms*

SMALL, USUALLY LESS THAN 4 MM. INTESTINE NOT THREE-BRANCHED

1. Pharynx bulbous proximally (Fig. 37.1).
   Neorhabdocoela. A very large group. A few species up to 6 mm.
2. Pharynx plicate.
   Allocoela. Mostly marine; a few aquatic species.
3. Pharynx simple
   Catenulida (Fig. 37.2). Slender, threadlike worms, usually white; often eyeless. They usually reproduce by fission, forming chains. Common in stagnant water. *Stenostomum* is often found in abundance in beds of

---

* Difficult for the beginner.

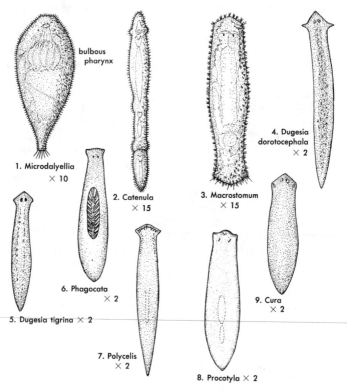

bulbous
pharynx

1. Microdalyellia
× 10

2. Catenula
× 15

3. Macrostomum
× 15

4. Dugesia
dorotocephala
× 2

6. Phagocata
× 2

5. Dugesia tigrina × 2

7. Polycelis
× 2

8. Procotyla × 2

9. Cura
× 2

Fig. 37. Flatworms (6 after Hyman)

Spirogyra; Catenula in decaying organic matter. Other genera.

Macrostomida (Fig. 37.3). Flattened or cylindrical worms; white or slightly pigmented, usually with pigmented eyes. Differ from *Catenulida* in having two protonephridia instead of one (a difficult character for the nonspecialist). *Microstomum* is often a mass of stinging cells from the hydras on which it feeds; it sometimes forms chains.

LARGE, USUALLY MORE THAN 5 MM. INTESTINE THREE-BRANCHED

Triclada. Planarians.

Planarians, order Triclada. Planarians are grayish brown or white. They are mostly easily recognized by the "apparent" head. This head may be truncate or triangular and often bears a pair of small earlike *auricles* and sometimes a pair of pigmented eyes; it may also bear an adhesive organ near the anterior margin. The three-branched gastrovascular cavity has one branch extending forward and two branches to the rear.

Locomotion. Most planarians do not swim. They glide over the substratum by means of slight muscular contractions and the activity of the thousands of microscopic cilia that cover the body.

Food. The mouth is located at the end of a short, muscular, protrusible *pharynx* on the ventral side of the body. Planarians feed upon living and dead organisms, and in turn are eaten by other worms, insects and crustaceans.

Reproduction. Planarians reproduce by fission. Under certain conditions of poor nutrition, they may do this so rapidly that proper growth does not take place. Most species also reproduce sexually (they are hermaphroditic), producing stalked egg-filled cocoons which they attach to the substratum. The eggs may hatch in about two weeks or may overwinter in the cocoon. Planarians have remarkable powers of regeneration; when snipped in two with a sharp knife the head end will grow a new posterior end and the posterior end a new head. Many interesting types of cuts can be made and the regenerative possibilities explored.

Planarians are rare in the tropics but abundant in temperate and cold regions where they are to be found in well-oxygenated water in all seasons of the year.

Grouping of Genera of Planarians

Many planarians can be identified only after sectioning. The following grouping may be of some help.*

PLANARIANS WITH TWO EYES OR WITH NONE

1. Head triangular. Colored.

* These belong to the two families, Planariidae and Dendrocoelidae. The black *Rectocephala* from Washington, D. C., and the *Dendrocoelopsis* from Alaska are not included. Modified from Hyman.

Balls of the bryozoan *Pectinatella*, as large as watermelons.

Planarians, *Dugesia*, with their pedicellate cocoons.

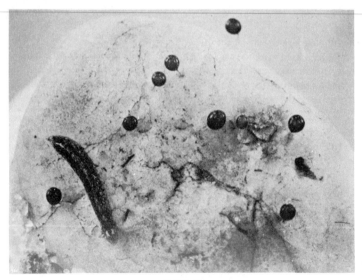

PLATE 11

Dugesia. Up to 30 mm. Head strongly triangular with prominent auricles.

Cura. Head a low triangle with low auricles; auricles with a white dash. In cool creeks and rivers, Can. south to Mich. and N. C.

Hymanella. Much like *Cura* but lacking white dash on auricles. In ponds and swamps, Mass. to N. C.

2. Head truncate. Colored or white.

    a. With an anterior adhesive organ.

        Procotyla. Eyeless. Whitish. Va. and Fla.

        Dendrocoelopsis. With two eyes. Mont.

    b. Without adhesive organ.

        Phagocata, several eastern and midwestern species, one of which, *P. gracilis,* has many pharynges; and *Planaria* with one species, Va. and Fla.

PLANARIANS WITH NUMEROUS EYES

Sorocelis. With numerous eyes in two longitudinal rows. Whitish. Ozarks.

Polycelis. Eyes as in Fig. 37.7. Brown to black. Hill and mountain streams S. D. to Pacific and Alaska.

Procotyla. With 2 to 7 eyes on each side. Whitish. Va. and Fla.

Proboscis Worms—Phylum Nemertea
Fig. 38

Most of the 600 or so known proboscis worms are marine. In N. A. there is only one freshwater species: *Prostomum rubrum.* When young it is white or yellowish but on becoming mature it changes to deep yellow or red. One rare green variety is also known.

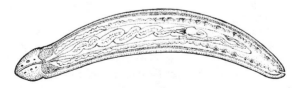

Fig. 38. *Prostoma rubrum,* $\times$ 4.

It feeds on small, live animal organisms and occasionally on dead ones. It, in turn, is eaten by worms, crustaceans and insects. Although widely distributed it is seldom abundant. It is most likely to be found in the fall when one is examining algae from well-oxygenated, shallow water, or the scrapings from under lily pads. It glides, by means of tiny cilia, along a track of slime of its own secreting. In the winter it migrates to deeper water but under adverse conditions may roll up in a mass of mucus which hardens to form a resting cyst that can withstand desiccation.

Specimens may be kept alive in an aquarium with rooted plants if fed bits of liver or earthworms, or minute living organisms.

Gordian Worms—Phylum Nematomorpha
Fig. 35

These are the "horsehairs" that (so the legend goes) mysteriously come to life in the town watering trough. They are unsegmented, hard, opaque, wiry worms, usually tannish to brown or black in color. In their writhing and undulating they often become entangled with one another, forming the knotted mass responsible for their common name (after the knot tied by Gordius, King of Phrygia). Each worm is cylindrical with a slight tapering at each end.

The eggs are laid in a long, gelatinous string which later breaks into pieces an inch or so in length. The miniature worm that emerges from the egg swims about for a short time and then encysts upon the vegetation or debris along the bank, where it is engulfed by certain crustaceans, molluscs or insects (mainly beetles, crickets or grasshoppers) within whose bodies the immature form lives parasitically until mature.

The adults, after leaving the body of these hosts, do not feed. They live in standing or running water, in puddles, tanks or ditches, usually in water up to 8 inches deep. They are most frequently seen in the spring and early summer and then not until later in the fall.

The genus *Gordius* is cosmopolitan. The most widely distributed of our species are *Gordius robustus* and *Paragordius varius*. The former has the posterior tip of the body rounded in the female, bilobed in the male; the latter has it trilobed in the female and with two long lobes in the male.

Thread Worms—Phylum Nemata
Fig. 39

Old textbooks frequently cited the description of a world devoid of all living substance except that of the nematodes, and yet a world that showed the outline of all previously existing organisms delineated by the nematodes that had infested them, with even the grasses of the meadows still standing in ghostly rows. This dubious but highly spectral picture indelibly impressed the minds of students with the abundance and widespread prevalence of nematodes both as parasites and as free-living forms, in the soil, in the sea, and in fresh waters. The thousand or more species described from fresh water probably represent but a fraction of those that actually exist. They thrive on lake shores where the bottom is stony, muddy or rich in vegetation; they live in swift mountain streams, glued to the substratum by secretions of their tail tip and by adhesive glands; and they live in ice pools and hot sulphur springs. In fact, they live in all kinds of water, the same species often occupying quite widely different habitats.

Locomotion. Nematodes are most easily recognized by their

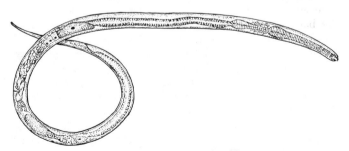

Fig. 39. A thread worm, × 85.

almost continual whiplike motion, the whipping occurring in a dorsoventral plane without an accompanying change of shape. Progression is accomplished chiefly by friction between the body and the surface over which it moves.

Food. Their food consists of detritus, dead and living plant material, and dead and living animal material, with an apparent preference for nematodes, rotifers, gastrotrichs and protists. A few cause damage to crops in lowlands near the water. Many live within the bodies of molluscs, crustaceans, worms and vertebrates.

Reproduction. Eggs are laid sometimes one or two at a time, sometimes in vast profusion. The complete life cycle, from egg to egg, may be completed in as few as 20 days.

Collecting. Any scraper that brings in mud, sand, debris or vegetation from the margins or bottom will bring in nematodes. If the material is left standing in a shallow pan of water the worms will soon wiggle out and can then be picked up with pipette or lifter. The great majority will, of course, be found only with the microscope. Washing and then straining the material through successively finer-meshed sieves will bring them, as well as many other small organisms, to light more quickly.

Segmented Worms—Phylum Annelida
Fig. 40; Pl. 12

The familiar earthworm, or night crawler, is composed of a series of segments or rings. Its basic body plan is that of a tube within a tube, the outer one being the cuticle-covered body wall which contains muscles, and the inner one the digestive tract that leads from mouth to anus. Each individual is hermaphroditic. The male sex cells from one worm are transferred to internal receptacles of another worm and later gathered, along with the eggs of the second worm, into a "napkin ring" secreted by a glandular area, the *clitellum.* When this ring slides forward it is pushed off the body of the worm, and its ends sealed off to form a cocoon. Fertilization, and the subsequent development of the embryo, takes place within the cocoon. Three classes of annelids are distinguished in Fig. 35.

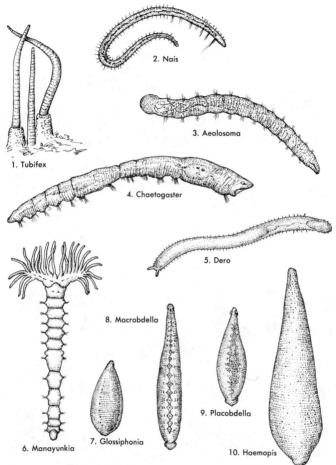

Fig. 40. Segmented Worms (4 and 6 after Ward and Whipple)

Bristle worms, class Oligochaeta (Fig. 40.1–5). The bristle worms are characterized by the bundles of bristles, or *setae*, present on each side of each segment after the first. (Setae are not present in one family that live attached to crayfish.)

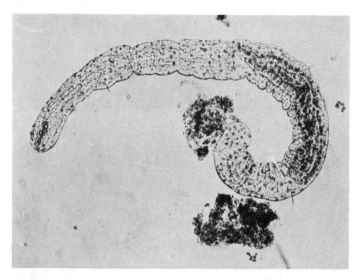

Aeolosoma, a bristle worm that contains red oil droplets

The leech *Haemopsis,* sometimes nearly a foot long

PLATE 12

These worms have a distinct head region followed by a variable number of segments ranging from 7 to 5,000.

Oligochaetes are common in the mud and debris of the substratum of stagnant waters everywhere. They often live in tubes and are sometimes present in mats of filamentous algae or on aquatic vegetation. Little *Dero* is commonly found on the undersides of the fronds of the duckweed *Lemna*. The Tubificidae occur even in the deepest parts of lakes. *Tubifex*, for example, is able to live without oxygen for some time and thus can survive periods of stagnation. During such periods, however, it may exhibit considerable agitation, waving the projecting posterior end of its body as though to create currents which might bring oxygen to it. It also grows abundantly in the shallow water of ponds and streams where there is considerable organic decay and pollution. The waving bodies as well as the many small casts on the surface of the muddy substratum show how very abundant it sometimes becomes. *Tubifex tubifex*, 30–100 mm., has been reported in numbers up to 8,000 per square meter. Its bright red color comes from the oxygen-bearing pigment *erythrocruorin* in the blood. (One must be careful not to confuse it with the red tendipedid midge larva. The midge larva differs in having prolegs at both ends of the body.)

Locomotion. Oligochaetes move, as do the terrestrial earthworms, by contractions of the muscular body wall which push them through the substratum. The setae along the side provide the necessary purchase, and the angle at which the setae are held determines the direction in which the body will move. A few species swim in the water with a serpentine motion.

Food. Except for the carnivorous *Chaetogaster* and for *Aeolosoma* whose waving cilia draw food particles to the mouth, these worms feed, as do terrestrial earthworms, by ingesting large quantities of the medium through which they are moving, extracting the organic material from it as it passes down the digestive tract, and discarding the remainder through the anus. Their nourishment comes chiefly from algae, diatoms and other miscellaneous organic substances. In this way they are of tremendous value in cleaning up masses of dead and decaying vegetation. As they work through the mud and detritus the head is held downward so that in ejecting the material they have ingested they are turning over subsurface material.

Grouping of Families of Bristle Worms

ATTACHED TO BODY OF CRAYFISH BY CAUDAL SUCKERS

Branchiobdellidae. 1–2 mm.

FREE-LIVING, WITHOUT SUCKERS. LESS THAN 25 MM. REPRODUCTION BY FISSION TO FORM CHAINS

Aeolosomatidae, *Aeolosoma* (Fig. 40.3; Pl. 12). Usually less than 5 mm. and more or less translucent. Often contains pigmented oil globules. Clitellum, if present, anterior to segment 8.

Naididae (Fig. 40.4,5). 5–25 mm. Without pigment and more or less opaque. With well-developed setae. *Chaetogaster, Dero* and *Aulophorus* have ciliated anal gills. They rest with anterior part of body concealed in substratum or in tubes. Other genera.

FREE-LIVING, WITHOUT SUCKERS. USUALLY MORE THAN 25 MM. Clitellum posterior to segment 8. (Identification dependent upon setae pattern.)

Haplotaxida. Threadlike, 100–300 mm. Semi-aquatic in wet earth, marshes, ditches or under rocks.

Enchytraeidae. 10–30 mm. Whitish or pinkish, aquatic or terrestrial; common in detritus and on snow.

Lumbriculidae and Tubificidae. Up to 200 mm. Usually reddish or brownish; often in a tube. About a dozen genera including the widespread *Tubifex* (Fig. 40.1), *Limnodrilus* and *Lumbriculus*. Their identification requires dissection.

Terrestrial earthworms. Sometimes in mud, debris and sewage by accident. Thick-bodied, with a mature length of 5–30 cm.

Polychaetes, class Polychaeta (Fig. 40.6). These are mostly marine or brackish-water worms. In North America there are only seven species described from fresh waters; they are of local distribution and seen infrequently, often only near the seacoast. Polychaetes are distinct from other annelids in having paired, muscular, lateral appendages, called *parapodia*, and in sometimes having other appendages at the anterior end of the body. Most species are colonial, living in the mud or sand; a few construct burrows or temporary tubes. The tube-dwelling *Manayunkia*, 3–5 mm., is known from Penn., N. J. and the Great Lakes; *Neanthes* is from Calif.

Leeches, class Hirudinea (Fig. 40.7–10). Leeches are predominantly creatures of fresh waters, though a few are marine and a few are terrestrial (mostly in the tropics). They are usually dorsoventrally flattened, sometimes to a considerable degree, and may be smooth, wrinkled or tubercled. They are often brightly colored and patterned in greens and black. The number of body segments is constant at 35 but each segment may have apparent subdivisions which make the number of segments seem greater.

Locomotion. Leeches have an anterior and a posterior sucker by means of which they creep across the substratum with a looping "inchworm" type of motion, sometimes stretching their bodies to incredible lengths. Some species swim well; others poorly if at all, tending to roll into a ball when loosened from the surface to which they have been attached. All species when not in motion cling, by at least one sucker, to vegetation or substratum.

Food. Most leeches are predators on snails, insect larvae, crustaceans and worms, or are general scavengers. Only a comparatively few feed on warm blood.

In Europe the bloodsucking *Hirudo medicinalis* has been used extensively for bloodletting and millions are still being sold for that purpose each year. In this country they have never been used so widely although *Macrobdella decora*, one of our native species, has at times sold as high as $100 a thousand.

A bloodsucking leech makes a lesion in the victim's skin by a back-and-forth rotary motion of the jaws, or by digesting away the superficial layers of the skin with a digestive enzyme. It then draws in the blood through a long, muscular, sometimes protrusible, proboscis. Since the leech is firmly attached to the victim by its anterior sucker it is able to remain in position until engorged. When it leaves the host it may have taken in sufficient blood to increase its weight five times. Leeches inject the wound with their saliva which contains an anticoagulant, *hirudin;* this not only retards clotting of the victim's blood but preserves the blood within the leech so that, when concentrated by the dehydrating action of the kidneys, it can be stored for a long period of time. Leeches have been known to live 18 months or so on one good blood meal. *Macrobdella* and *Philobdella,* our common bloodsucking leeches, leave a characteristic incision where the three jaws have pierced the tissues.

Reproduction. Leeches are hermaphroditic. Most species lay their eggs between May and August, depositing them in a cocoon which they fasten to some submerged object or bury in the soft mud. They often remain with the cocoon for 2 or 3 months. The Glossiphonidae carry their eggs in a membrane or gelatinous capsule attached to the ventral side of the body. The emerging young may remain attached to the parent for several days.

Leeches may be a great nuisance to bathers; but, other than the daily use of lime, there is little that can be done to rid an area of them. If in the fall, the water is lowered a few feet after the leeches have begun to hibernate in the soil along the margin, the drying out of the banks will kill many of them.

Collecting. Leeches, especially *Macrobdella,* are very sensitive to vibrations or to the presence of any foreign substance introduced into the water, so just walk in and they will attach themselves to your boots or legs. More elusive ones can be found by turning over rocks, logs and debris and picking the leeches off with forceps. A dip net will catch the rapid swimmers as well as those that roll into a ball when loosened from their position. Baiting with raw meat will attract many others. They may be kept in an aquarium if the water is clean and cool, the light dim, and a wire-screen cover fastened on *tightly.* Some species will need some projection from the water onto which they may crawl.

Grouping of Families of Leeches

BLOOD COLORLESS. PHARYNX PROTRUSIBLE. WITH-
OUT JAWS

Glossiphoniidae. Body flat. Poor swimmers.

1. Body excessively flat; mouth not within sucker cavity
though it may be on its rim; one pair of eyes. *Placob-
della* (Fig. 40), up to 90 mm., has three annuli per
segment; it feeds on fish, frogs, turtles and occasionally man. *P. parasitica* is very common, clinging to
legs of the common snapping turtle; it may leave the
turtle to swim free and feed on snails and worms.
Smooth, greenish marked with yellow. Other species.
Other genera, with 2 to 6 annuli per segment.

2. Body not excessively flat; mouth within sucker cavity.
Theromyzon has 4 pairs of eyes; body translucent and
gelatinous after egg-laying. *Glossiphonia* (Fig. 40),
the common leech of running water, has 3 pairs of
eyes; up to 30 mm.; greenish often spotted or striped
with yellow. *Helobdella*, 5–20 mm. has 1 pair of eyes;
very common, occasionally on fish and frogs, rarely
on man. *H. stagnalis* is the most distinctive of our
leeches, having a brown chitinous plate on the dorsum of the 8th segment. Other species. Other genera.

Piscicolidae. Body cylindrical, often with narrow anterior and wide posterior region. 6–30 mm. These
are the fish leeches, seldom harmful except in hatcheries. Widespread in east and north.

BLOOD RED. PHARYNX FIXED

Erpobdellidae. Without jaws: 3 or 4 pairs of eyes.
Erpobdella, up to 100 mm., usually has 3 (occasionally 4) pairs of eyes. Brownish. Feeds on invertebrates, fish, frogs and occasionally man; sometimes
a scavenger. *Nephelopsis*, up to 100 mm., has 4 pairs
of eyes. Gray to brown, spotted with black; has all
annuli of middle of body subdivided. Widespread on
vertebrates; occasionally a scavenger. Other genera.

Hirudidae. With jaws (except some species of *Haemopsis*); 5 pairs of eyes. Strong swimmers.

1. Jaws with saw teeth in a single row. *Hirudo medici-*

nalis, up to 100 mm., usually green with brown stripes; each jaw with about 50 teeth; northeast. *Macrobdella decora* (Fig. 40), up to 230 mm., dull green above with red and black spots, reddish orange beneath; each jaw with about 65 teeth. Feeds chiefly on vertebrate blood though it has been reported eating frog's eggs, tadpoles and insect larvae. Very common in ponds and ditches in northern part of country. Other species and genera.

2. Jaws without teeth, or with teeth in two rows. *Philobdella*, the common striped southern bloodsucker. *Haemopsis* (Fig. 40), with very small jaws or none at all; widely distributed in northern states at edge of ponds. *H. marmoratus*, the horse leech, up to 160 mm., is green blotched with brown or black. When small it sucks blood from any vertebrate, including man, but also feeds on worms and molluscs. *H. plumbeus*, up to 160 mm., has a red or orange band on the side. *H. grandis*, up to 300 mm., is greenish or gray with blotches. Other species. Other genera.

CHAPTER 10

Crayfish and Shrimp—
Class Crustacea

Figs. 41–45; Pl. 13

E VERYONE knows what a crayfish looks like; and many people have sat on a beach watching hard-shelled "fleas" snap in and out of pools on the sand, or have floated on an air mattress on the water, basking under a summer sun and pondering on the fate of the tiny side-swimming shrimp that were trapped in the folds of the canvas. These enticing little creatures, and some 30,000 other species, are crustaceans. About 800 species live in fresh water, developing in numbers sufficient to make them of great importance in the economy and biology of ponds, lakes and streams.

Crustaceans belong to the Arthropoda, the phylum which comprises about four-fifths of all animals known. It is characterized by having the body divided into a linear series of segments which are grouped into a *head*, *thorax* and *abdomen*; in having paired, jointed *appendages*; and in having the body protected by a hard, durable covering, the *exoskeleton*, to which the muscles are attached. This skeleton is molted at intervals to permit the growth of the individual, and its sclerotization interrupted at the joints to insure motility. The sexes are usually separate.

The segmentation of the arthropods, especially in such creatures as the millipedes, is reminiscent to the most untutored of us of the segmentation of the earthworm. But in the Crustacea, as well as in the Insecta, the segments are no longer all alike; they have become differentiated both in structure and in function.

135

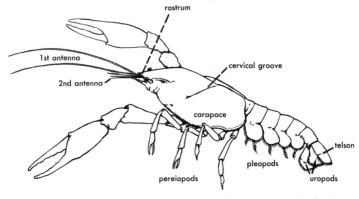

Fig. 41. A Decapod

Crustaceans differ from the others of the phylum in having *two* pairs of antennae, and in usually having the head and thorax more or less fused to form a *cephalothorax*. Furthermore, they breathe by means of gills, for all species except a few sow bugs that live on the damp forest floor are aquatic or marine.

The head is often prolonged into a *rostrum*. The *antennae*, typically long and tenuous, usually have a sensory function, but they vary; the normally small second pair, for example, may sometimes be larger than the first pair and specialized for food-getting, for swimming, or, as in the male fairy shrimp, for grasping the female during copulation. *Mandibles* and two pairs of *maxillae* (one pair in the water fleas) comprise the paired mouthparts. Of the variable number of paired appendages on the thorax one or more pairs are often modified for food-getting and called *maxillipeds*; those used for walking are the *periopods*. The abdominal appendages used for swimming are the *pleopods*; occasionally they are modified for reproductive purposes. The last pair of abdominal appendages (the last three pairs in the scuds) are called *uropods*; they combine with the terminal *telson* to form a strong propeller.

Gills are usually concealed beneath a *carapace*, the roof-

Grouping of Orders of Fresh Water Crustaceans*

	Shape** of body	Carapace	Pairs of trunk appendages	Eyes	Size in mm.
Fairy shrimp	Cyl.	Absent	11–19 leaflike	Stalked	5–100
Clam shrimp	Comp.	Bivalve	10–28 leaflike	Sessile together	2–16
Tadpole shrimp	Dep.	Covers thorax	35–71	Sessile together	10–58
Water fleas	Comp.	Appears bivalve	4–6 leaflike	Single	.2–18
Seed shrimp	Comp.	Bivalve	2–3	Sessile together	.3–7
Copepods	Cyl.	Short	5–6	Variable	.3–3.2
Fish lice	Dep.	Expanded	4–5	Sessile	5–25
Oppossum shrimp	Cyl.	Covers thorax	2 + 6 + 6***	Stalked	15–30
Sow bugs	Dep.	Absent	1 + 7 + 6	Sessile	10–20
Scuds	Comp.	Absent	1 + 7 + 6	Sessile	10–25
Crayfish	Cyl.	Fused with thorax	3 + 5 + 6	Stalked	15–130

* The first four orders listed belong to the subclass Branchiopoda; the last four to the Malacostraca; the other three are each a separate subclass.
** *Cyl.* = cylindrical. *Comp.* = laterally compressed. *Dep.* = dorsoventrally flattened.
*** Thoracic appendages used for food-getting, plus thoracic legs, plus abdominal appendages.

like chitinous covering of the cephalothorax, and are often fastened to the leg bases (as one who has sucked many a lobster leg in childhood well knows). Thus the movement of the legs increases the circulation of water over the gills.

Collecting. Many crustaceans can be collected by gathering masses of vegetation or debris, or by skimming off the top layer of the substratum. This material should be placed in pans of water and slowly separated so that the organisms can swim out into open water and be picked up with pipette or lifter. Plankton or open-water forms may be caught in a tow net or Birge cone net. The bottom sprawlers of shallow water can often be sucked up with a large pipette. Many species will live in a balanced aquarium.

Fairy Shrimp—Order Anostraca
Figs. 42, 43.1

As their name indicates (*anostraca*, without a shield), the fairy shrimp lack the carapace. They vary in color, ranging from translucent whitish to blue, green, orange or red. (I vividly recall a little red, white and blue *Eubranchipus* from an isolated pothole in the Finger Lakes region.) A single species may vary also, its color apparently depending upon its food and stage of development and, according to Dr. Roman Vishniac, upon the bacterial content of the water. Although the average length is 20–25 mm., *Eubranchipus floridanus* is only 5–6 mm. and *Branchinecta gigas*, 60–100 mm.

Locomotion. Fairy shrimp are remarkably graceful, swimming usually on their back, beating their many long, leaflike gill feet in a series of wavelike motions which pass rearward; then drifting along lazily for a moment only to dart forward again, with a flash, to come to rest upon the substratum.

Food and importance. They feed on bacteria, protists, rotifers, or bits of detritus, filtered out of the water and brought to the mouth by the beating of the legs. They are, in turn, especially relished by amphibians, caddis larvae and dytiscid beetle larvae. Since the water in which they live is often temporary, as well as alkaline, they do not form an important item in the diet of fish. In many regions they have disappeared by the time the birds are abundant, and so are of little significance as food for them, although flamingos are said to scoop up the Brine Shrimp, *Artemia salina,* with seeming enjoyment. The Brine Shrimp were also harvested by the Indians.

Reproduction. In any population females are usually more abundant than males. When males are present each is usually paired with a female. The eggs may be produced by parthenogenesis or by fertilization. They are carried in a brood sac on the ventral side of the female's body, and are released in clutches at intervals of 2 to 6 days, with 10 to 250 eggs in a clutch. The eggs, their development already started, drop to the bottom. Each eventually hatches into a *nauplius,* an immature stage with three pairs of appendages, which must undergo several molts before becoming adult. There are two types of eggs: thin-walled summer ones and thick-shelled winter, or resting, eggs. The latter are able to withstand cold and desiccation and are the means of survival when the temporary pools disappear. Winter eggs may hatch as early as January if water is present, the brightly colored fairy shrimp sometimes swimming about beneath the ice. Other species may not hatch until May.

Habitat. With the exception of the Brine Shrimp of Great Salt Lake and of brine pools the world over, fairy shrimp live in temporary bodies of water, pools formed by melting ice, small potholes that contain water only in the early spring, pools where water gathers only after a rain, or in ditches. They seem to spring to life almost overnight, growing to maturity and reproducing in a few short weeks.

Although they are fairly common their discovery always seems to mark an occasion for the collector. One cannot expect to go back again and again to the same place to find the same species. Fairy shrimp are extremely local in distribution, one species being present in one pool and a quite different species in a pool close by. Furthermore, they appear sporadically, the species that is abundant one year sometimes being completely absent the next.

Grouping of Families of Fairy Shrimp

WITH 17 TO 19 PAIRS OF SWIMMING APPENDAGES
Polyartemiidae. *Polyartemiella* from Alaska and Northwest Terr.

WITH 11 PAIRS OF SWIMMING APPENDAGES

1. Second antennae of male with long, folded outgrowth on terminal segment; head with small frontal outgrowth (Fig. 42).

   Streptocephalidae. *Streptocephalus.*

2. Second antennae of male not as above; head without frontal outgrowth.

   Artemiidae. Second antennae of male with terminal segment platelike. *Artemia salina* lives in salt lakes sometimes of such density that salt crystallizes on its body.

   Branchinectidae. Second antennae of male serrate on inner margin, or with a knob or spur at base of inner margin, or slender with outturned tips. *Branchinecta* (Figs. 42, 43), west of the Miss. R.

   Chirocephalidae. Second antennae not as above; sometimes without appendage. Appendage small and blunt in *Pristocephalus* of Calif.; long, ribbonlike and serrate in *Chirocephalus* (Fig. 42) of northern states; long, coiled and with fingerlike processes in *Eubranchipus*

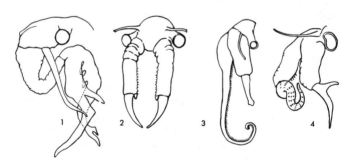

Fig. 42. *1*, Lateral view head and appendages *Streptocephalus seali*. *2*, Head of male, anterior view, *Branchinecta paludosa*. *3*, Head of male, lateral view, *Chirocephalus bundyi*. *4*, Head of male, lateral view, *Eubranchipus holmani*. (1, 2 and 4 after Pennak; 3 after Ward and Whipple.)

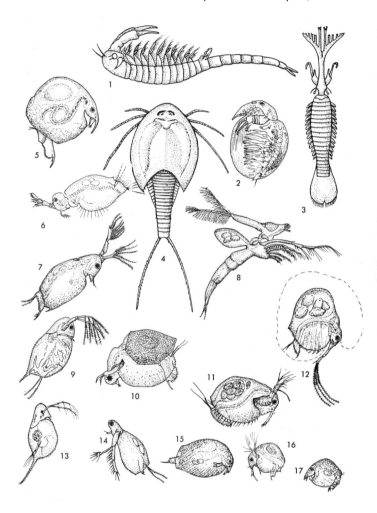

Fig. 43. Crustaceans. 1. *Branchinecta*. 2. *Lynceus* with shell removed. 3. *Thamnocephalus*. 4. *Triops*. 5. *Chydorus*. 6. *Latona*. 7. *Sida*. 8. *Leptodora*. 9. *Daphnia pulex*. 10. *Ceriodaphnia*, with ephippium. 11. *Macrothrix*. 12. *Holopedium*. 13. *Daphnia longiremis*. 14. *Diaphanosoma*. 15. *Acroperus*. 16. *Bosmina*. 17. *Alonella*. (After Pennak, Ward and Whipple and various authors.)

(Fig. 42); and absent in *Artemiopsis* of Alaska and Northwest Terr.

3. Second antennae of male not as any above. Frontal appendage present, branched in male.

Thamnocephalidae. *Thamnocephalus* (Fig. 42) of west and southwest; and a rare genus from Ga.

Clam Shrimp—Order Conchostraca

· Fig. 43.2

The little clam shrimp are covered with a bivalved carapace and thus really do resemble tiny clams. Most species live in the littoral zone of lakes, ponds and temporary pools, preferring warmer water than do the fairy shrimp. A few live in muddy water, and a few in alkaline pools. They swim backside up with a rowing motion of the two long, biramous second antennae; or they burrow in the substratum or move clumsily over the bottom, tumbling on their sides if their antennae stop waving. The reproductive cycle is similar to that of the fairy shrimp except that they carry their eggs in a mucous mass on the back, between the body and the shell. They are often extremely local in distribution.

Grouping of Families of Clam Shrimp

SHELL WITHOUT GROWTH LINES
Lynceidae (Fig. 43). *Lynceus* is cosmopolitan.

SHELL WITH CONCENTRIC GROWTH LINES
Limnadiidae. With a poduncled structure on middorsal surface of head. Two genera, N.E. to Colo., south to Texas.

Leptestheriidae. Rostrum with a conspicuous spine. *Leptestheria*, west and southwest.

Cyzicidae. Without head structure and without spine on rostrum. Several genera, west from Ky. and Texas.

Tadpole Shrimp—Order Notostraca

Fig. 43.4

The flattened tadpole shrimp, each with a large, shield-like carapace over the head and thorax, bear a remarkable resemblance to tiny horseshoe crabs of the sea beach. They swim backside up in a graceful, gliding manner and may even creep over the bottom or burrow in it. Some species are hermaphroditic. The eggs, borne on the 11th pair of appendages, hatch into *nauplii*. Food consists of earthworms, molluscs and even frog's eggs and dead tadpoles, as well as their normal diet of microscopic organisms. In California, *Triops* may be a serious pest in the rice fields, eating the young leaves and stirring up silt; but in Mexico, it is valued as food.

Triops, of the west and the tropics, has 34 to 44 body segments. *Lepidurus,* of the west and far north, has only 25 to 34 segments and has the telson expanded to form a flat paddle.

Water Fleas—Order Cladocera
Fig. 43.5–17

The many widespread species of water fleas are compressed from side to side. Most species have a shell which is a single folded piece, gaping ventrally and not covering the head. This shell may be oval, round, elongate or angular and may bear a characteristic posterior spine. The head is often bent down and birdlike in profile; it sometimes develops grotesque and helmeted extensions. Plankton species are darker in color than littoral ones, with tinges of yellowish brown, reddish brown or even black. A few pond species have pink blood but the majority have pale yellowish blood.

Water fleas are a joy to watch through the microscope; the large oval heart can be seen beating through the carapace, and the large conspicuous, compound eye jerking and rotating with every movement of the body.

Locomotion. The biramous second antennae are long and fringed for swimming. A single vigorous stroke of these antennae will send a quietly resting *Latona* (related to *Sida*) off in a sudden leap. A series of rapid, jerking strokes will be used to propel a *Daphnia* along on its irregular course. Other species toddle along unsteadily like high-heeled teenagers over cobblestones. The gelatinous-cased *Holopedium* and the spine-tipped daphnid, *Scapholeberis,* are the only ones to swim upside down.

Food and importance. The larger cladocerans, *Polyphemus* and *Leptodora*, are primarily carnivorous, rowing rapidly about in pursuit of smaller water fleas, rotifers and protists, and seizing them with specially modified legs. The majority, however, feed on organic detritus, bacteria and protists. Some plankton species may even be able to separate colloidal organic material from the water. Some species of *Daphnia* and *Bosmina* are algal feeders and are of distinct value in holding in check the growth of algae in reservoirs and water supplies.

Water fleas are an important link in the food chain, serving as food for hydras, insects, wading birds and for fish, for whom they may supply 90 percent of the diet. Rotifers are often attracted to them (especially to *Daphnia*), possibly because of the oscillation of the appendages. *Vorticella* and *Epistylis* often live upon them, feeding on the bacteria brought in on the currents set up by the waving antennae.

Reproduction. In the early spring only a few cladocerans are about, but by the time the water has reached a temperature of 6–12° C, reproduction proceeds at such a rate that the numbers increase strikingly, reaching 200 to 300 individuals in a liter of water. By midsummer the numbers will have been greatly reduced but a second pulse will occur in the fall. Lake species do not show the same fluctuation.

Females may carry from 2 to 40 parthenogenetic eggs in a dorsal cavity. The young remain in this chamber for about two days after hatching and when released must undergo several molts before becoming fully mature. By the time they are adult their own first clutch of eggs is ready in the brood chamber. Adults may molt as many as 25 times and each time a new clutch of eggs is produced. Males do not appear in any number until late spring, sometimes then reaching 5 percent of the population and sometimes more than 50 percent. Development of males is probably induced by the crowding of the females, which results in a lessening of the food supply and an accumulation of excretory products, and possibly by the attainment of a certain thermal condition (probably 14–17° C). If these same conditions continue the females begin to produce only one or two, or very few, eggs instead of their usual number, and these will be fertilized by the males and stored in the thickening, darkening brood chamber. At the next molt of the female the brood chamber is released as an *ephippium* which, with its contained eggs, either drops to the bottom or floats upon the surface. In the family Chydoridae it remains attached to the molted female skeleton. The ephippia are highly resistant to drying and freezing and thus survive adverse conditions of drought and of winter. If the pool becomes filled again with water in the fall the ephippial eggs hatch into females that reproduce parthenogenetically. If the population again becomes large the same cycle will ensue and more ephippial eggs will be produced for wintering over.

Habits. Species of *Daphnia* that live in the plankton of open waters have an interesting diurnal migration pattern, rising at dusk, going down during the night, rising at dawn and going down again during the daytime hours. They ordinarily swim away from light of any intensity, so there must be a combination of factors of temperature, pressure and carbon dioxide concentration, etc., to produce this pattern. Another type of activity studied in some *Daphnia* has been their tendency to dance up and down in water from which blue light has been removed, or, in other words, in red light areas; and their corresponding tendency to move in a horizontal direction in blue light areas. Thus in areas rich in green algae, where much of the blue light has been removed, they will remain to enjoy the fruits available; but in open water where the blue has not been subtracted, they move out horizontally until by chance they reach a nutrient-rich area.

Cladocerans are abundant in all types of water except rapid streams and polluted waters. *Holopedium* lives in calcium-poor water; some live in acid bog waters; but many prefer the weedy margins of ponds. *Macrothrix* and *Camptocercus* skim over the substratum; *Ilyocryptus* burrows in the mud; while many genera live in the plankton of open lakes.

Grouping of Families of Water Fleas

BODY AND APPENDAGES NOT COVERED WITH A FOLDED SHELL

Leptodoridae. With 6 pairs of appendages. *Leptodora kindtii* (Fig. 43.8) of northern lakes is the largest freshwater cladoceran; females 7–18 mm.

Polyphemidae. With 4 pairs of appendages. *Polyphemus pediculus*, 1½ mm., in northern lakes, ponds, marshes.

BODY AND APPENDAGES ENCLOSED IN A FOLDED SHELL. Less than 6 mm.

1. With 6 pairs of legs, all similar except the last pair, flat, foliaceous.

   Sididae (Fig. 43.6,7,14). Not in a gelatinous case. Several genera.

   Holopedidae (Fig. 43.12). In a gelatinous case. *Holopedium*, 1–2 mm., N.E. to Col. and Texas.

2. With 5 or 6 pairs of legs; first and second pairs prehensile.

   a. First antennae covered by ridges of top of head which unite with rostrum to form a beak.

      Chydoridae (Fig. 43.5,15). Several genera, including *Camptocercus*.

   b. First antennae attached to ventral side of head, not covered.

      Daphnidae (Fig. 43.9,10,13). With 5 pairs of legs. Several genera of which the commonest is *Daphnia* which has a rostrum and a cervical sinus.

      Bosminidae (Fig. 43.16,17). With 6 pairs of legs. First antennae fixed.

      Macrothricidae (Fig. 43.11). With 5 to 6 pairs of legs. First antennae freely movable. Several genera, including *Macrothrix* and *Ilyocryptus*.

Seed Shrimp—Subclass Ostracoda
Fig. 44.1

Seed shrimp resemble tiny clams, as do the clam shrimp. Their bivalve shell lacks growth lines; it is held together on the back by a band of elastic tissue which permits the ventral side to gape and the appendages to protrude. Although marine forms may reach a length of 21 mm., and one South American freshwater species is 8 mm. long, all North Ameri-

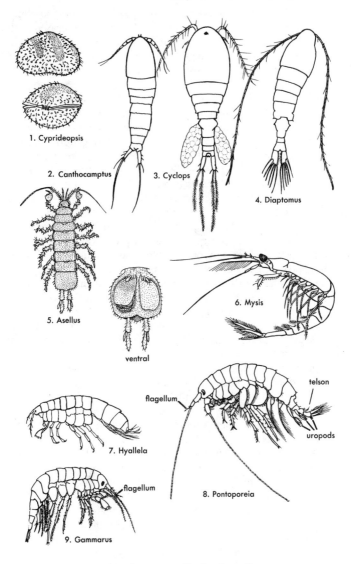

1. Cyprideopsis

2. Canthocamptus

3. Cyclops

4. Diaptomus

5. Asellus

ventral

6. Mysis

7. Hyallela

flagellum

telson

uropods

8. Pontoporeia

flagellum

9. Gammarus

Fig. 44. Crustaceans (8, after Pennak)

can freshwater forms average 1 to 3 mm. They may be white, yellow or gray-green, red, brown or black. The thorax usually has three pairs of legs and the head region four pairs. The abdomen has no appendages but terminates in two long *rami*.

Locomotion. These active "seeds with legs" creep along the bottom in an unsteady manner, sometimes scurrying rapidly and sometimes stopping to introduce a little dance step into their gait. Their antennae are in almost constant motion.

Food and importance. For the most part they are scavengers, feeding on bacteria, molds, algae and general detritus and on dead animal matter. They themselves are eaten only to a very small degree by fish; but a few species do serve as an intermediate host of certain fish tapeworms and of an Acanthocephala that parasitizes fish. Several live on fish, amphibians and crayfish although possibly not as parasites.

Reproduction. The majority of all individuals collected are females. In some species no males are known; in most cases males are present but only in very small numbers. Certain European ostracods are notorious for the size of their long-headed sperm cells which may be up to 10 times as long as the males themselves and longer than the sperm of whales or elephants. There is some question whether these excessively long sperm cells are functional since most of the eggs develop parthenogenetically. In North America, with the exception of one ovoviviparous *Darwinula,* all species lay their eggs singly or in clumps or rows along twigs, rocks or plants. The *nauplii* that emerge from the eggs must undergo about 8 molts before becoming adults.

Habitat. Ostracods are found in all types of fresh waters but are seldom found more than 1 meter deep, although *Cypridiopsis vidua* has been collected at 300 meters. Most species creep about in the algae or over vegetation or burrow in the mud and ooze of the bottom, but a fairly large number are free-swimming. One rare cyprid *Notodromas monacha* clings upside down to the surface film in open water. One Puerto Rican species lives only in the water of bromeliads. Several cyprids can survive long periods of stagnation with little oxygen. Ostracods of some species or another can be found at most any time of year.

Grouping of Families of Ostracods

ALL LEGS SIMILAR. OUTER BRANCH OF SECOND
ANTENNAE A LONG BRISTLE

Cytheridae. Several genera, including *Entocythere* that
lives on gills of crayfish.

LEGS DISSIMILAR. OUTER BRANCH OF SECOND AN-
TENNAE ABSENT OR PLATELIKE

Darwinulidae. 2nd and 3rd legs similar, the latter directed ventrally. *Darwinula,* on muddy bottom of
lakes.

Cypridae. 2nd and 3rd legs dissimilar, the latter directed
dorsally and backward. About 20 genera many of
which, including *Cypris* and *Cypridiopsis* and *Can-
dona,* are common.

Copepods and Fish Lice—Subclasses Copepoda and Branchiura

Fig. 44.2–4

Copepods are most easily recognized by their cylindrical
shape, greatly narrowed abdomen and two setae-bearing
caudal *rami* (branches). The single-eyed *Cyclops,* bearing
two egg sacs, is probably the most familiar member of the
group.

The great majority are less than 2 mm. long, whitish,
grayish or brownish in color. Littoral species, as well as those
at higher altitudes, tend to be brighter; in the spring some
species along the weedy margins of ponds may be bright
pink, green or blue. The bright reddish color sometimes seen
in *Diaptomus* is due to oil globules stored within the body.
Deep-water species tend to be smaller, more slender, and
translucent.

Locomotion. The three orders (see below) are different
in many of their habits. The harpacticoids crawl or run
over the substratum, but the calanoids and cyclopoids swim
freely. The movements of the antennae and the feeding
activities of the mouthparts account probably for their slow
forward movement. The antennae also aid in equilibrium and

depth adjustment; but it is the backward movements of the hind legs that produce their jerky forward progression.

Food and importance. Most species feed primarily on organic detritus that they scrape or rake from the bottom, or upon small organisms that they can seize with their mouthparts. The calanoids, however, feed only on plankton filtered out by the mouthparts from the currents of water brought toward them by the waving of the antennae. Although free-living forms are eaten to some degree by larger animals they are of no great significance in the aquatic food chain. They are of some importance in other ways since several species serve as the alternate host of some tapeworms, flukes and nematodes. In Africa, Asia and the West Indies it is *Cyclops* that is the intermediate host of the Guinea Worm, *Dracunculus medianus,* a serious parasite of man; and, here at home, *Cyclops* and *Diaptomus* that are intermediate hosts of the fish tapeworm that may infest man.

Many species are parasitic on the body, fins or gills of fish, obtaining nourishment from the tissues of the host; but they are rarely present in sufficient numbers to be a serious pest except in fish hatcheries. Some of these are placed in a separate subclass, Branchiura.

Reproduction. Mating pairs are often seen swimming together. The sperm are transferred to the female in small packets; the actual fertilization of the eggs may take place in a few minutes or not for several months. The eggs are carried on one or two sacs attached to the ventral side of the body, 5 to 40 eggs in a sac. In *Cyclops* the newly hatched larvae leave the sac in 12 hours to 5 days after hatching, but the disintegrating sacs are almost immediately replaced and filled with a new clutch of eggs. Since this may be repeated from 7 to 13 times at intervals of 1 to 6 days, the females have egg sacs attached more often than not. Some species of *Diaptomus,* as well as of a few other genera, sometimes produce thick-walled resting eggs that withstand adverse conditions. The *nauplius* that hatches from the egg may become an adult in a week or not for several months or even a year.

Some cyclopoids encyst under adverse conditions. This not only enables them to survive periods of drought but facilitates their dispersal by the wind.

Habitat. Copepods are widespread and common in all quiet waters; they occasionally inhabit lotic waters. Limnetic species may be found in tremendous aggregations numbering 100 per liter of water, but such aggregations usually contain few species. A greater variety of species live in the littoral vegetation but they occur in fewer numbers of individuals.

Temperature plays an important part in the distribution of copepods. Many species prefer the cold water of arctic and deep-water lakes; others, the warmer water of small pools.

Grouping of Suborders of Free-living Copepods

ANTERIOR PART OF BODY MUCH BROADER THAN POSTERIOR

1. First antennae long, with 22 to 25 segments, reaching to end of broad part of body or beyond.

   Calanoida. With a movable articulation between segments 6 and 7. Females usually have a single egg sac. Of the seven or eight genera *Diaptomus,* with the first leg 2-segmented, is the largest and most widespread; in plankton of ponds and lakes. *Senecella* of the deep cold water of the Great Lakes has the left antenna of the male geniculate; all others have the right antenna geniculate.

2. First antennae with no more than 17 segments, never reaching beyond the wide part of the body.

   Cyclopoida. Females usually with two egg sacs. Several genera of which the most common and widespread is *Cyclops*; mostly littoral, a few in plankton.

ANTERIOR PART OF BODY NOT MUCH WIDER THAN POSTERIOR PART

   Harpacticoida. Antennae short, not reaching beyond end of head segment. Females with a single egg sac. The 27 genera, belonging to 12 different families, are mostly littoral, in vegetation, woodland pools, mud and debris of the shore, even between sand grains on damp beaches. Some are in brackish water. *Bryocamptus* and *Canthocamptus* are common and widespread.

Grouping of Suborders of Parasitic Copepods and Branchiurans (free-swimming at some stages)

NO MOVABLE ARTICULATION BETWEEN SEGMENTS 5 AND 6

1. Long and wormlike.

   Caligoida. *Lernaea*, 7–15 mm., on gills and skin of fish. Leave host for a free-swimming life for a short time, returning to another host.

2. Cephalothorax a broad, flat disc.

   Celigoida. *Lepeophtheirus*, 6–16 mm., on salmon recently returned from the sea.

3. Body not as in 1 and 2. Legless.

   Lernaeopodoida. Males small, clinging to females. Attached to gills and fins of fish.

WITH MOVABLE ARTICULATION BETWEEN SEGMENTS 5 AND 6

   Branchiura. *Angulus*, .5–25 mm., body greatly flattened. In branchial chambers or on skin of fish.

   Cyclopoida. *Ergasilus*, .6–1 mm., body not flattened. On gills of fish.

Oppossum Shrimp—Order Mysidacea
Fig. 44.6

Most of the oppossum shrimp live in the sea; only one is found commonly in fresh waters of North America although two are known from brackish and coastal waters and several from caves. They resemble miniature crayfish differing in having a short carapace that is not fused with the thorax; in having long, slender 2-branched, many-segmented appendages, none of which are walking legs and none of which are chelate (having pincers); and in not having gills.

Mysis relicta, 15–30 mm., is probably evolved from *M. oculata* of the Arctic Ocean; it is circumpolar, living in this country in the cold, deep waters of the Great Lakes, some of the Canadian lakes, Green Lake of Wisconsin, and the Finger Lakes of upper New York State. In warm weather it withdraws to the deeper parts where temperatures may be as low as 4° C, migrating to the surface at dusk where it can endure a temperature of possibly 20° for a few hours.

Food. Mysis is an important food for fish, sometimes making up 80 percent of the stomach content of such fish as the Lake Trout. It feeds on plankton and detritus, filtering it out of the water by means of the *maxillipeds.*

Reproduction. Breeding occurs during the colder months. The eggs are never laid in water above 7° C. They are carried in a *marsupium* on the ventral side of the body, 40 in a clutch, and there they hatch, remaining within it for from one to three months after oviposition.

Groupings of Species of Opossum Shrimp

TELSON WITH WIDE BIFURCATE TIP
    Mysis relicta, 15–30 mm. Northern lakes east of the
        Great Plains.
    Taphromysis louisianae, 8 mm. Gulf coast.
TELSON WITH NARROW TRUNCATE TIP
    Acanthomysis awatchensis, 15 mm. Brackish and coastal
        ponds of Pacific coast.

Sow Bugs—Order Isopoda
Fig. 44.5

Sow bugs, sometimes called pill bugs, are chiefly terrestrial or marine but about 50 species live in springs, spring brooks, wells and subterranean waters. They are flattened dorsoventrally and do not have a carapace. The head is fused with the first two thoracic segments; the seven remaining thoracic segments are similar to each other and expanded on each side to cover the leg bases; the last four abdominal segments are fused with the telson to form a shield that gives them a distinctive appearance. The abdominal appendages are modified as respiratory organs. Most species are uniformly black or gray; a few are brown, reddish or yellowish; and a few are mottled.

Locomotion. Sow bugs crawl slowly over the bottom or

over vegetation. The Sphaeromidae roll into a ball when disturbed in much the way many of the terrestrial species do.

Food and importance. All are scavengers on dead or injured animals but some feed on plant tissues at times. *Sphaeroma terrebrana* may bore into the timbers of wharves and pilings, and some species of *Lirceus* become pests on water cress. Sow bugs are of little importance as food for fish. Several species are the intermediate host for certain nematodes of birds, fish and amphibians.

Reproduction. Breeding may take place throughout the year. The male carries the female, ventral side down, beneath his body for several hours, performing bilateral copulation. The eggs and newly hatched young are retained in a brood pouch for 20 to 30 days. This brood pouch, or *marsupium,* is a shallow area on the female's venter, formed by inward projections from several of the anterior legs. It is aerated by the up-and-down motion of the legs and mouthparts.

Habitat. Preferring to hide in vegetation or under logs and rocks, isopods are seldom out in open water, and they are seldom in water more than one meter deep, although *Lirceus lineatus* has been found down to 55 meters. They can withstand stagnation and often live in refuse and trash where no other living creatures are to be found. Swirling aggregations of *Asellus* have been reported from small streams but they were probably swept out of seclusion by the current. Some live in temporary pools, burrowing into the bottom during a drought; some live in quite acid waters. They are often seen in midwinter clustering beneath the ice, and again in early spring in incredibly large numbers.

Grouping of Families of Isopods

PARASITIC ON SHRIMP

    Bopyridae. *Probopyrus* of Gulf States is parasitic on Palaemonidae.

FREE-LIVING. UROPODS LATERAL IN POSITION

    Sphaeromidae. Abdomen with only 2 segments. Up to 70 mm. *Sphaeroma,* with outer margins of uropods toothed, bores in timbers and mangrove roots, etc., in brackish waters of Gulf States. *Exosphaeroma,* with outer margins of uropods smooth, lives in warm springs of southwest and Pacific coast.

Cirolanidae. Abdomen with 6 segments. Springs of Texas.

FREE-LIVING. UROPODS TERMINAL. COMMON AND WIDESPREAD

Asellidae. *Lirceus,* up to 25 mm., has margins of head produced laterally to cover the leg bases; east of Great Plains. *Asellus,* our commonest genus, up to 20 mm., does not have margins of head produced. Many common species as well as many blind, cave forms.

Scuds, Sideswimmers—Order Amphipoda

Fig. 44.7–9; Pl. 13

Like the isopods, the amphipods have no carapace; but unlike the isopods, their body is laterally compressed. They are chiefly marine, only about 50 species having taken up life in fresh waters.

Locomotion. They move about actively at night, walking, crawling or "skittering" on their sides by flexing and extending the entire body, and frequently rolling up on their sides or back. When swimming they hold the body out straight.

Food. They are omnivorous scavengers, feeding on both plant and animal material and browsing over aquatic vegetation for the microscopic film of organic material to be found there. They are preyed upon by fish, birds, insects and amphibians.

Reproduction. The males transfer their sperm to the females where it mixes with the eggs that have been placed in a *marsupium.* The eggs may range in number from 1 to 50. In species of *Gammarus, Hyallela* and *Synurella,* the males carry the females on their back during mating, swimming about in that position sometimes for as long as a week. They separate to give the female an opportunity to molt if the need arises, and then come together again for the trans-

Hyallela, a common amphipod

A female *Cambarus* with her young attached to her swimmerettes

PLATE 13

fer of the sperm. The newly hatched young remain in the marsupium for several days. Each female may have several broods a season, a new copulation being necessary for each brood.

Habitat. The common and widespread *Hyallela azteca, Gammarus limnaeus, G. fasciatus* and *Crangonyx gracilis* live in clear, unpolluted waters in enormous numbers. The less common species are more restricted; some are found only in deep, cold water or in caves or springs. Except for the deep lake species of *Pontoporeia* they are seldom found more than one meter below the surface. In general, they flourish in cold waters the year round, hiding in vegetation or under debris in both quiet and lotic waters.

The many blind species (and blind forms of normal species) of caves and underground springs may appear in woodland seepages. The gammarid *Synpleonia,* completely without eyes, is often found as far north as New York and Connecticut.

Grouping of Families of Amphipods

FIRST ANTENNAE WITHOUT ACCESSORY
FLAGELLUM
>   **Talitridae.** *Hyallela azteca,* 4–8 mm., is widely distributed in springs, brooks, pools and lakes where there is submerged vegetation.

FIRST ANTENNAE WITH ACCESSORY FLAGELLUM
>   **Haustoriidae.** First antennae slightly shorter than second; 5th pair of legs much shorter than 4th. *Pontoporeia affinis* is found in deep cold water only, on the bottom or in plankton of such lakes as Nipigon, Green (Wisc.), Washington (Seattle), the Great Lakes and some Finger Lakes.

>   **Gammaridae.** First antennae usually longer than second; 5th pair of legs as long as or longer than 4th.

>   1. Accessory flagellum with 3 to 7 segments. The widespread and common *Gammarus,* up to 25 mm., has inner branch of 3rd uropod more than half as long as the outer branch; but the northwestern *Anisogammarus,* 11 mm., has the inner branch very small.

2. Accessory flagellum with one short and one long segment, or rudimentary. Several genera; the largest in number of species and the most widespread are *Crangonyx* and *Synurella*.

Crayfish, Shrimp—Order Decapoda
Figs. 41, 45; Pl. 13

Crayfish and shrimp are mostly marine but about 160 species are found in fresh water. They resemble the oppossum shrimp in having the carapace covering most of the thorax and in having the eyes stalked. They are much larger, however, and differ in having the carapace fused dorsally with all of the thoracic segments and extended forward to form an elongated, spined *rostrum*. They also differ in having three pairs of the thoracic legs modified to form maxillipeds. The remaining five pairs of legs are walking legs, at least 2 pairs of them chelate (with a movable finger).

The highly sclerotized exoskeleton bears a conspicuous *cervical groove* across the dorsum of the carapace. Some species are translucent, others are heavily pigmented with

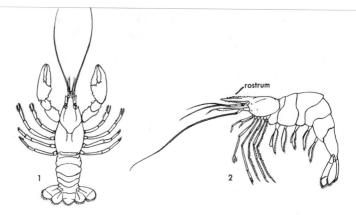

Fig. 45. Crustaceans. *1. Procambarus*, showing three pairs of chelate walking legs. *2. Palaemonetes*, showing two pairs of chelate legs (after Pennak).

black, brown-red, orange-red or blue, occasionally with mottling. They may show considerable color variation. *Oronectes immunis,* for example, ranges through all the colors listed above. Often the shade and even the hue is influenced by the background; this is the result of the ability of the light-sensitive color cells, the *chromatophores,* to open and close, thus exposing varying amounts of the red, yellow, blue or white pigment granules they contain.

Locomotion. Decapods swim, walk or climb about slowly, moving with equal facility backward, forward, or sideways. When alarmed they dart quickly backward, swimming with a vigorous downward stroke of the tail. The Palaemonidae are fairly good swimmers.

Food and associates. They are omnivorous predators and scavengers but they also eat a variety of vegetation. They are eaten by fish, wading birds, frogs, turtles, racoons, otter, mink, etc. Algae and protozoa of many species live growing upon them; the ostracod *Entocythere* lives as a commensal on their gills and the leechlike oligochaetes of the Branchiobdellidae live in the gill chambers.

Reproduction. Mating in some species occurs in the fall; in others, the year round. The males seem unable to distinguish the sexes, for in breeding season they try to mate with whichever they encounter. During copulation, which may last several hours, the female is held with her back down; the sperm, guided by the first pair of abdominal appendages of the male, are then deposited in an orifice between the 4th and 5th walking leg of the female. Several weeks after copulation the female secretes a sticky covering, or *glair,* over the ventral surface of her body. Into this the sperm, as well as her own eggs, are released; and here fertilization takes place. A single female may produce as few as 10 or as many as 800 eggs, all of which are carried fastened to her abdominal appendages, for from 2 to 20 weeks. The newly hatched young remain attached to the mother until they have undergone 2 or 3 molts (Pl. 13).

Habitat. Some crayfish burrow in wet meadows, never actually going into the water. Others prefer muddy ponds and ditches, burrowing into the banks if the water dries up. Still others live always in the water of lakes and slow rivers or swift streams. They seldom are in water over 5 feet deep. Crayfish are active primarily at night, although in shady streams or on cloudy days they may come out into the open. The burrows vary in size and complexity of structure; they range in depth from a few inches to 8–10 feet, depending upon the water level, since the terminal chamber in which the crayfish spends the day must be wet. The excavated soil is piled up around the entrance, sometimes forming chimneys of considerable height.

In Europe, crayfish are eaten extensively. They have never become as popular in America although species in Louisiana and in Oregon have been eaten to some extent, as have those from the Great Lakes and the Mississippi drainage system. In the south, they sometimes become a nuisance. They denude young grain, sugarcane and cotton seedlings, and they burrow in dams and dikes. Furthermore, the chimneys of their burrows often clog farm machinery. Several eastern species serve as intermediate host to the lung fluke *Paragonimus westermani*, which is parasitic in man and other carnivores, so crayfish must be thoroughly cooked before being eaten.

Grouping of Families of Decapod

BODY LATERALLY COMPRESSED. WITH FIRST TWO PAIRS OF WALKING LEGS CHELATE

> **Palaemonidae.** Second chelate leg larger than the first. No spine above the eye. The southeastern river shrimp, *Macrobrachium*, 9–240 mm., have a palp on the mandible. The eastern and southern prawns and grass shrimp. *Palaemonetes*, 25–55 mm., have no palp on the mandible.
>
> **Atyidae.** First and second pair of chelate legs subequal. With a spine above the eye. *Syncaris*, 20–50 mm., Calif.

CEPHALOTHORAX CYLINDRICAL, ABDOMEN FLATTENED. WITH FIRST THREE PAIRS OF LEGS CHELATE

> **Astacidae.**
>
> 1. West of continental divide. *Pacifastacus*, up to 110 mm.

2. East of continental divide. *Cambarus* and *Oronectes* males have the tip of the first abdominal appendages ending in two parts, which in the former are short and bent at right angles; in the latter, short or long but if short never bent at right angles; 50–130 mm. *Procambarus* and *Cambarellus* males have the tip of the first abdominal appendages ending in 3 or more parts; the former genus has hooks on basal segment of the 3rd or the 3rd and 4th thoracic appendages; the latter has hooks on basal segment of 2nd and 3rd thoracic appendages. *Procambarus* ranges in size from 50–130 mm.; *Cambarellus,* from 15–30 mm.

CHAPTER 11

Spiders and Mites—
Class Arachnida

Fig. 46; Pl. 14

ARACHNIDS differ from other arthropods in having *no* antennae, *four* pairs of long, six-segmented legs, and only *two* pairs of mouthparts.

None of our spiders are truly aquatic although a few are consistently associated with fresh waters, chiefly the fisher spiders of the family Pisauridae. *Dolomedes,* for instance, may run out on the surface film and occasionally dive beneath, covered with a silver coating of air trapped in the body hairs. Although normally insectivorous they sometimes capture small fish and tadpoles. In Europe the famed *Argyronecta aquatica* spins a flat web in vegetation beneath the surface and then carries air bubbles down into the water, releasing them beneath the web. She then sits, air-enveloped, beneath the ballooning bell-shaped web, viewing the submerged life around her, exploiting the aquatic environment but not aquatic herself. No American species has been found to be so daring. Only the mites of the order Hydracarina have become at home in the water.

Water mites are usually globular in shape, though some are depressed and slightly elongated and some are compressed. They differ from the spiders in having the cephalothorax and abdomen fused and unsegmented. Their mouthparts consist of a pair of mandibles that are small (unlike their spider counterparts, the *chelicerae*) and are kept withdrawn in the *capitulum* when not in use; and a pair of *pedipalps* that may be scissorslike at the tip or merely clawed or pointed. The two eyes are double; they may be widely separated with sometimes a third median eye, or they may lie close together on the midline of the dorsum. The body may be soft and leathery or may bear heavily sclerotized plates. It is usually bright scarlet red or orange, sometimes blue, yellow or tan, and occasionally brown. Stream species are likely to be brownish. They tend to be flatter and smaller than pond species, and lack swimming hairs on the legs, though they may have strong claws for clinging to submerged vegetation or substratum.

Respiration. A pair of spiracles is located on the dorsal surface of the capitulum near its base, but respiration is probably mostly through the body wall, for mites apparently seldom come to the surface for air.

Locomotion. Mites creep about on the bottom and on vegetation. Although they swim, their swimming is awkward and uncertain, since their legs are poorly coordinated. If they stop swimming they sink to the bottom. That is probably why they seem to scurry through the water in such a purposeful manner.

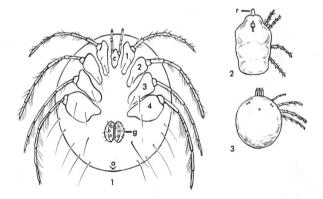

Fig. 46. 1. Diagram to show mite structures, ventral side; c, capitulum; 1, 2, 3, 4, epimera of the four legs; g, genital field; a, anus. 2. Dorsal view of *Limnochares* showing two pairs of eyes on an ocular plate. 3. Dorsal view of *Hydrachna* showing eye arrangement; r, rostrum.

Dolomedes sexpunctatus, a fishing spider capable of catching small fish.

Eggs of the fish fly *Nigronia,* on a *Typhus* leaf. Top of stem is to the right.

PLATE 14

Food. Mites are carnivorous or parasitic, feeding on insects and worms, piercing their victim to draw out the juices. It has been suggested that they may be of some value in controlling mosquitoes, for a mosquito carrying a load of five or more mites is indifferent to eating and without a blood meal is unable to reproduce. A few mites are cannibalistic and a few feed on dead animals. They are preyed upon by hydras, insects and fish, sometimes being one of the main items to be found in fish stomach contents.

Reproduction. The eggs are usually bright red. They are laid in groups of 20 to 200, often in a gelatinous matrix, on vegetation and debris, hatching in from 1 to 6 weeks. Some are laid within plant tissues; others are deposited in the tissues of sponges or in the gelatinous matrix of colonial protozoa.

The larvae are probably at first free-swimming but soon attach themselves to the bodies of aquatic insects, especially to stoneflies, dragonflies, flies and bugs. After feeding upon these for a while they may undergo a resting period of from 5 days to 6 months, during which they slowly shrink inside their outer skin. The *nymph* that eventually emerges is similar to the adult but is not sexually mature. It may enjoy a carnivorous, free-swimming life for a short time and then again settle down. This time it attaches itself to algae or other plants for a resting period of 7 to 10 days before finally emerging as a mature adult.

A few species are never parasitic; a few are parasitic for their entire lives within the bodies of mussels or sponges. Undoubtedly there are other variations from the normal pattern. Mites have been taken from within the bodies of dragonfly nymphs where they were packed beneath the exoskeleton in great numbers, and have been gathered from the adult dragonflies as the dragonflies emerged from their nymphal skin.

Mites are found in all seasons of the year, even under the ice. They are most abundant in the spring and autumn. They live in all kinds of water, even in temporary pools and hot springs, and in the wet moss and algae along the shores. *Unionicola crassipes* is apparently the only species to be found normally in plankton.

Collecting. Mites are usually collected by dragging a dip net or plankton net through vegetation in shallow water, especially in temporary pools. David Cook advises placing the vegetation thus gathered in a water-filled, white pan, leaving a large clear space out into which the mites can swim; or sinking a pan in the vegetation and then sucking into a pipette the mites that swim out. In lotic waters he finds the best technique to be that of removing a stick or stone from the water and then, just as it begins to dry, to pick up the wiggling mites with a toothpick.

Anyone who has observed water striders skating about on the surface film, laden with the bright red bodies of mites, will know where collecting will be productive.

Grouping of Families of Aquatic Mites*

LATERAL EYES CLOSE TOGETHER AT MEDIAN LINE
1. Mouth at tip of protruding rostrum. Eyes on elongated plate.
   Limnocharidae. *Limnochares,* up to 5 mm., a soft red creeper; often on Hydrometridae.
2. Mouth not at tip of rostrum. Eyes connected by a narrow bridge.
   Eylaidae. *Eylais,* up to 7 mm., soft, red swimmers in quiet water, often on aerial insects.
LATERAL EYES WIDELY SEPARATED
1. Pedipalps scissorslike (4th segment extending beyond insertion of 5th so that the two can cut on each other).
   a. With swimming hairs on legs.
   Hydrachnidae. Rostrum protruding well beyond body (Fig. 46,C). Mandibles straight and stilettolike, 1-segmented. Median eye present.
   Hydrachna, 1–8 mm., soft, globular, red, orange or brown; in standing water.
   Diplodontidae. Rostrum not protruding. Mandible 2-segmented with tip curving and clawlike. No median eye. *Diplodontus,* 2 mm., soft, red. Common.
   Hydryphantidae. Rostrum not protruding. Mandible

*Adapted from Pennak. Identification is not practicable for anyone but the specialist.

2-segmented. Median eye present. *Hydryphantes* 1–2.5 mm., red. Often on mosquitoes or midges.

b. Without swimming hairs on legs.

Protziidae. Last two pairs of epimera widely separated from first two. Soft forms on bottom in cold water.

Thyasidae. Last two epimera not widely separated. Northern. Uncommon.

2. Pedipalps not scissorslike, 5th segment pointed, clawlike and opposable to 4th.

Arrenuridae. Genital field posterior to 4th epimera. *Arrenurus* is the largest American genus; heavily sclerotized, red, green or with blue-green and orange. Common in vegetation.

Athienemanniidae. Genital field between 4th epimera. Midwestern. Uncommon.

3. Pedipalps not scissorslike. 5th segment not opposable to 4th.

a. Legs crowded together at anterior end of body. Body laterally compressed.

Lebertiidae. Several genera. Uncommon.

b. Legs not crowded together. Body not laterally compressed.

1) First epimera fused on midline. Dorsum without large sclerotized plates.

Hygrobatidae. Genital field posterior to 4th epimera. Common.

Libertiidae. Genital field between 4th epimera. Cold waters.

2) First epimera fused on midline. Dorsum with a large sclerotized plate.

Atractideidae. First epimera projecting beyond anterior margin of body.

Thermacaridae. In hot springs of Nev.

Mideidae. Genital field bounded by all epimera. Rare, Wisc.

Axonopsidae. Genital field near posterior margin.

Unionicolidae and Mideopsidae. Not as above.

3) First epimera not fused on midline. Genital field between 4th epimera or anterior to them.

Sperchonidae, Tyrelliidae and Limnesiidae. The latter with swimming hairs but no terminal claws on legs.

4) First epimera not fused. Genital field posterior to 4th epimera.

Unionicolidae and Prionidae. Widely distributed and common.

CHAPTER 12

Insects—Class Insecta

Figs. 47–71; Pls. 1–5, 14–18

INSECTS are the dominant animals of any freshwater environment and are often the most conspicuous and most easily caught. Yet, of the more than 700,000 species of insects known, comparatively few are aquatic. Insects first became established on land; their occurrence in water is secondarily derived. They all, even those that are truly aquatic, have a tracheal system of respiration which is an oxygen-carrying set of tubes with external openings called *spiracles*. But insects have ever been opportunists and when there has been an unexploited area they have taken advantage of it. Thus it is that many species and some entire orders have moved into fresh waters for at least a part of their existence. Thirteen orders have aquatic representatives and four orders have become truly aquatic, laying their eggs in the water and spending their entire larval life there, using oxygen dissolved in water.

Insects, in common with all other arthropods, have a segmented body and jointed legs, and are covered with a chitinous *exoskeleton* which must be periodically shed (molted) as the animal increases in size. The body is divided into *head, thorax* and *abdomen*; but these differ from those of other classes in the phylum in that in the adult stage the head bears *one* pair of antennae only, the thorax has *three* pairs of legs and usually *two* pairs of wings, and the abdomen *no* true appendages other than occasional, greatly modified terminal *cerci*, or reproductive structures.

The mouthparts typically consist of a stout pair of jaws,

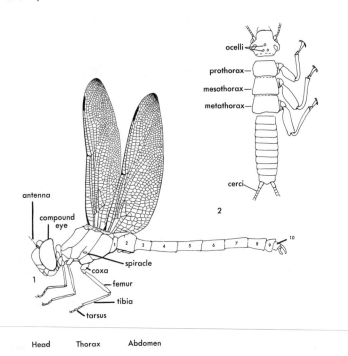

Fig. 47. Parts of an insect. 1. An adult dragonfly. 2. A stonefly
nymph.

mandibles, one on each side of the mouth; a pair of sharp
maxillae, bearing palps; an upper lip, the *labrum;* and a
lower lip, the *labium,* which sometimes bears palps. These,
however, are greatly and variously modified. Most insects
have a pair of compound eyes made up of many small visual
units and many also have tiny simple eyes, the *ocelli.* Typically they have two pairs of spiracles on the thorax and eight
pairs on the abdomen but these have become greatly reduced
in number.

The immature forms often vary considerably from the
adults and may not have these distinguishing characteristics.
In fact, no group of animals shows as much diversification

as the insects. This diversification as well as their ability to exploit nearly every possible environment and every type of food has largely been made possible by their *metamorphosis*.

Metamorphosis is a series of changes which permits an animal to have a different form and even a different way of life at successive periods of its existence. The insect that hatches from the *egg*, except in a few groups, does not resemble the adult; it is called a *larva*. After a series of molts the larva will undergo a decisive molt which transforms it into an *adult*, or *imago*; or it may pass through an intermediate, semiquiescent stage, the *pupa*, which permits an even greater change in internal structure to take place, with a subsequent transformation to an adult of very different form. The function of larval life is nourishment and growth; that of the pupa, when it occurs, is change; and that of the adult is the distribution and reproduction of the species. Metamorphosis with a pupal stage is said to be *complete*. When there is no pupal stage the metamorphosis is described as *incomplete*, and the larva is called a *nymph*.

WHERE INSECTS ARE TO BE FOUND

The secondary invasion of the water by insects is by no means recent in geological history. (The Paleodictyoptera, known only from the Upper Carboniferous, are believed to have had aquatic larvae.) Yet insects have not conquered the problems of life in very deep water or in the oceans. Only a few species of midges are to be found in the deep water of lakes, and only a few bugs, flies, and dragonflies tolerate the conditions of brackish waters and salt lakes, although in New Zealand there is one caddis fly that seeks saline waters. Bugs of one family, the Halobatidae, are to be found skipping over the surface of the ocean, sometimes far from land, but they are probably not physiologically aquatic. Nevertheless insects are to be found in many unusual aquatic environments, such as hot springs, alpine pools, tree holes, flower vases, leaves of pitcher plants, bases of epiphytes, sewage, petroleum beds, subterranean streams and caves, as well as in a great variety of open waters.

1. *On the surface of the water.* Whirligig beetles gyrate in the surface film, with occasional forays beneath the water; water striders run lightly over the surface, dimpling the film but never breaking through; marsh treaders creep slowly out, never venturing far from vegetation; and springtails in enormous numbers mill about in quiet coves. A few hydrophilid beetles creep up to the surface film from beneath, pierce it with their tarsal claws, and run about suspended upside down.

2. *Submerged but coming to the surface for air.* Many aquatic beetles and bugs, as well as the larvae of many flies and a few moths, live this way. (See paragraph on respiration below.)

3. *Submerged, living on oxygen dissolved in water.* Here are found the larvae of the four so-called aquatic orders: the stoneflies, mayflies, dragonflies and caddis flies. Here also are found the larvae of Spongilla flies, alder and fish flies, blackflies and midges; the larvae of a few moths and beetles; and a few rare bugs.

PROBLEMS OF AQUATIC LIFE

The chief problems for insects living in the water are those concerned with respiration, food-getting, locomotion, anchorage, oviposition and emergence.

Respiration. Obviously, surface-living insects have no problem. Those that come to the surface to get air use it as do their terrestrial relatives but they have a variety of ways for breaking through the surface film and for transmitting the air to the spiracles. Those that remain submerged have developed special devices for availing themselves of the oxygen beneath the surface. These can be grouped briefly:

1. *A spiracle-bearing tube for piercing the surface film.* Mosquito larvae project a respiratory tube, or siphon, through the film, then hang suspended by means of hydrofuge hairs that spread out on the film. A *Culex* larva may obtain enough oxygen in this way to permit its subsequent submergence,

without activity, for ten minutes or more. Several other groups of dipterous larvae, notably the false cranefly larvae and the rat-tailed maggot, have a long, spiracle-bearing tube for reaching up through the surface film; so also do the water scorpions.

2. *A device for carrying air on the outside of the body.* The insect must first come to the surface and break the film. Water boatmen do this with their head; giant water bugs with straplike flaps at the end of the abdomen; hydrophilid beetles with the unwettable clubs of the antennae; most other beetles with the tip of the abdomen. The air is then drawn in through any exposed spiracle and is also channeled to spaces under the wings or to the ventral side of the body where it is held in place by minute hydrofuge hairs, coating the body with a silver sheen. In certain bugs these hairs are said to number 250,000,000 per square centimeter. The spiracles lying under this coat of air draw upon it as air is needed. The silver coating is known as an *air plastron* and may sometimes act as an air gill, an exchange of gases taking place through the film of the plastron.

Plastron respiration is more common than hitherto suspected. Many bugs and bettles stay submerged for longer periods of time than the amount of air in the jacket would permit if further exchange were not taking place. Professor G. A. Edwards[*] has pointed out that a notonectid bug may remain submerged for six hours; that a dytiscid beetle may stay beneath as long as 36 hours, although its normal period of submergence is not over 20 minutes; and that certain small beetles of the genus *Helichus* are able to remain submerged for weeks. Probably any plastron, no matter how seemingly permanent, has to be replenished at the surface or from bubbles of oxygen from submerged plants, or, in the winter, by bubbles trapped beneath the ice; but its efficiency as an "organ" of respiration has been an important factor in making life beneath the surface possible for many species of air-breathing insects.

3. *Tracheal gills.* These are thin-walled cutaneous outgrowths that contain many air-filled trachea. Oxygen diffuses

[*] In Roeder.

into them from the water, and carbon dioxide diffuses out. Stonefly nymphs have tufts of gill filaments on the thorax. Mayfly nymphs have pairs of platelike or filamentous gills along the sides of the abdomen. Alder fly and fish fly larvae have paired lateral abdomenal filaments and sometimes anal filaments as well. Caddis larvae have variously placed filaments, and some aquatic caterpillars have hundreds. Caddis larvae and odonate nymphs have rows of tracheal gills in the lining of the rectum. Damselflies do also, but they have, in addition, three conspicuous caudal gill plates. Mosquito and a few fly larvae have anal gills, though they may be more concerned with diffusion of ions than of oxygen.

4. *Blood gills.* These are thin-walled cutaneous outgrowths of the larval body wall that are continuous with the blood cavity. They are present in nonbiting midges, a few caddis flies, a few psychodid caterpillars and a few exotic beetles. Insect blood, since it contains haemoglobin, can carry oxygen. Insects having blood gills usually live in waters of low oxygen concentration.

5. *Special structures for chewing or piercing submersed plants to obtain oxygen from their tissues. Donacia,* a chrysomelid beetle and *Lissorhaptus,* a weevil, pierce the tissues with sharp spines. The larvae and pupae of *Mansonia,* a mosquito, pierce the tissues with a respiratory siphon. Other dipterous larvae use a spine on the tip of the abdomen. A few tendipedid midges and nepticulid moths spend their larval life as miners within the leaves of aquatic plants, and both beetle and moth larvae of a few species live as borers in the stems. Several moth larvae make a case out of green leaves and use the oxygen produced by the photosynthesis of the living plant tissues.

Locomotion. Most aquatic adult beetles and bugs are more streamlined than their terrestrial relatives. The body is often keeled and boat-shaped, and may have a smooth, slippery cuticle. The antennae are sometimes folded back into grooves on the sides of the head. One or more pairs of legs may be flattened and fringed with long hairs. The hind legs of many beetles have the basal segment (*coxa*) greatly expanded and closely adherent to the body, or so attached to the subsequent segments as to permit them to pivot on each other. In the gyrinid beetles the segments of the flattened, paddlelike hind legs are hinged fanlike at one side.

Water striders have long slender legs that spread out spiderlike as the insect runs over the surface film. Their bodies as well as their legs are covered with a water repellent. The tarsal claws are well back from the tip so do not pierce the film. The Broad-shouldered Water Strider, *Rhagovelia*, has a fanlike tuft of hairs on the middle tarsus which spreads out to make a paddling device.

Submerged larvae swim by lateral undulations of the body, sometimes aided by a rudderlike motion of the tail. The Odonata dart ahead by "jet propulsion," accomplished by sucking water in through the anal opening and then expelling it with such force that the body shoots forward.

Anchorage. Because of their air-filled trachea, insects have a problem not shared by most other aquatic organisms, that of anchorage. Many bugs and beetles have to cling to vegetation by means of their tarsal claws, lest they rise to the surface. Water pennies are greatly flattened with expanded hind margins and are thus held by "suction" to the rocks in waterfalls and fast streams where they live. Lotic mayflies are also flattened, sometimes with lateral abdominal gills overlapping, first and last pairs extended inward to form a suction area beneath. The larvae of net-veined midges are held to the rocks by a row of small suction discs; the pupae are cemented down by their flat, moist ventral surface, thus exposing to the current only the hard, slippery, seedlike dorsum. Caddis fly larvae are held down by the weight of their cases, many of which are also glued to the substratum. Blackfly larvae are held fast to rocks by means of a terminal adhesive disc and by silken threads, and they securely fasten down the cocoon which they spin for their pupae. A roll call of aquatic insects would be necessary were one to attempt to cover all the devices they employ in securing anchorage.

Oviposition. Water-dwelling adults usually glue their eggs to rocks, to vegetation or to other submerged surfaces. Some pierce submerged plant tissues with an ovipositor and then insert their eggs. One little haliplid beetle bites out a hole for this purpose. Some nonaquatic adults drop their eggs into the water as they fly overhead. The eggs drop singly or in clusters, and sink to the substratum where they may become anchored by discs or adhesive filaments. *Anopheles* and *Culex* mosquitoes lay their eggs on the surface. Those of *Anopheles* are laid singly and held afloat by two floats on each egg; those of *Culex*, in clusters that form flat, floating rafts. One nonbiting midge deposits a gelatinous clump of eggs which remains suspended, several inches below the surface, by a slender thread attached to a transparent disc which catches upon the surface film.

Females of some mayflies and some caddis flies wrap their wings about their body and go beneath the surface to deposit their eggs upon submerged objects, directed by some impelling, unrecognized maternal urge into this unnatural medium from which they may not emerge alive. One water boatman, *Ramphocorixa*, fastens her eggs to the back of the crayfish *Cambarus*. Giant water bugs of two genera lay them on the back of their own long-suffering mate who must bear the eggs as well as the offspring that hatch from them.

But many of the nonaquatic adults either oviposit on land, on rocks, bridges, pilings and branches overhanging the water or on, or in, emergent plants.

Grouping of Orders of Aquatic Insects

INSECTS WITH WELL DEVELOPED WINGS. ADULTS
1. With one pair of wings. Hind pair absent or rudimentary.

> **Diptera.** Hind wings replaced with rodlike balancing organs. Fig. 65.

> **Ephemeroptera.** Hind wings rudimentary. Abdomen with long tails. Fig. 54.

2. With two pairs of membranous wings. Abdomen petiolate.

> **Hymenoptera.** Rarely in water.

3. With two pairs of membranous wings. Abdomen broadly joined to thorax.

> a. Antennae short and bristlelike.

> > **Odonata.** Fore and hind wings more or less similar. Fig. 57.

Ephemeroptera. Hind wings much smaller than fore wings. Fig. 54.

  b. Antennae long and threadlike, or massive.

    1) Wings not covered with hairs or scales.

      Neuroptera and Megaloptera. Tarsi 5-segmented. Figs. 49, 50.

      Plecoptera. Second and third tarsi 3-segmented. Fig. 51.

    2) Wings covered with scales. Tarsi 4–5-segmented.

      Lepidoptera. Mouthparts forming a long coiled tube.

    3) Wings covered with hairs. Tarsi 4–5-segmented.

      Trichoptera. Mouthparts reduced. Fig. 69.

  4. First pair of wings, at least the basal half, horny, leathery or parchmentlike.

    1. Entire fore wing horny, without veins, forming a shell-like covering.

      Coleoptera. Mouthparts for biting; with palps. Fig. 63.

    2. Fore wings with only basal half thickened, with veins.

      Hemiptera. Mouthparts forming a sucking beak; without palps. Fig. 62.

    3. Fore wings parchmentlike, with veins.

      Orthoptera. Mouthparts for biting, with palps. Rarely in water.

PUPAE, ENCASED IN A HARD SHELL, OR MUMMY-LIKE

  1. Pupa encased in a hard capsule.

    Diptera.

  2. Pupa mummylike with appendages free.

    a. Thorax with one pair of wing pads.

      Diptera. Fig. 67.

    b. Thorax with two pairs of wing pads.

      Hymenoptera. Abdomen petiolate.

      Trichoptera. Mandibles crossing each other. Usually in a web or case.

      Coleoptera. Pads of front wings thickened. Antennae usually 11-segmented.

      Neuroptera and Megaloptera. Not as in above three

orders. Neuroptera are small, 10 mm. or less, and in a cocoon above ground. Megaloptera are 12 mm. or over and in burrows in the ground or in wood.

3. Pupa mummylike with appendages fused with the body.

Diptera. With one pair of dorsal breathing tubes near the front of the body and a pair of terminal leaflike gills.

Lepidoptera. Not as above. Sclerotized.

INSECTS WITHOUT WINGS OR WING PADS. THORAX WITHOUT SEGMENTED LEGS. Larvae (see PUPAE above)

1. With a distinct head capsule.

Diptera. With gills or breathing tube at end of body. Figs. 66, 68.

Coleoptera. Without gills or breathing tube. Weevils. Rare.

2. With head capsule indistinct.

Diptera. Fig. 65.

Hymenoptera. Less than 2 mm. long. Rare.

INSECTS WITHOUT WINGS OR WING PADS. THORAX WITH SEGMENTED LEGS

1. Head with a pair of compound eyes, each with 100 or more facets (see group with external wing pads).

2. Head with only a few separated eye facets.

a. Abdomen with never more than 6 segments.

Collembola. With a ventral spring.

b. Abdomen with more than 6 segments, usually 10 to 11. Larvae.

Neuroptera. Living in sponges. 10 mm. or less. Mouth beaked. Fig. 49.

Lepidoptera. Abdomen with several pairs of prolegs each with a ring of hooks. Fig 71.

Trichoptera. Apex of abdomen ending in 2 lateral lobes each with one hook. Usually in a case or web, Fig. 70.

Megaloptera. Apex of abdomen ending in 2 lateral lobes each with 2 or more hooks. Family Corydalidae. Fig. 50.

Megaloptera. Apex of abdomen terminating in a long tail. Family Sialidae.

Coleoptera. Apex of abdomen ending in one lobe with 4 hooks. Family Gryinidae. Fig. 64.

Coleoptera. Apex of abdomen with no terminal hooks. Fig. 64.

INSECTS WITH EXTERNAL WING PADS

1. Active, with freely movable legs and antennae.

a. Abdomen with paired, horny plates. Pupae.

Trichoptera. Usually in a case or web. Antennae with 25 segments; tarsi with 5.

b. Abdomen not so.

Hemiptera. Mouthparts a beak. Antennae with 10 or fewer segments.

Odonata. Lower lip hinged and extensile. Figs. 59, 60.

Ephemeroptera. With two or three long, terminal tails. Sides of abdomen usually with paired gills. Tarsi with 2 claws. Figs. 55, 56.

Plecoptera. Abdomen terminating in 2 short cerci. Antennae with 25 or more segments. Tarsi not more than 3-segmented, with 2 claws. Fig. 53.

Trichoptera. Antennae of 25 segments or more. Tarsi 5-segmented. Usually in cases or webs. Pupae.

Orthoptera. Hind leg for jumping. Rare.

2. Mummylike or in a hard covering. See Pupae, above.

Springtails—Order Collembola
Fig. 48

The tiny springtails, usually less than 3 mm. long, are wingless. They are often found on the surface film in whirling aggregations of many hundreds, an occasional individual darting beneath the surface, then rejoining the mass immediately or remaining submerged for a considerable period of time. When disturbed the entire group may burst into the air, only to drop back and resume its endless milling about.

Their leaping is made possible by a forked spring, or *furcula*, that rises from the ventral side of the 4th or 5th segment of the abdomen and projects forward, catching in a clasplike structure, the *tenaculum*, on the 3rd segment, much

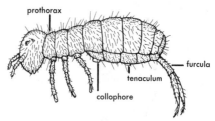

prothorax

furcula

tenaculum

collophore

Fig. 48. A Springtail, *Podura*.

like the spring of a mousetrap. When released it exerts a force that propels the insect into the air.

Eggs and immature forms. Eggs are probably laid in the vegetation along the shore. The young that emerge differ in appearance from the adults only in having less pigmentation and less differentiation of appendages. Springtails are thus without metamorphosis.

Food. Food consists of decaying animal or vegetable matter and possibly some living plant material.

Habitat. Many species are terrestrial, living in damp vegetation, rich humus and forest litter; and one species lives on the snow. Aquatic species are common in stagnant water, rain pools, intertidal zones or in quiet backwaters of ponds and streams. They hibernate during the winter, probably in the debris of the substratum, and often become reactivated on warm days. They may be among the first signs of animal life in the spring.

Collecting. Springtails may be dipped out with fine-mesh net or gathered by shaking moss and trash into a pan and then picked out with brush or pipette.

Grouping of Families of Aquatic Springtails

BODY ELONGATE. THORAX AND ABDOMEN SEGMENTED
1. Prothorax well developed, hairy. Cuticle granular.
   a. Thorax and abdomen without ocelli.
      Poduridae. Furcula extending to or beyond the collophore on abdominal segment 1. Ocelli present on back of head. *Podura aquatica*, 1–1.5 mm., is

the commonest aquatic species. It is dull, reddish brown or bluish black. In stagnant water. Cosmopolitan.

Hypogastridae. Furcula not extending beyond the collophore. Ocelli, if present, on front of head. Several genera. *Anurida maritima* is cosmopolitan in intertidal zone.

   b. Thorax and abdomen with ocelli.

Onychiuridae. *Onychiuris armatus* is cosmopolitan in rain pools and stagnant water. The furcula does not extend beyond the collophore. Other genera.

2. Prothorax reduced, usually hidden, not hairy. Cuticle smooth.

Entomobryidae. 4th abdominal segment at least twice as long as 3rd. Inner edge of claw with basal groove.

Isotomidae. 4th abdominal segment not twice as long as 3rd. Inner edge of claw without basal groove. *Isotomurus palustris* is cosmopolitan in stagnant water. Other genera.

BODY SUBGLOBULAR. SEGMENTS USUALLY NOT DISTINCT

Smynthuridae. Several cosmopolitan genera. *Smynthurus* is occasionally aquatic.

Spongilla Flies—Family Sisyridae, Order Neuroptera
Fig. 49.

The order Neuroptera contains many families of great diversity. The larvae are all predacious; their elongate, usually sicklelike mandibles are so grooved as to channel the flow of the blood and juices of their pierced victims. Only one family has aquatic larvae: the Sisyridae. These larvae live in or on sponges.

Spongilla flies are 6–8 mm. long, yellow or brownish in color, with two similar pairs of wings, long antennae, and biting mouthparts. They have complete metamorphosis. The adults may be seen all summer long but each individual probably lives only a few days. There may be several gen-

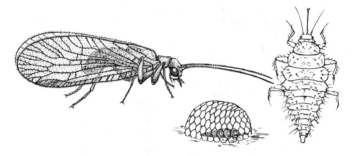

Fig. 49. Spongilla fly, *Climacia*. Adult × 6, pupal case, and larva × 7. (Pupal case after Brown.)

erations a year. Hibernation is believed to take place in the cocoon before pupation.

Eggs. The eggs 2 to 5 together, and covered by a silken blanket, are laid in vegetation or on bridges or other objects overhanging streams, so that the larvae fall to the water when they hatch some 8 days later.

Larvae. The larvae often have trouble breaking through the surface film and, when finally they do, seem quite ill at ease, swimming jerkily and apparently aimlessly until by chance they come in contact with a sponge. One might well ask what happens if they do not chance upon a sponge. Presumably they die; but it is to be remembered that the presence of egg-laying adults in that particular environment implies that they had transformed from sponge-inhabiting larvae, so unless something cataclysmic in the life of the stream has occurred, sponges are there. The larvae, upon finding the right species of sponge, will rest on its surface or actually enter the ostioles. When full grown they are 4 to 6 mm. long, pale greenish or yellow, stout and bristly. The stiff bristles catch bits of debris and sponge to such an extent that the larvae are often concealed and camouflaged.

Food. The elongate, apically curved larval mouthparts, when held together, form a tube that is inserted into the sponge tissue for extraction of its juices. The digestive tract is closed between mid and hind guts, so undigested material is retained.

Respiration. Paired, segmented, tracheal gills are located on the ventral side of the first 7 abdominal segments.

Pupation. Pupation takes place on shore or on emergent vegetation. The larva constructs a loose, dome-shaped net which in *Sisyra* is a crisscross mesh, but in *Climacia* is made of loose open hexagons. Within this it spins a tight-fitting cocoon in which it eventually pupates.

Both the larvae and the pupae may be parasitized by the chalcid wasp, *Sisyridivosa cavigena*, which is able to pierce the pupal net and the cocoon to oviposit on the organism within.

Collecting. Adults may be collected at lights or by sweeping the vegetation near sponge-inhabited streams. Larvae are taken by collecting the sponges. *Spongilla*, especially *S. fragilis*, and *Meyenia* are most likely to contain species of *Sisyra*.

Two genera, *Sisyra* and *Climacia*, are widespread. The larvae of the latter have conspicuous setae-bearing tubercles on the dorsum; those of the former have setae but no tubercles.

Alder Flies, Fish Flies—Order Megaloptera
Fig. 50; Pls. 5, 14

These awkward flying insects seldom go far from water and fly only short distances at a time. They are most easily recognized by the two similar pairs of large, membranous wings laid flat or rooflike over the body when at rest; by the long, many-segmented antennae; and by the biting and chewing mouthparts. They have complete metamorphosis. The smoky or black-winged Alder Fly, *Sialis*, 10–15 mm., is diurnal; it tends to run when disturbed rather than to fly. The fish flies or dobson flies, 25–70 mm. long and with a wingspread of 40–160 mm., are nocturnal, often lumbering into lights at night. When collected they should be handled with care, for they are capable of giving a quite sharp nip. Although all species have stout mandibles, those of *Corydalus* are exceptional; in the female they are about as long as the head and sharply toothed, but in the male they are two or

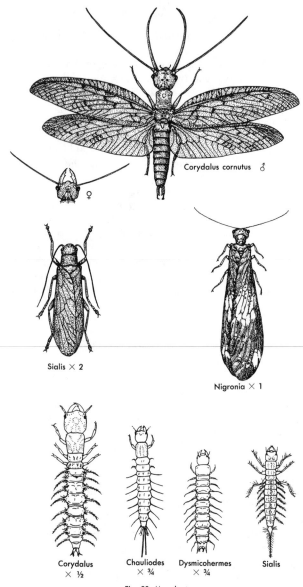

Corydalus cornutus ♂

♀

Sialis × 2

Nigronia × 1

Corydalus
× ½

Chauliodes
× ¾

Dysmicohermes
× ¾

Sialis

Fig. 50. Megaloptera

three times as long, and are slender and curved, and of little use other than for holding the female during mating.

Eggs. The eggs are deposited in rows of several thousands on vegetation (Pl. 14), bridges or other objects overhanging streams. They hatch during the night, in from 5 to 10 days.

Larvae. The hatching larvae drop into the water where they lead extremely predacious and cannibalistic lives for 2 to 3 years, seeking their prey on the bottom or in the mud under stones. *Corydalus*, the Hellgramite, is primarily nocturnal; it seems to swim backward as easily as forward.

Respiration. Respiration is by lateral filamentous gills or gill tufts, on the abdomen; and in *Sialis* by anal filaments as well. They also have spiracles so can remain alive out of water for some time.

Food. The larvae are of great importance in the ecology of the stream. They are secondary consumers feeding upon small animals and serving as food for still larger ones. They are thus "middlemen" in the food chain, changing small units into larger ones. Since they can survive exposure, especially if kept damp, they are useful as fish bait.

Collecting. Megalopteran larvae can be collected by dip net, apron net or scraper along the margins of ponds and lakes or from among the stones of the stream bed.

Grouping of Larvae

WITH LONG ANAL FILAMENT. WITHOUT ANAL PROLEGS
> **Sialidae.** Up to 30 mm. With 7 pairs segmented, lateral filaments. *Sialis.*

WITHOUT ANAL FILAMENT. WITH HOOKED ANAL PROLEGS
> **Corydalidae.** Up to 90 mm. With 8 pairs lateral gill filaments.
> 1. With tufts of filamentous gills at base of each lateral filament.
>   *Corydalus.* East and southwest.
> 2. Without gill tufts.
>   *Chauliodes.* 8th abdominal segment with long, contractile, spiracle bearing respiratory tubes

extending past end of terminal claws. Eastern and central states and Canada.

Nigronia. Respiratory tubes of 8th segment not reaching middle of 9th segment; half as long as wide. East.

Dysmicohermes. Respiratory tubes of 8th segment not reaching middle of 9th segment, about as long as wide. West.

Neohermes. Tubeless, having spiracles on margin of 8th segment. West and south.

Protochauliodes. As above. West and Canada.

Stoneflies—Order Plecoptera
Figs. 51–53

Adult stoneflies are mostly shade-loving, seeking seclusion in shrubbery and vegetation not far from the water from which they emerged. Occasionally, however, some of the capnids may be seen in bright sunlight on the winter snow. The wings, though sometimes rudimentary, are usually long and held folded back lengthwise over the body when at rest. At such times the insect has an elongate appearance as it sits thus wing-garbed, with two long antennae pointing forward and two fairly long abdominal cerci directed rearward. Adult mouthparts are greatly reduced; most species do not feed at all during that stage of their life, although a few feed on algae or nibble on pollen.

Eggs. Eggs are usually laid in the water, sometimes dropped in packets while the female flies overhead, and

Fig. 51. Adult stonefly × 3.

sometimes deposited in the water as she alights upon the surface. In a few species they are placed on objects just above or below the waterline by the crawling female.

Nymphs. Nymphs are similar in appearance to the adults except for their lack of wings, the structure and development of the mouthparts and, in some cases, the possession of tufts of filamentous gills. The wing pads, however, are to be seen conspicuously developing on the back of the thorax. The gills may be on the thorax at the "neck," at the base of the legs, on the base of the abdomen, and occasionally at the anus. They are often profusely branched and tufted. Nymphs show a considerable range in size; some species of *Capnia* may be only 6 mm. long, whereas the blackish *Pteronarcys* may be up to 60 mm. The latter are clumsy when removed from the water and often curl up motionless.

Food. Nymphs feed mainly on algae and plant debris, although most of the Perlidae, Perlodidae and some Chloroperlidae feed on insects, especially mayfly nymphs and fly larvae. Stoneflies are of enormous economic importance as

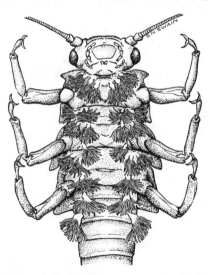

Fig. 52. Ventral view of *Pteronarcys* nymph, showing gills on thorax and first two abdominal segments.

food for fish and are even considered the most valuable item in the diet of young trout.

Stonefly nymphs, as a rule, are sluggish, resting in the debris or algae or clinging to the undersides of rocks in swift water. They are seldom found where the water is poorly oxygenated or polluted. They live as nymphs 1 to 3 years, crawling out of the water to transform in the early spring or in the late fall; a few species emerge in midsummer and a few in warm days during the winter.

Collecting. Nymphs are most easily collected by turning over stones in swift water and picking them off by hand; or by agitating stones, gravel and debris upstream of a hand screen held across the current. If they are to be transported alive they should be carried in damp cotton or moss rather than in water. They cannot be kept in an aquarium without an oxygenating device.

Grouping of Families of Stonefly Nymphs*

GILLS PRESENT ON VENTRAL SURFACE OF ABDOMEN

Pteronarcidae (Fig. 53.8). These are the giant stoneflies found in small, upland streams amid decaying vegetation. They usually emerge in late spring and early summer. *Pteronarcella* has gills on third abdominal segments; *Pteronarcys* does not.

GILLS NOT PRESENT ON VENTRAL SURFACE OF ABDOMEN

1. Body flat, broad and roachlike.

   Peltoperlidae (Fig. 53.5). With distinctive shieldlike thoracic plates. *Peltoperla.*

2. Not roachlike. Glossa and paraglossa of labium of equal length (*g* and *p* in Fig. 53).

   Nemouridae. Top of head with three ocelli. The winter stoneflies, Taeniopteryginae, live in large streams and rivers, emerging from January to April; they can be distinguished from others in having the 2nd tarsal segment as long as the first, instead of much shorter.

---

* A key to the genera of stonefly nymphs will be found in the Appendix.

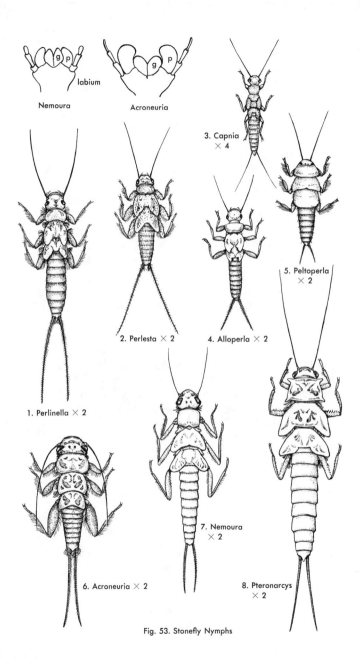

labium

Nemoura

Acroneuria

3. Capnia × 4

2. Perlesta × 2

4. Alloperla × 2

5. Peltoperla × 2

1. Perlinella × 2

6. Acroneuria × 2

7. Nemoura × 2

8. Pteronarcys × 2

Fig. 53. Stonefly Nymphs

The Nemourinae (Fig. 53.7), the spring stoneflies, live in small, sandy streams; they differ from the two following groups in having wing pads divergent instead of parallel. The Capninae (Fig. 53.3) and Leuctrinae are the smallest of the stoneflies, the former emerging in the late winter months, the latter from February to June but usually living only in hilly or mountainous streams.

3. Not roachlike. Paraglossa much longer than glossa.

Perlidae (Fig. 53.1,2,6). Profusely branching gills on ventral side of all thoracic segments. Many genera.

Perlodidae. Gills, if present on thorax, are single or double. Hind wing pads divergent. Many genera.

Chloroperlidae (Fig. 53.4). Gills, if present, are single or double. Hind wing pads nearly parallel. Many genera.

Mayflies—Order Ephemeroptera
Figs. 54, 55, 56

The cloud of mayflies dancing over a stream on an early summer evening may cause dismay to the motorist as the slender bodies hit against his windshield; and the swarming millions, attracted to the lights of a lakeside town, litter the streets as their dead bodies and cast skins fall to the

Fig. 54. Adult mayfly.

ground beneath lampposts and lighted windows. But the aquatic nymphs from which these short-lived adults emerged have been an important link in the chain of life that goes on beneath the surface of the water.

The winged form that first emerges, leaving its cast skin floating on the surface or clinging to floating vegetation or some waterside object, is not a true adult; it is a *subimago* and must, with but few exceptions, molt again. Then, as an adult, its one purpose is to mate and, if a female, to lay her eggs. This it does within a few hours or a few days, after which it dies, never having eaten and never having gone far from the water in which it spent its long larval life. The dancing swarms of newly emerged adults are called nuptial flights and consist mainly of males awaiting the emergence of the females. Many of them are eaten by dragonflies and birds.

Eggs. Eggs are laid a few at a time as the female dips the tip of her abdomen into the water between her gentle up-and-down dancing flights, or they may be dropped haphazardly into the water as well as onto wet roads or shining car tops. Sometimes they are placed on submerged objects by the female who crawls beneath the surface. She may be held by the accompanying male and be jerked back to the surface by him; or she may enter the water alone, search carefully for a suitable place, and then float back to the surface on an air bubble escaped from beneath her wings. Occasionally, however, she may not survive her journey into this unnatural medium.

The eggs are delicately contrived; they are sometimes embedded in a gelatinous matrix and are usually equipped with tiny knobs or with long, coiled filaments which anchor them to vegetation or debris. Many are washed away, if the current is swift, and many will be eaten by caddis larvae, snails, etc.

Nymphs. Mayfly nymphs are most easily recognized by the gills on the sides of the abdomen; the long, sweeping, filamentous tails (usually 3 in number; occasionally 2); and the single-clawed tarsi.

BURROWING FORMS (Fig. 55.1–7). The burrowers live in the banks or muddy bottoms of shallow lakes and rivers, digging in with the flattened, shelflike anterior margin of the head, the large mandibular tusks, and the flattened, fossorial front legs. Their long plumose gills are situated well around upon the back, and thus are not injured during burrowing. The gills are kept in almost constant motion in order to keep a current of water flowing through the open-ended burrows. Burrowers are usually less than 2 inches below the surface of the substratum but they have been found as deep as 5½ inches. Occasionally they dig into wet banks above the waterline by the hundreds, leaving their long, sweeping tails projecting from the burrows. These are the largest of the mayfly nymphs, 25–40 mm. long, and are the ones that emerge from lake waters in late spring and early summer in such enormous numbers that the subimaginal skins and the bodies of the adults lie deep upon the streets and sidewalks.

CLINGING, LIMPETLIKE FORMS (Fig. 55.8,14). These fast-water nymphs are greatly flattened. They cling so tightly to the surface of stones, especially to the undersides out of the light, that it is sometimes difficult to dislodge them. Their legs are flattened, knife-edged and sharp-clawed; their tails are held outspread in a horizontal plane; their gills are platelike, tending to overlap to form a ventral suction disc. Members of this group abound in running water, especially in cold mountain streams, often so attuned to cold that they remain active all winter. Their life cycle is shorter than that of the other groups, usually being completed in a single year.

FREE-RANGING FORMS (Figs. 55.13; 56.4). These nymphs have a more cylindrical body. The lentic water species have heavily fringed tails that give propulsion in swimming. They climb about in the vegetation, dart in and out of shelter and occasionally swim out in open water with considerable agility. The lotic water species do the same and, when at rest, head upstream into the current. Most of these forms emerge rather early in the season.

SPRAWLERS (Figs. 55.11,12; 56.1–3). The sprawlers are stiff-legged, thin-tailed and often slightly depressed of form. They walk about in the trash and debris or sit, silt-covered, on the bottom. The gills are often reduced in number and are dorsal in position; the foremost pair is often thickened

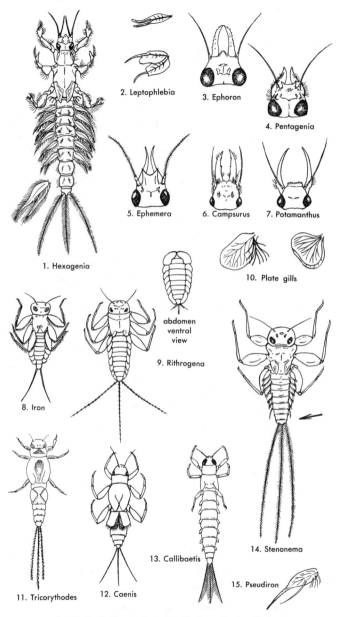

2. Leptophlebia

3. Ephoron

4. Pentagenia

5. Ephemera

6. Campsurus

7. Potamanthus

1. Hexagenia

10. Plate gills

abdomen
ventral
view

9. Rithrogena

8. Iron

14. Stenonema

11. Tricorythodes

12. Caenis

13. Callibaetis

15. Pseudiron

Fig. 55. Mayfly Nymphs (1–7 after Needham; 11 after Klots)

and platelike, forming an *operculum* under which the remaining gills may be concealed. Sometimes the gills bear marginal fringes that help in straining out the silt.

Food. Since the adults do not eat, the nymphal life beneath the waters is of importance. There, feeding upon diatoms and other microscopic plant organisms, and occasionally chewing the tissues of higher plants, the nymphs spend from one to four years. They contribute enormously to the economic life of fresh waters by changing plant material into animal tissue which can then serve as food for larger insects such as dragonfly larvae and beetles, as well as for many fish.

Emergence. When ready to emerge the nymphs crawl out of the water onto the bank, vegetation or pilings. Some swift water forms come to the surface of the water and molt as they break through the surface film; the emerging subimago is thus imperiled and must take instantly to wing.

Collecting. Mayfly nymphs are collected with apron net or scraper from the vegetation and substratum of ponds, lakes and slow streams. Lotic water forms may be collected from a hand screen held downstream in the current (see Appendix) or may have to be picked individually from stones. The delicate bodies must be handled with forceps and care taken not to injure the gills.

Grouping of Families of Mayfly Nymphs*

MANDIBLES WITH LARGE TUSKS PROJECTING FORWARD
1. Gills tuning-fork shaped, not fringed.
   Leptophlebiidae. This family does not belong in this group but the western *Paraleptophlebia* does have flattened, blunt, bare tusks.
2. Gills not tuning-fork shaped, with fringed margins.
   a. Gills lateral, outspread. Sprawlers. South and east.
      Potamanthidae (Fig. 55.7). Fore tibiae long and slender. *Potamanthus.*
   b. Gills dorsal, curving up over abdomen. Fore tibiae modified for digging.

* A key to mayfly genera will be found in the Appendix.

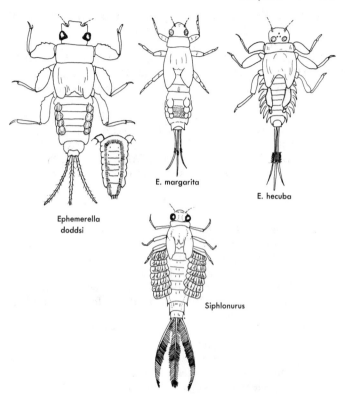

E. margarita

E. hecuba

Ephemerella
doddsi

Siphlonurus

Fig. 56. Mayfly nymphs. Three western species of *Ephemerella* show the variation in the dorsal gills. *Ephemerella* usually sits silt-covered on the substratum, but *E. doddsi* has the knife-edged femur and ventral suction disc (formed of hairs) that enable it to cling to rocks in lotic water. *Siphlonurus occidentalis* has large, heavily veined lateral gills. (After Klots.)

Polymitarcidae (Fig. 55.3,6). Head usually rounded in front, without a frontal process (except in *Ephoron*, which has tusks downcurved). *Campsurus.*

Ephemeridae (Fig. 55.1,4,5). Head with a frontal process. Tusks curving upward apically. Several genera.

MANDIBLES WITHOUT TUSKS. THORAX COVERED
WITH SHIELDLIKE CARAPACE
   Baetiscidae. *Baetisca.*
MANDIBLES WITHOUT TUSKS. BODY FLATTENED.
EYES AND ANTENNAE DORSAL. Lotic forms
   Leptophlebiidae. Gills forked, or ending in a filament,
   or in clusters. Several genera.
   Heptageniidae (Fig. 55.8–10,14). Gills a single plate,
   usually with a tuft near the base. Several genera.
MANDIBLES WITHOUT TUSKS. BODY NOT FLAT-
TENED. EYES AND ANTENNAE NOT DORSAL
   1. Anterior lateral margins of head with conspicuous crown
      of setae.
      Behningiidae. Gills ventral with fringed margins.
      Dolania.
   2. Not as in 1. Gills on segment 1 ventral.
      Oligoneuridae.
   3. Not as in 1. Gills dorsal, those on segment 2 operculate.
      Outer tails fringed on both sides.
      Tricorythidae. Opercula triangular. *Tricorythodes.*
      Neoephemeridae. Opercula quadrate, fused on midline.
      Neoephemera.
      Caenidae (Fig. 55.12). Opercula quadrate but not fused.
      Caenis, Brachycerus.
   4. Gills dorsal, those on 2 not operculate. Outer tails
      fringed on both sides (almost bare in *Baetodes*).
      Leptophlebiidae. Gills on segments 1 to 7. Several
      genera.
      Ephemerellidae. Gills on segments 3 to 7 or 4 to 7, first
      pair sometimes operculate. *Ephemerella* (Fig. 55.11).
   5. Gills dorsal, those on 2 not operculate. Outer tails
      fringed heavily on inner side only (Fig. 55.13).
      a. Claws all similar, shorter than tibiae.
         Baetidae. Postero-lateral angles of apical abdominal
         segments not prolonged. Front margin of labrum
         notched. Many genera.
         Siphlonuridae. Postero-lateral angles of apical abdomi-
         nal segments prolonged. Several genera.
      b. Claws of middle and hind legs as long as the tibiae.
         Metropidae. Claws of foreleg bifid. *Metretopus, Acan-
         thametropus.*

Ametropidae. Claws of foreleg slender, curved. *Ametropus.*

Dragonflies and Damselflies—Order Odonata
Figs. 57–60; Pls. 2, 4

Most of the myths that have grown up around these beautiful "darning needles" are apocryphal. Dragonflies do not sting; they do not sew up bad boys' ears or mouths; they do not kill snakes; neither are they "snake doctors." Actually they are highly beneficial insects, eating tremendous numbers of small insects which they catch on the wing and seem to relish with voracious appetite. Their mouthparts, though powerful, could scarcely nip a human being; they do not possess a sting. Although the big aeschnid, *Coryphaeschna ingens* of the south, nearly 4 inches long, sometimes captures bees, especially the queens; and though the libelluline, *Lepthemis vesiculosus,* has been observed many a time with remnants of butterfly and day-flying moth wings in its jaws, the great majority limit their bill of fare to the small, swarming midges and mosquitoes.

Odonata do have outstanding characteristics which make them fearsome in appearance and which certainly help explain their success as predators. Their bulging compound eyes are enormous, each one containing from ten to twenty thousand facets (each facet represents the outer face of a visual unit). The loosely jointed head rotates freely, giving the insect a broad field of vision. The long, spiny legs are held basketlike beneath the mouth when the insect is in flight; they serve to scoop up the small creatures on which the odonate preys and to hold the victim as the meal progresses. The large, membranous, conspicuously net-veined wings are controlled by powerful muscles packed within the large "skewed" thorax. Thus some species are capable of strong sustained flight (dragonflies have been captured many miles at sea); others are capable of great agility and speed.

Damselflies differ from dragonflies in several ways. The compound eyes project from the sides of the head instead of overspreading it as they do in dragonflies. The base of the hind wings is more or less the same size as that of the fore wing, instead of being broader. Their wing, when at rest, are held parallel to the body or tilted obliquely upward, seldom outspread. Damselflies are considerably more fluttering and uncertain in flight.

No visitor to fresh water can fail to be attracted by the grace and beauty of the dragonflies hovering along the shore, swooping over the water, or soaring overhead; or to be intrigued with the manner in which many species patrol a regular beat, returning again and again to the same perch. Identification of genera is dependent upon an understanding of wing venation, but one can quickly learn to recognize the small (wing expanse 50–78 mm.), red-bodied *Sympetrum*

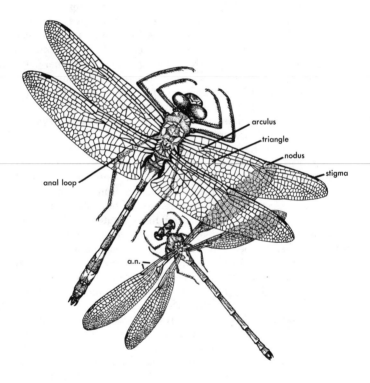

Fig. 57. Adult dragonfly and damselfly; a.n., antenodal cross veins.

flying in great numbers about ponds and swales in early autumn; the black-bodied, white-faced *Leucorrhinia;* or the hairy-bodied, darting, pugnacious *Tetragoneuria.* The large (expanse 80–122 mm.), strong-flying, blue darners, *Aeschna;* and the soaring, agile, green darners, *Anax* (Pl. 2), with swollen, light green or blue thorax, are common everywhere, often flying far from water, cruising along an arid bench or down a forest trail. The yellow- or green-bodied *Gomphus,* often conspicuously patterned with brown or black, and often with the tip of the abdomen expanded, are widespread but less seldom captured. The genus *Libellula* has many common species, some with black spots on the wings and some with brown or reddish-golden bands. *L. pulchella* is widespread and conspicuous, with three large, brown spots on each wing and, when mature, with additional spots of chalky white, two on each fore wing and three on each hind wing. *L. quadri-maculata* has a small basal spot on each wing; it frequently evokes the comment "No, not again," for it seems to turn up everywhere, sometimes with spots greatly reduced, sometimes with an additional spot at each wing nodus or a streak of yellow along the costa. The tiny (expanse 38 mm.), fluttering *Perithemis* has amber wings; and the related, but larger, *Celithemis* has wings marked with gold and brown.

Everywhere in and around the emergent vegetation of quiet waters one sees the slender, bright blue damselflies *Enallagma* and *Ischnura,* often in mated pairs (the female is dull in color); or a blue or violet *Argia;* and along the shaded margin or by a trickling brook, the brilliantly metallic, blue-bodied *Calopteryx maculatum,* with black wings.

Dragonflies range in size from the voracious *Epiaeschna heros* of the east, with a wing expanse of 116 mm., and the less common *Anax walsinghami,* from Calif. and the southwest, with wing expanse of 122 mm.; to *Nannothemis bella,* the pruinose blue, low-flying dragonfly of temporary pools and marshes from Ont. to Fla., with a wing expanse of 32 mm. Damselflies are all very much more slender and delicately built. The largest is the western *Archilestes grandis,* with wing expanse of 82 mm.; the smallest may be one of the species of *Neoneura* having a wing expanse of only 26 mm., though some species of *Ischnura* may be as small.

Eggs. The eggs of most species are scattered as the female skims over the surface dipping her abdomen periodically into the water. She is sometimes accompanied by the male riding in tandem. He may stay with her as she swoops down to the water or he may release her, waiting overhead until she once again soars upward. Damselflies and those dragonflies having an ovipositor (Cordulegasteridae) lay their eggs in the tissues of submerged green stems, in submerged logs or in the mud and sand of the bottom.

Nymphs. The nymphs are aquatic, burrowing in the soft substratum, crawling silt-covered, or algal-covered (or even coated with bryozoans) over the bottom, or lurking in the vegetation. They are voracious carnivores, feeding on insects and other small creatures, even small tadpoles and fish, which they catch by shooting out the double-hinged lower lip, or *labium*. This lip when in repose lies folded back against the ventral side of the head and thorax, with the broad, flat or scoop-shaped *mentum* concealing, or partially concealing, the lower part of the face. The labium is variously armed with sharp, jagged, toothlike incisors, movable hooklike teeth, or sharp bristles; so once the victim is caught it is impaled and held in place beneath the mouth of the captor whose strong mandibles can then chew at leisure. The jet-

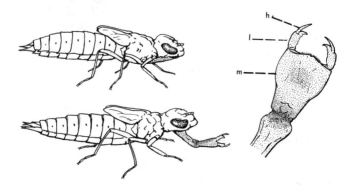

Fig. 58. A dragonfly nymph, *Gomphus*, with labium in position, and extended. Enlargement of labium showing, *l*, lateral lobe; *h*, movable hook; *m*, mentum.

propulsion type of locomotion, described earlier, can be demonstrated by placing a few drops of India ink in the water near the tip of the abdomen.

Respiration. (See page 174.)

Emergence. Emergence takes place sometime between early spring and early fall depending upon the species. Although some damselflies, such as *Enallagma* and *Ischnura,* may complete their life cycle in a year, most Odonata take longer, the nymphs hibernating in the mud and debris of the bottom. When they are ready to transform they crawl up onto the shore or onto bank, bridge or vegetation, as is evidenced by the cast skins so frequently found. The adults are at first soft-bodied, with shriveled abdomen and crumpled wings. Before they can take flight they must extend the abdomen and expand and dry the wings. For this reason transformation often takes place in the early morning before the predatory birds are abroad.

The transformation process is worthy of careful observation from the time, several days before, when the nymph ceases feeding and climbs up some appropriate object. Sometimes the nymph only partially emerges from the water, leaving the tip of the abdomen submerged. This position permits the continuance of normal aquatic respiration through the rectal gills; at the same time it enables the mesothoracic spiracles to open and gradually accustom themselves to the aerial environment. The splitting of the nymphal skin down the middorsal line, the emergence of first the thorax and then the head and legs, and then, when the legs have grasped a firm support, the withdrawal of the long abdomen, are but the prelude to the magic moment when air is gulped in, the abdomen is stiffened, and the shivering of the wings indicates that blood is being pumped into the wing veins. At last, extended and dried, the adult takes flight.

Collecting. As in collecting mayflies, the equipment used depends upon the habits of the nymphs. An apron net is good for those crawling in the vegetation, a scraper or garden rake for those in the mud and trash of the bottom, and an ordinary dip net for those along the margins of the shore. If the catch is emptied into a white pan or onto a piece of canvas the nymphs will soon wiggle into view. The collector will gain great pleasure from bringing home odonate nymphs alive and keeping them in aquaria under conditions as near like their natural environment as possible. Full-grown, or nearly full-grown, nymphs are recognized by their thickened and sometimes darkened wing cases; they will often transform in captivity if emergent stems or twigs are provided. (See, also, use of the pillow cage, in Appendix.) Nymphal skins (exuvia) may be gathered in numbers where they have been discarded on emergent or shoreline vegetation, or on bank or piling. A pillow cage, with bottom open and edges turned inward, can be inverted on a stick thrust into the mud in the midst of emergent vegetation. This will often trap nymphs that are crawling upward to transform if it is set out at the height of the transformation period. Or the early riser may get out and pick off the nymphs that have crawled out; or, if not early enough for that, collect the shivering, teneral adult and its outgrown exuvium. In warm waters where dragonfly nymphs are abundant they sometimes can be lured in at night to a light held close to the water, and then caught with a dip net.

Grouping of Families of Odonate Nymphs*

BODY TERMINATING IN THREE FLAT GILLS. Sub-order Zygoptera, damselflies. To 25 mm. (to 40 in *Archilestes*).

1. First antennal segment as long as or longer than the rest of the antenna.

    Calopterygidae (Fig. 60.4). Living in clear streams and woodland pools, clinging to submerged vegetation. The median cleft of the labium extends nearly half-way to the base in *Calopteryx*; to the level of the lateral lobes in *Hetaerina*.

2. First antennal segment much shorter than the rest of the antenna.

    Lestidae (Fig. 60.3,6). Lower lip with its hinge reaching to or past the base of the middle legs; spoon-

---

* A key to the genera of odonate nymphs will be found in the Appendix.

shaped, narrowed in the middle but tapering back regularly to the hinge. Each caudal gill with small tracheae running perpendicular to main axis of gill. In ponds, small lakes and streams with marshy edges, concealed in vegetation by their slender size and delicate coloring. *Archilestes* differs from the more common and widespread *Lestes* in having 2 well-defined dark cross bands on each caudal gill.

Agrionidae (Fig. 60.1,2,5). Lower lip flat, not greatly narrowed in the middle, with hinge reaching only to or slightly beyond the base of first pair of legs. In a great variety of unpolluted waters. Many genera, including the common *Enallagma* and *Ischnura*.

BODY WITHOUT EXTERNAL GILLS. Suborder Anisoptera, dragonflies. To 45 mm.

1. Lower lip flat, or nearly so (Fig. 58).

Gomphidae (Fig. 59.2). Antennae short, thick, of four segments. Front of head often flat and wedge-shaped. Stiff-legged burrowers and sprawlers in mud and sand of shallow waters. Transform on logs and stones rather than on weed stems. Many genera.

Petaluridae. Antennae short, thick, hairy, of 6 to 7 segments. Sluggish nymphs with short, twisted legs; in soft, muddy bottoms of spring-fed or boggy, woodland waters.

Aeschnidae (Fig. 59.4). Antennae slender, bristlelike, of 6 to 7 segments. Body cylindrical, sometimes slightly wider beyond the mid-length. Head more or less flattened. Abdomen with lateral spines on segments 8 to 9 and sometimes also on 5 to 7. Clean, active climbers in vegetation of shallow waters. Voracious. Many genera.

2. Lower lip spoon-shaped, covering face up to eyes (Fig. 59.1).

a. Distal edge of each lobe of lower lip deeply incised to form teeth.

Cordulegasteridae (Fig. 59.7). Body heavy and hairy; head broad, flat, and shelflike, with eyes prominent and well forward. Lie in soft mud and muck of slow, woodland streams, often lying buried up to

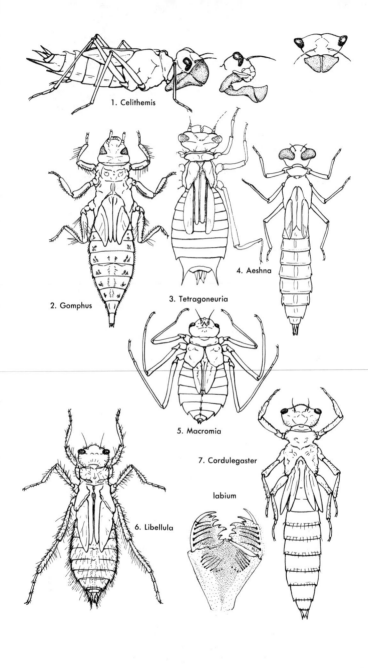

1. Celithemis

2. Gomphus

3. Tetragoneuria

4. Aeshna

5. Macromia

6. Libellula

7. Cordulegaster

labium

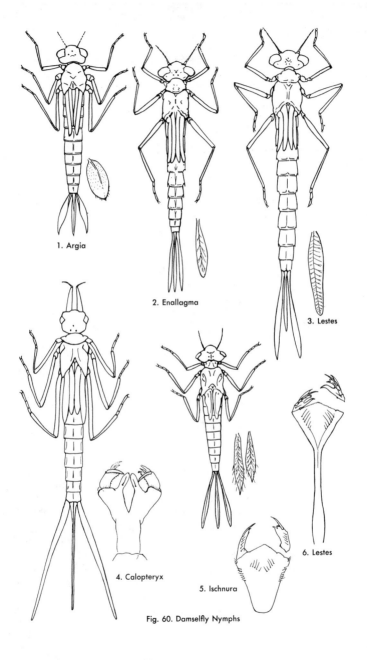

1. Argia

2. Enallagma

3. Lestes

4. Calopteryx

5. Ischnura

6. Lestes

Fig. 60. Damselfly Nymphs

the high peaked tips of the eyes. When disturbed, squirm and kick with hind legs. Several genera.

b. Distal edge of each lobe of lower lip smooth or evenly crenulate.

Macromiidae (Fig. 59.5). Head with a prominent, upcurving, frontal horn between the antennae. Abdomen very flat with a median row of high, flattened hooks. Legs long and sprawling. Sedentary; on bottom of shallow parts of lakes or wide streams, often silt-covered.

Libellulidae (Fig. 59.6). Head without a frontal horn. Nymphs of the Subfamily Cordulinae (Fig. 59.3) differ from the Libellulinae in having hind femur longer than width of head and in having big, cultriform dorsal hooks on the abdomen *if* the lateral spines are long; but the distinction is not always sharp. The cordulines are hairy sprawlers on the bottom but some climb on trash and vegetation; they are often prettily patterned in brown and green. The libellulines are stockier; some sprawl silt-covered on the bottom, others are climbers. In a great variety of waters; *Erythrodiplax berenice* and *Macrodiplax balteata* are in brackish water. Many genera.

Bugs—Order Hemiptera
Figs. 61, 62; Pls. 3, 15–16

The aquatic representatives of this very large order belong to families that are almost entirely aquatic or semiaquatic. Many of the latter merely live in very damp places or along the shoreline, occasionally running out on aquatic vegetation or onto the surface film. Several families, however, are permanent residents of fresh waters, even though they are air-breathing and occasionally take flight.

For the most part aquatic bugs have but a single generation a year, usually hibernating as adults in the mud at the bottom or in debris and vegetation, often becoming active very early in the spring when they can be seen swimming

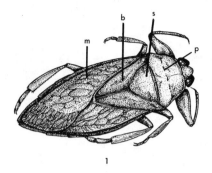

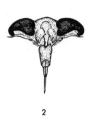

Fig. 61. *1.* An adult bug, *Lethocerus; p,* pronotum; *s,* scutellum; *b,* thickened basal portion of fore wing; *m,* membranous portion of fore wing. *2.* Ventral view of head showing beak.

beneath the ice, especially the Corixidae and Notonectidae. Many are able to make a chirping sound by rubbing one part of the body against another, and many have scent glands which produce a characteristic odor.

Their mouthparts are modified to form a jointed beak, consisting usually of 3 or 4 segments, used for piercing and sucking. It normally projects rearward along the ventral side of the thorax. The fore wings, called *hemelytra,* are leathery at the base and membranous at the tip. Metamorphosis is incomplete but of a gradual type. The young nymph that hatches from the egg develops gradually by a series of molts into the adult, without undergoing a marked change. Thus nymphs and adults live and look very much alike.

Collecting. Water bugs are most abundant in protected spots where there is an abundance of vegetation. They can be collected with dip net, kitchen sieve or dredge, and then transported fairly easily if kept moist. They will live in aquaria containing aquatic plants; but remember that most of them are predacious.

Grouping of Families of Aquatic Bugs*

ANTENNAE SHORTER THAN HEAD
   1. Living in the water. Without ocelli.

* Adapted from Usinger.

A water boatman, swimming. Note the tarsus of the foreleg.

A backswimmer at the surface film.

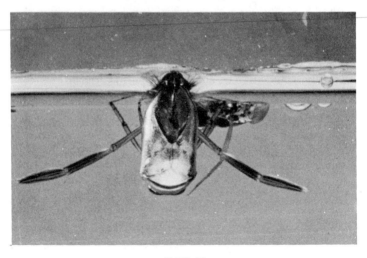

PLATE 15

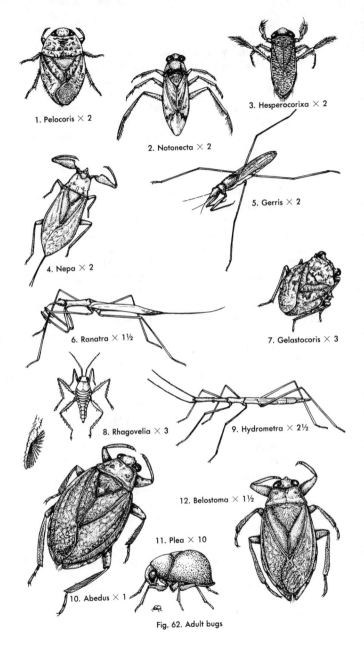

1. Pelocoris × 2

2. Notonecta × 2

3. Hesperocorixa × 2

4. Nepa × 2

5. Gerris × 2

6. Ranatra × 1½

7. Gelastocoris × 3

8. Rhagovelia × 3

9. Hydrometra × 2½

10. Abedus × 1

11. Plea × 10

12. Belostoma × 1½

Fig. 62. Adult bugs

    a. Hind tarsi with 2 claws.

      Nepidae. Apical appendages drawn out into 2 long filaments that come together to form a tube. Fig. 62.4,6.

      Belostomatidae. Large, 20–70 mm. Membrane of fore wings veined. Figs. 61, 62.10,12.

      Naucoridae. Size moderate, 5–16 mm. Membrane of fore wings not veined. Fig. 62.1.

      Pleidae. Very small, 1½–2½ mm. Body almost spherical. Fig. 62.11.

    b. Hind tarsi without claws.

      Notonectidae. Beak distinctly segmented. Eyes prominent. Backswimmers. Fig. 62.2.

      Corixidae. Beak not distinctly segmented. Base of head overlapping pronotum. Swim normally. Fig. 62.3.

  2. Semiaquatic, living on the shore. With ocelli.

    Gelastocoridae (Fig. 62.7). Antennae concealed; forelegs raptorial.

    Ochteridae. Antennae exposed; forelegs not raptorial.

ANTENNAE LONGER THAN HEAD

  1. Head as long as thorax. Body greatly elongate.

    Hydrometridae (Fig. 62.9).

  2. Not as above

    a. Tarsal claws inserted before apex of tarsus. Striders on surface.

      Gerridae. Hind femur reaching beyond tip of abdomen. Beak 4-segmented. Fig. 62.5.

      Veliidae. Hind femur not exceeding tip of abdomen except in *Microvelia longipes*. Beak 3-segmented.

    b. Tarsal claws apical. Semiaquatic.

      Hebridae. Antennae 5-segmented, the two basal segments swollen. Tarsi 2-segmented.

      Macroveliidae. Antennae 4-segmented, base not swollen. Membrane of fore wing with 6 cells. Legs without black bristles.

      Mesoveliidae. Differs from above in having membrane of fore wing without cells, and legs with stiff black bristles.

      Saldidae. Membrane of fore wing with 4 to 5 cells.

Habitat Grouping of Families of Bugs*

AQUATIC, LIVING IN THE WATER

1. Break surface film with pronotum. **Corixidae.**
2. Break surface film with tip of abdomen.

   Backswimmers. **Notonectidae.**

   Swim normally. **Naucoridae.**
3. Break surface film with abdominal tube or flaps.

   Awkward swimmers, living in trash or vegetation. **Nepidae.**

   Strong swimmers, hiding in protected places. **Belostomatidae.**

SURFACE BUGS

1. On surface of open water.

   On quiet water. **Gerridae.**

   In riffles. **Veliidae.**
2. At water's edge, or on floating vegetation, running when disturbed.

   Treaders on long legs, in protected places. **Hydrometridae.**

   Skaters on short legs, in open places.

   Resting on film near shore; gregarious. **Veliidae.**

   Resting on floating leaves; solitary. **Mesoveliidae.**

SHORE BUGS

1. Walking or running bugs.

   Swift runners, beneath stones. Rare. **Dipsocoridae.**

   Slow walkers, at edge, on stones, in moss.

   Capable of skating on water when disturbed. **Mesoveliidae.**

   On dry land near water. **Macroveliidae.**

   At water's edge, under stones, moss and algae. **Hebridae.**
2. Jumping bugs, concealed by coloration, on sand or mud. **Gelastocoridae.**
3. Jumping and flying bugs.

   Moving by quick, short jump-flights. **Saldidae.**

   Moving by longer flights. **Ochteridae.**

* Based on Hungerford.

Nepidae, water scorpions (Fig. 62; Pl. 3). Inconspicuous and dull in color, sluggish in behavior, and secretive in habits, these large-eyed bugs tend to lurk in the trash, mud or vegetation of ponds and streams, sometimes remaining motionless for an hour or more. Occasionally they back slowly up a plant stem to thrust their long respiratory tube through the surface film and then rest for some time in that position.

Respiration. Two long filaments at the tip of the abdomen are grooved on the inner surface and, when brought together, became fastened by interlocking bristles to form a respiratory tube for conducting air into the caudal spiracles.

Food. They seldom swim and then slowly, for they do not pursue the small insects on which they feed but lie in wait for them, usually head downward and forelegs held out in raptorial position. The long, stout femur is so hinged as to permit the razor-edged tibia and tarsus to fold back upon it like the blade of a knife.

Eggs. The eggs are inserted singly in the stems and leaves of submerged plants, usually an eighth of an inch or more apart and in a straight row. Each egg has long filaments at one end, 7 in *Nepa* and 2 in *Ranatra*. These remain projecting from the plant tissue and usually from the water also; they undoubtedly have a respiratory function.

Ranatra, 20–40 mm. exclusive of the tube, is extremely long and cylindrical, with prothorax narrower than the head. *Nepa,* 17 mm., is broader and flatter, one-third as wide as long; eastern. *Curicta,* 16–22 mm., is intermediate in shape; southwestern.

Belostomatidae, giant water bugs (Fig. 62; Pls. 3, 16). These large bugs, 20–70 mm. long, live in ponds and quiet pools, resting inconspicuously on the bottom or sitting in the vegetation with the tip of the abdomen projecting through the surface film. Their large flat, oval bodies are brown or dull greenish in color. The front legs are raptorial, the knife-edged tibiae and tarsi folding back on the flattened femora. The hind legs are flattened and fringed for swimming.

Respiration. Giant water bugs, on rising to the surface, break the film with two straplike, retractile appendages at the tip of the abdomen. The air then fills the tracheal system

A male giant water bug, *Belostoma fluminea*, carrying eggs.

A whirligig beetle, *Dineutes*, carrying a bubble of air beneath the surface.

PLATE 16

directly through the spiracles at the base of these two appendages. At the same time air enters the space beneath the hemelytra, forming a glistening, silvery bubble.

Food. They are fiercely predacious, attacking insects and crustaceans and even tadpoles, frogs and fish several times their size. They may at times be a serious pest in fish hatcheries. Occasionally one will give a bather a sharp stab (hence the name "toe-biters"). Undoubtedly the toxic substance causing the sting that accompanies this stab is an aid to them in capturing prey.

Eggs. The females of *Abedus* and *Belostoma* cement their eggs, in clusters of 100 or more, to the back (hemelytra) of the male. He carries them until they hatch a week later and may even continue to carry the emerging nymphs. Females of other genera fasten their eggs to cattails or other submerged plant stems.

These bugs are sometimes called "electric-light bugs" because of the frequency with which they come wham-banging into lights at night. When held in one's hand they may chirp, or they may eject a fluid smelling faintly of apples. They may also at such times put on a death-feigning act, assuming a rigid position which they may hold for 15 minutes or more. In China, *Lethocerus* is sold for food and is munched on by children as a sweetmeat.

Grouping of Genera of Giant Water Bugs

ANTERIOR FEMUR WITH INNER SURFACE NOT GROOVED
  Benacus, over 40 mm. Eastern.
ANTERIOR FEMUR WITH INNER SURFACE GROOVED FOR RECEPTION OF TIBIA
  1. Head produced conically; rostrum with basal segment long and thin.
    Abedus, over 27 mm. Membrane of hemelytra reduced. 3rd thoracic segment with midventral keel. Southeastern and southwestern.
    Belostoma, less than 22 mm. Membrane of hemelytra not reduced. 3rd thoracic segment without midventral keel. Widespread.

2. Head not produced conically; rostrum with basal segment thick and short.
Lethocerus, more than 40 mm. Cosmopolitan.

Naucoridae, creeping water bugs (Fig. 62; Pl. 3). These bugs
half creep, half swim over the dense vegetation in quiet
waters, sometimes even in hot springs and saline pools. They
are 5–16 mm. long, broad, flat and with a very broad head.
They are fiercely predacious, as is evidenced by the raptorial
fore legs with especially enlarged femora. Their eggs are
laid on stones in shallow water.

Grouping of Genera of Creeping Water Bugs*

ANTERIOR MARGIN OF PRONOTUM, BEHIND IN-
TEROCULAR SPACE, STRAIGHT OR NEARLY SO
Usingerina. Inner margins of eyes anteriorly divergent.
Western.
Pelocoris. Inner margins of eyes anteriorly convergent.
Eastern.
ANTERIOR MARGIN OF PRONOTUM DEEPLY CON-
CAVE BEHIND INTEROCULAR SPACE
Cryphocricos. Prothorax completely exposed ventrally.
Southern Texas.
Ambrysos. Prothorax with posterior part ventrally cov-
ered by lateral plates. Western.

Pleidae, pigmy backswimmers. These are the small bugs, 1½–
2½ mm., with deeply arched, grayish yellow bodies, often
found clinging to dense mats of *Chara, Anacharis* and
Myriophyllum. They swim for short distances only, with
even, rapid strokes and looking for all the world like tiny
beetles. Their eggs are laid on plant stems. *Plea striola* is the
commonest and most widespread.

Notonectidae, backswimmers (Fig. 62; Pls. 3, 15). Backswimmers are a common sight in most quiet ponds the world
over. They are often strikingly colored, pearly white, yellowish gold, green or bluish black; with large, sometimes red,

* After Usinger.

eyes. They swim about for short distances with powerful oarlike strokes and then come to rest, clinging to vegetation in characteristic position with long swimming legs outstretched; or they rise to the surface where they lie obliquely, ventral side up, and tip of abdomen through the surface film. *Buenoa* swims smoothly, often schooling in open water some distance beneath the surface. *Notonecta,* however, swims jerkily and has difficulty maintaining its position when at rest, unless clinging to something. These bugs are deep-bodied, convex dorsally, keeled ventrally, with sides sloping rooflike on the back. The hind legs are long and fringed for swimming; the first two pairs of legs are short and raptorial.

Respiration. When beneath the surface, backswimmers carry air in the space beneath the hemelytra and in two troughs on the ventral side of the abdomen. These troughs, formed by three fringes of hair, one median and two lateral, are connected with the abdominal spiracles. *Notonecta* has been known to remain beneath the surface as long as 6 hours, so undoubtedly has plastron respiration also. *Buenoa* contains an oxygen-bearing pigment, giving it a reddish blush and increasing its respiratory efficiency.

Food. Backswimmers are predators, attacking even small fish. They can inflict a painful sting. *Buenoa* has front legs so spined that when held together they form a basket for holding the prey.

Eggs. Eggs are laid in the spring and summer, fastened to plant stems or stones or inserted in plant tissues. There is more than one brood a year.

The worldwide *Notonecta,* over 10 mm., has 4-segmented antennae. *Buenoa,* 5–9 mm., has 3-segmented antennae; it is limited to the western hemisphere and Hawaii.

Corixidae, water boatmen (Fig. 62; Pl. 15). Boatmen are extremely common in the shallow water of ponds, lakes, streams and even muddy pools. At night they fly into lights, sometimes in enormous numbers. Their large-eyed, flattened bodies are dark grayish, often mottled and faintly cross-lined with yellow. The middle legs are extraordinarily long; the hind legs are flattened and fringed for swimming, propelling the bug along with strong oarlike strokes.

Corixids occur in the tropics, the subarctic, below sea level in Death Valley and up to elevations of 15,000 feet. Species of *Corisella* and *Trichocorixa* live in brine pools along with the brine shrimp and brine flies; and *Corisella* has been reported from sewage tanks.

Respiration. When the bugs are submerged, air is held beneath the hemelytra as well as in a film enveloping the body. They may remain submerged for long periods but when they do come to the surface to replenish the plastron they break the surface film with the head and the edge of the pronotum.

Food. The forelegs are short, with broad, scooplike, 1-segmented tarsi, fringed and spined for scooping up and sifting out minute organisms from the water. Boatmen are the only bugs that are not wholly predacious. They do eat some microscopically small animals such as protists, and possibly mosquito and midge larvae, but most of their food is plant debris from the muddy bottom, or green algal filaments whose cells they pierce with their piercing and rasping beaks. In spite of the scent glands that give them an unpleasant taste, as well as a distinctive odor, they are eaten in large quantities by fish and are thus important converters of plant material into animal tissue.

Eggs. These are on pedicels, attached to aquatic plants, usually on the stems. Those of *Ramphocorixa acuminata,* an eastern and southern species, are fastened to the bodies of the crayfish *Cambarus.* This relationship is probably not an obligatory one, for if the eggs are deposited on plants under artificial conditions they develop normally. Since the two species are often in close proximity, the relationship is probably one of chance, and certainly one of convenience.

Many males stridulate by rubbing a patch of pegs on the base of the first femur against a scraper on the side of the head. During mating the males, recognized by the asymmetry of the abdomen, hold the females with a comblike structure of the 6th abdominal segment.

In Mexico, species of *Corisella* are cultivated by placing reeds in the water to encourage egg-laying. The eggs are then collected and eaten. The adults also are collected, dried and packaged for bird, fish and turtle food.

There are about 20 genera and 115 species in the U. S. *Sigara* and *Hesperocorixa* are the most common and widespread, the former ranging from 3 to 9 mm., the latter from 6 to 11.

Hydrometridae, marsh treaders (Fig. 62). Marsh treaders, sometimes called water measurers, are the walking sticks of the aquatic world. The attenuated head, with long, elbowed antennae, and the greatly elongated, brownish to greenish body with long slender legs, all tend to make this insect nearly invisible as it sits motionless on the vegetation or walks slowly and deliberately across a tangle of weed stems or out on a floating leaf. Occasionally one will walk out across the surface film but never far from shore, for its sharp claws break through the film easily, and when in the water it is extremely awkward.

Food. They stalk small animal organisms with apparent alertness, spearing them with their long beaks. They are preyed upon, in turn, by fish, for they lack the scent glands that protect many bugs.

Eggs. The long, stalked, spindle-shaped eggs are laid on plant tissues just above or below the surface. They are about six times as long as broad, brown, and longitudinally fluted. There may be several broods in one season, for the adults become active very early in the spring.

The one genus, *Hydrometra*, is 8–11 mm. long.

Gerridae, water striders (Fig. 62). Water striders, 2–15 mm. long, live on the surface film of quiet waters, drifting aimlessly or running rapidly about. Some are gregarious and gather in large aggregations along the margin of backwaters or in shady spots, only to scatter in all directions when disturbed. One genus, *Metrobates*, of the eastern and central states, prefers rapid water; and one genus, *Halobates*, is marine, sometimes being found far out on the surface of the sea.

The last two pairs of legs, two or three times as long as the body, are spread far apart. When the insect runs over the water, the tarsal claws do not break through the surface film, for they are set well back from the tip. Often the dimpled footprints can be seen reflected from the substratum, a challenging sight for the amateur photographer.

Food. The forelegs are raptorial, seizing hold of any terrestrial insect that may fall into the water and even catching crustaceans and small aquatic insects that venture too near the surface film from below.

Eggs. Eggs are laid throughout the spring and summer, glued in long, parallel rows to floating objects or to objects at the water's edge. They are usually deposited just below the surface of the water.

Grouping of Genera of Water Striders*

INNER MARGINS OF EYES SINUATE OR CONCAVE BEHIND THE MIDDLE

    Gerris. Pronotum dull. Widespread.

    Limnogonus. Pronotum shining. Eastern and southern.

INNER MARGINS OF EYES CONVEXLY ROUNDED

1. First antennal segment as long as rest of antenna.

    Metrobates. Swift streams. East of Rockies.

2. First antennal segment shorter than rest of antenna. Eastern and southern.

    Rheumatobates. Third antennal segment with several stiff bristles.

    Trepobates. Third antennal segment with fine pubescence.

Veliidae, broad-shouldered water striders. These bugs, 1.6–5.5 mm., also run about on the surface film without breaking through. Some of them, however, swim quite well. They feed on any small creatures that they can capture. Their eggs are laid singly or in clusters, usually beneath the surface film, on floating objects or at the water's edge.

The cosmopolitan *Rhagovelia* prefers the swift riffles of streams for which it is especially equipped with a paddlelike tuft of fringed hairs sprouting from a deep cleft in the tarsi. The cosmopolitan *Microvelia* and *Velia* live in quiet waters. The former has the first antennal segment the same length as the other segments; the latter has it distinctly longer.

* After Usinger.

Hebridae, velvet water bugs. The hebrids, less than 2.5 mm.,
live along the margins, beneath stones or in trash, feeding on
any small creatures they can capture. They are covered with
a dense, water-resistant, velvety pile. The elongate, oval
eggs are laid in moss and vegetation. There are two cosmopolitan genera. *Merragata,* with 4-segmented antennae,
runs out onto floating plants and mats of *Spirogyra;* if it becomes submerged it can respire through the silvery plastron
that is trapped in the velvety pile. *Naeogeus,* with 5-seg-
mented antennae, is more likely to remain on shore.

Macroveliidae. The one genus *Macrovelia* is never found
actually in or on the water but always within a few feet of
it, in mosses at the water's edge, behind rocks or logs, or
in debris.

Mesoveliidae, water treaders. This family contains one widespread genus, *Mesovelia,* 4–5 mm. It is greenish yellow and
usually wingless, though winged forms do occur. They
scamper about at pond edges, occasionally running out onto
floating objects, feeding on living or dead terrestrial insects
that fall into the water or upon aquatic ones that come near
the surface. Eggs, laid in the tissues of emergent or shore
plants, are narrowed at the micropylar end which is bent to
form a curved neck, the flat surface of which is left exposed.

Saldidae. These bugs live on the beach and shoreline of
lakes, streams and oceans, as well as of marshes, bogs and
springs, but an occasional ducking in the water would not
be harmful because the body is covered with a fine pu-
bescence. Eggs are laid at the base of clumps of moss or
grass, out of water.

Gelastocoridae. Toad bugs live in the mud and sand at the
water's edge; they are not really aquatic. Their squat, nubbly
bodies are protectively mottled to resemble the background.
Gelastocoris lays its eggs amidst the sand grains. *Nerthra*
places them in small holes in the mud several feet up on the
shore, and remains to guard them.

Ochteridae. Members of this shore-living family of bugs are
more oval in shape than their relatives the toad bugs. The

immature stages often carry small sand grains attached to their body, and some species construct a small sand cell in which to molt. The eggs are laid in clumps on grasses and roots.

Beetles—Order Coleoptera
Figs. 63, 64; Pls. 3, 16, 17

Beetles represent the largest group of insects on land, so it is not surprising that they are similarly abundant in the water, possibly 5,000 species having taken up an aquatic mode of life. Beetles have complete metamorphosis, which permits the exploitation of different environments at different stages in the life cycle. They have primitive, chewing mouth-parts, which make it possible for them to feed on a wide variety of solid foods. They have hard, shell-like fore wings, called *elytra*, which protect the body and the folded, membranous hind wings. These characteristics may be the key to their success.

Respiration. The adults, as well as the pupae, all breathe atmospheric air. They draw it into the space beneath the elytra and sometimes also cover the ventral surface of the body with a plastron. The little Haliplidae carry an additional store of air beneath their greatly expanded hind coxae. The larvae, except for a few species that have filamentous gills, respire by diffusion through the skin or come to the surface; some even pierce plant tissues, withdrawing the air from hollow cells or from stems and roots.

Locomotion. Most aquatic beetles have a hard, smooth, streamlined body. Many have modifications of the hind pair of legs, and sometimes also of other legs, into flat, often fringed, oarlike paddles which would be useless on land but make excellent swimming organs. For the most part aquatic beetles are also able to fly, frequently coming into lights at night.

Most aquatic beetles hibernate as adults, burrowing in the debris and mud of the substratum.

Collecting. An ordinary kitchen sieve dipped into shallow, weedy water usually brings up a few shining, black beetles. Sieves of various sizes attached to poles of differing lengths, a dip net, or the Needham scraper are all good for collecting beetles, depending upon the type of water in which one is collecting. Large pans or, better yet, a piece of white canvas, 4 x 5 feet or so, to spread on the ground for receiving the catch will be useful. If the latter is used the water can drain off and the beetles, as they emerge from the trash, can be picked up with lifter or forceps. In moving water the two-handled screen can be held downstream of a likely area. Violent stirring back and forth with a net handle with vigor enough to dislodge stones and debris should also dislodge beetles, which will then be washed down into the net. Lotic water larvae that cling to the rocks will have to be dislodged individually.

Habitat Grouping of Families of Beetles*

	Amphizoidae	Chrysomelidae	Curculionidae	Dryopidae	Dytiscidae	Elmidae	Gyrinidae	Haliplidae	Helodidae	Hydraenidae	Hydrophilidae	Hydroscaphidae	Noteridae	Psephenidae
Lakes														
Rocky shores					x	x								x
Shallow, weedy inlets	x	x					x				x			
Ponds														
Weedy ponds	x	x			x		x	x	x	x	x	x	x	
Woodland ponds									x					
Streams														
Backwaters					x		x	x			x			
Fast water				x	x									x
Wet wood and leaves	x			x	x				x	x	x			
Sandy or rocky shores										x	x			
In algae								x			x	x		
Swamps	x	x									x			
Cold springs				x			x		x		x			
Hot springs				x	x					x	x	x		
Tree holes									x					

*Based on material given by Leech and Chandler in Usinger.

Grouping of a Few Families of Aquatic Beetles—Adults

FIRST ABDOMINAL SEGMENT DIVIDED ON THE VENTRAL SIDE BY THE HIND COXAE, SO NOT VISIBLE ITS ENTIRE LENGTH.* Suborder Adephaga

1. Eyes divided by the margins of the head, making four eyes.

    Gyrinidae. On the surface. Hind tarsal segments hinged fanwise. Fig. 63.

2. Eyes two, normal. Hind coxae expanded to form large plates covering the bases of the hind legs.

    Haliplidae. Antennae elongate. Fig. 63.

3. Eyes, two, normal. Hind coxae not as above.

    a. Hind legs adapted for swimming.

    Dytiscidae. Hind tarsi with a single claw. Common. Fig. 63.

    Noteridae. Hind tarsi with 2 equal claws. Uncommon.

    b. Hind legs not adapted for swimming.

    Amphizoidae. Uncommon.

    Other families. Occasionally stray into the water.

FIRST ABDOMINAL SEGMENT NOT DIVIDED VENTRALLY BY HIND COXAE. SEGMENT VISIBLE ITS ENTIRE WIDTH. Suborder Polyphaga

1. Hind legs adapted for swimming.

    Hydrophilidae. Antennae clubbed, often concealed beneath the prothorax; club with three hairy segments. Labial palpi long, often projecting and thus mistaken for antennae. Figs. 63, 64.

2. Hind legs not adapted for swimming.

    Hydroscaphidae. Elytra truncate. Tiny, .5–1 mm. Southwest, uncommon.

---

* I recall my difficulty in seeing this character clearly when I was a beginning student in entomology and have tried to avoid it; but it is a basic characteristic of the suborder. All aquatic families falling in this category have the hind legs modified for swimming except the uncommon Amphizoidae. However, the very common Hydrophilidae also have swimming legs and they are not in this group. The Gyrinidae seem to have the first segment undivided but that which at first glance appears to be the first is actually the second abdominal segment; they, however, are easily recognized by the divided eyes.

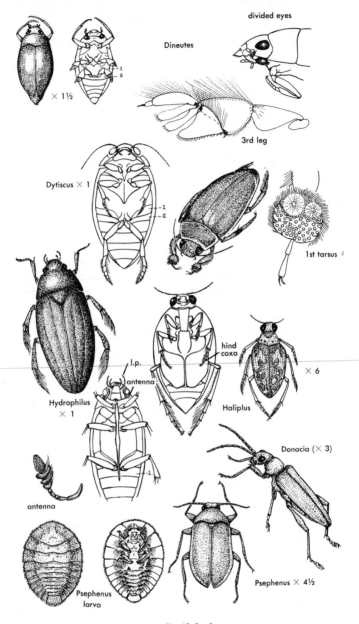

divided eyes

Dineutes

3rd leg

Dytiscus × 1

1st tarsus ♂

l.p.

antenna

hind coxa

Hydrophilus × 1

Haliplus × 6

antenna

Donacia (× 3)

Psephenus larva

Psephenus × 4½

Fig. 63. Beetles

Hydraenidae. Antennae with a club of five hairy segments. Head with Y-shaped line on vertex (as in Hydrophilidae). Seldom over 2.5 mm.

Curculionidae. Head drawn out into a beak. Not common in water.

Chrysomelidae. All tarsi 5-segmented (sometimes appearing 4-segmented) often with first 3 dilated and with adhesive pads beneath. On floating leaves or emergent vegetation. Not common in water. Fig. 63.

Helodidae. Front coxae more or less conically projecting. Hind margin of thorax never crenulate.

Psephenidae. Without any of the above characters. With 6 to 7 abdominal segments on ventral side. Enter water only to lay eggs. Fig. 63.

Dryopidae. With 5 abdominal segments on ventral side. First coxae transverse. Antennae short and pectinate, usually clubbed.

Elmidae. With 5 abdominal segments on ventral side. First coxae globular. Antennae slender.

Grouping of a Few Families of Aquatic Beetles—Larvae

LEGS WITH FIVE SEGMENTS PLUS TWO TARSAL CLAWS (One in Haliplidae)

1. Last abdominal segment with 4 hooks.
   Gyrinidae. Abdominal segments with lateral, fringed gills.

2. Last abdominal segment without hooks.
   a. Abdomen with 9 to 10 segments.
      Haliplidae
      Other families. Occasionally in water.
   b. Abdomen with 8 segments.
      Dytiscidae. Without characters of two following families. Common.
      Noteridae. With digging legs. Uncommon.
      Amphizoidae. Flat, with expanded sides. Uncommon.

LEGS WITH FOUR (OR FEWER) SEGMENTS PLUS CLAW

1. Tip of abdomen with segmented or movable cerci or filaments, often retracted.

Hydrophilidae. Without characters of two following families. Usually with 8 complete abdominal segments. Ocelli usually in groups of six. Common.

Hydraenidae. Last abdominal segment with pair of recurved hooks. With 9 complete abdominal segments.

Hydroscaphidae. Prothorax and abdominal segments with balloonlike appendages. Southwestern. Uncommon.

Other families.

2. Tip of abdomen with cerci firmly fused at base or absent.

Psephenidae. Body oval or circular, depressed; lateral margins expanded. Clinging to rocks in fast water.

Families difficult to identify.

Dryopidae. Body depressed, lateral margins excised as in Psephenidae but body more elongate. First 5 abdominal segments with median fold. 9th abdominal segment with a ventral, movable operculum exclosing a caudal chamber.

Elmidae. 9th segment with operculum, as above, but ventral side of abdomen flat or concave.

Chrysomelidae. Not as above. Without abdominal gills. Mandibles short and broad. On roots or on lily pads.

Helodidae. Gills in caudal chamber of 8th segment. Body depressed or flattened. Antennae longer than head plus thorax.

Other families.

Gyrinidae, whirligig beetles (Figs. 63, 64; Pls. 3, 16). The sight of whirling, spinning aggregations of gyrinids is often one's first introduction to pond life. In the early part of the day and of the season, they may be scattered along the margins of quiet ponds or lakes, in puddles or backwaters of streams. As the day and the season progress, they tend to move out into open water, often forming large gyrating masses which, at times, may be made up of several species. Some are nocturnal. They are the only beetles that swim in the surface film; there they dart back and forth and round and round with great rapidity, occasionally diving beneath

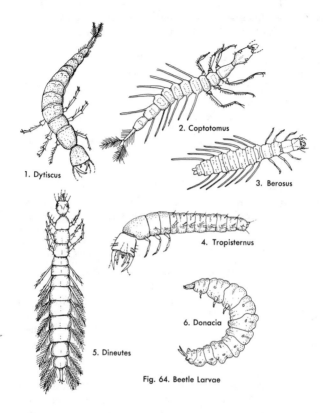

1. Dytiscus

2. Coptotomus

3. Berosus

4. Tropisternus

6. Donacia

5. Dineutes

Fig. 64. Beetle Larvae

with a bubble of air attached to the tip of the abdomen but soon rising to rejoin the group. Aside from their flattened, streamlined body they show a remarkable adaptation to aquatic life in their swimming legs (Fig. 63) and in the division of the compound eyes which permits simultaneous vision above and below the surface.

Respiration. When about to swim beneath the surface the adult beetle stores air beneath the elytra, drawing it in along a groove under the rear end of the lateral margins. It is a bit of this air that escapes as a bubble at the rear.

Food. They feed primarily upon insects caught on the surface film but may be scavengers to some degree.

Eggs. Eggs are attached to submerged plants. They hatch in about 3 weeks.

Larvae. The larvae, looking a bit like centipedes, hide and hunt on the bottom, breathing by means of long, fringed gills of which there is one pair on each of the first 8 abdominal segments and two on the 9th. They are cannibalistic and actively predacious, feeding on blood worms, nymphs and even small fish. Each slender, curved mandible is pierced by a tube through which poison is ejected into the victim and through which the victim's juices are sucked in.

Pupation takes place in a mud cell made by the mature larva on plants at the water's edge, or even several inches from the water. Adults emerge in about a month.

Adults frequently take flight. They have been known to mistake the shining tops of parked cars or of greenhouses for the surface of the water and have rained down upon them in numbers.

Gyrinus and *Dineutes* are cosmopolitan. They both have a glabrous dorsum. The former, 3–8 mm. long, has the elytral striae punctate and the scutellum visible. The latter, 9–16 mm. long, does not. *Gyretes,* a neotropical genus, has pubescent elytra. Identification of larvae is difficult. The head of *Dineutes* is subcircular; that of the other two, elongate.

Haliplidae, crawling water beetles (Fig. 63). One seldom collects in the vegetation of quiet waters without bringing up these little, 5.5 mm. or less, yellowish or brownish, blackspotted beetles. They are not particularly good swimmers, so are apt to be crawling on the vegetation or between the crevices in stones if the water is at all swift. They are characterized by enormous, platelike hind coxae covering the leg bases and by longitudinal rows of punctures on the elytra.

Food. They feed on algae and possibly on some animal material.

Respiration. The adults break the surface film with the tip of the abdomen to replenish the air carried beneath the elytra and the expanded hind coxae. An escaping bubble may protrude from the hind coxal cavities, serving as a hydrostatic organ as well as a store of oxygen. A beetle with such a bubble can rise to the surface at will but without it must climb back up the vegetation to reach the surface.

Eggs. Eggs are laid on aquatic vegetation such as *Anacharis* and *Ceratophyllum* and on various filamentous algae. *Haliplus* has been seen biting tiny holes in the plant tissues for the insertion of the eggs.

Larvae. The larvae crawl about on the vegetation. Since they respire through the skin they do not come to the surface. They feed primarily on algae, some seeming to prefer *Spirogyra,* others *Chara* and *Nitella.* When ready to pupate they crawl out on the shore where they prepare a cell in the mud beneath a stone or log. Larvae of *Peltodytes* are distinctive in having on each segment 2 or more long, curved spines each of which is half as long as the body itself.

Of the four U. S. genera, *Haliplus* is the most abundant, although *Peltodytes* and *Brychius* are also widespread and common. The large hind coxal plate covers all but the last segment in *Peltodytes.* In *Haliplus* and *Brychius* it leaves the last 3 segments exposed. *Haliplus* differs in having the sides of the pronotum widest at the base, converging anteriorly. *Apteraliplus* is a flightless genus of the Pacific coast.

Dytiscidae, predacious diving beetles (Figs. 63, 64.1,2; Pl. 17). These are the most commonly collected of all aquatic beetles, save possibly the ubiquitous hydrophilids. They include the largest aquatic beetles as well as the strongest swimmers. They are shining black or brownish black, sometimes marked with dull yellow or green, especially along the margins. They have slender antennae and widely spaced hind legs. Some species make stridulating sounds and some excrete a slightly offensive substance from prothoracic glands.

A few live in fast waters, others crawl upon the stones in quiet backwaters, but many live in weedy shallows where they may be observed floating slowly upward, abdomen tip foremost, or darting and diving with powerful oarlike strokes of the flattened, fringed hind legs.

Respiration. They break through the surface film with the tip of the abdomen, the last segment of which bears hydrofuge hairs as well as a pair of spiracles. They simultaneously

A beetle larva, *Coptotomus*, with lateral filaments.

Diving beetles, *Dytiscus*, strong swimmers and voracious predators.

PLATE 17

fill the tracheal system and draw air into the subelytral spaces. No air can be carried on the glabrous ventral surface and yet dytiscids have been known to stay beneath the surface for as much as 36 hours.

Food. Dytiscids are actively predacious, feeding upon any small animals they can capture. In turn they are relished by reptiles, amphibians, fish, wading birds, raccoons and skunks; they are host to protistan parasites, gordian worms, trematodes and mites. Even their eggs may be parasitized.

Eggs. The eggs are laid on or in emergent or shoreline plants.

Larvae. These "water tigers," or "dragons of the pond," are cannibalistic and voraciously predatory. They attack insects, crustaceans, leeches, snails, tadpoles and even small fish, hunting them actively or lurking in ambush to await their passing. They grasp their victim with strong, sharp jaws, through the channels of which a brown digestive juice flows, killing the prey and practically digesting it before the juices are sucked in. They swim by means of active up-and-down movements of the body. Most species have to come to the surface for air (only *Coptotomus* has gills) and can often be seen hanging from the surface film by means of their hairlike caudal cerci or by the tip of the abdomen. They draw in air through the caudal spiracles only.

Pupation takes place in damp soil or sand, under stones and logs, occasionally in more open spots.

The adults, emerging in about 6 weeks, appear to be long-lived, possibly living as long as 5 years. Some overwinter as adults and some as larvae, secreting themselves in the debris of the bottom or even remaining active beneath the ice.

There are about 40 genera of dytiscids. The species range in size from 1 to 40 mm. in length. Most of the large species are in the genus *Dytiscus,* although some species of *Cybister* may attain a length of 35 mm.

Noteridae. Noterids are strong, active swimmers resembling the dytiscids but more common in warmer parts of the country. Most species have a curved spine on the first tibiae. They are small, 5.5 mm., predacious beetles of weedy ponds and lakes. The larvae have strong digging legs and work their way rapidly through mud and debris. *Noteris capricornis* pierces the roots of *Iris, Alisma* and *Sparganium* for the air in the tissues. Several genera.

Amphizoidae. These are the reddish-brown to black beetles, 11–15 mm., that crawl over trash in backwaters and in log jams in the northern and western part of the country. When touched they eject a thick yellow fluid that stains the fingers. Both adults and larvae appear to have a predilection for stonefly nymphs. Eggs are laid in the cracks of logs. Young larvae float characteristically in quiet water with the abdomen horizontal to the surface, with the 8th pair of spiracles at the surface but with the head and thorax tucked under the abdomen. They pupate in crevices in damp wood. One genus, *Amphizoa.*

Hydrophilidae, water scavenger beetles (Figs. 63, 64; Pl. 3). Hydrophilids are common in marshy spots, weedy ponds, and flooded areas having emergent grasses; in saline and mineral water and even in running water if there is good algal growth. A few species live in compost or in the mud along the shore. They are the dominant beetles in warmer waters replacing the dytiscids that predominate in cooler waters.

Hydrophilids are usually black, sometimes with yellow or orange or red markings along the margin. They are often called "silver beetles" because of the glistening coat of air that covers the surface of the body when submerged. They are flatter beneath and more convex above than are the dytiscids; they are poorer swimmers.

Food. Hydrophilids are primarily herbivorous, scavenging on dead and decaying vegetation, especially algae and grasses, and occasionally on dead animal tissues. Since they do not have to pursue their prey, as do the dytiscids, their lack of speed and agility is not a serious handicap.

Respiration. They come to the surface for air, breaking the surface film with the hairy, unwettable club of the antennae, thereby making a funnel in the water through which the air may pass to the underside of the body where it is trapped in the thick pile of hydrofuge hairs. This air plastron is connected with air held in the subelytral spaces.

Eggs. Eggs are laid singly or in masses. They are enclosed in a case carried by the female beneath the abdomen or in a loose web or blanket fastened beneath leaves. The egg case of *Hydrophilus* bears a vertical mast or ribbon. The function of this mast has been highly debated, but it is probably concerned with respiration, since it apparently must protrude above the water's surface. In some species it may serve as an escape hatch for the emerging larvae.

Larvae. Most hydrophilid larvae are moderately sluggish. They crawl about on the vegetation in shallow water, or wander across the stony substratum. Occasionally one will swim out in the open water. Except for the algal-feeding *Berosus,* all are predacious and cannibalistic. When they come to the surface for air they protrude the tip of the abdomen; the surface film than causes the caudal cerci to spread apart, exposing the spiracles that lie between. *Berosus* has lateral, filamentous gills and thus, not needing to come to the surface for air, may live in deeper water.

There are more than 30 genera of hydrophilids. Two of the commonest are *Tropisternus,* 6–15 mm., and *Hydrophilus,* 30–45 mm.

Hydraenidae. These small, 1–2.5 mm., beetles resemble the Hydrophilidae. They cling to rocks and waterlogged wood in fast streams, or in the debris or sand along the shore, for they do not swim.

Food. The adults feed on plant material.

Respiration. They crawl to the surface, breaking the film with the unwettable clubs of the antennae and then, lying in a horizontal position, replenish the plastron of air.

Eggs. These, covered with a blanket of silk, are laid singly on stones, or in algae in shallow water, or in damp places on the shore.

Larvae. The larvae are carnivorous. Often they are more terrestrial than aquatic, making tunnels along the margins of ponds where filamentous algae are abundant, or using the tunnels of other insects such as the staphylinid beetle, *Bledius,* or the carabid, *Dyschirius.* They pupate in damp places nearby, sometimes in mud cells on the sides of stones.

Hydraena and *Limnebius* are common along streams and rivers. The former has the pronotum punctate. The southern

Ochthebius lives in ponds, lakes, saline waters and hot springs; its sculptured pronotum is transparent along the margin.

Psephenidae, long-toed beetles or water pennies (Fig. 63). Psephenids, 6 mm., are brown or black, sometimes variegated. They gather in numbers along the margins of clear, rapid streams, especially those having a gravel or rocky bottom. They enter the water only to lay their eggs. When submerged for this purpose they are enveloped by a film of air trapped in the dense body hairs.

Eggs. Eggs are laid on the undersides of stones that are in the water but near or protruding from the surface.

Larvae. The larvae, known as "water pennies," cling to the surface of the stones even in very fast water. They are broad and flat, with expanded lateral margins, and bearing tufts of gill filaments on the ventral surface. Pupation takes place on stones just in or out of the water. The pupae, too, are oval, flattened and tufted with gills.

Acneus and *Eubrianax* are known only from the west coast; *Psephenus* is from the west and northeast; *Ectoparia* from northwestern and north-central states.

Elmidae, riffle beetles or marl beetles. These small beetles, 2–3 mm., crawl over the bottom or cling to vegetation in streams, preferably cold, fast ones, and occasionally in ponds and lakes where there is some wave action. They do not come to the surface, for they have true plastron respiration, and yet they cannot swim. The eggs are laid on plants. The larvae respire by means of retractile gills located in a caudal chamber. They, like the adults, are herbivorous. Pupation takes place on stones and banks. About 24 genera.

Chrysomelidae (Figs. 63, 64.6). This large terrestrial family is included here because of three genera whose larvae are well known in aquatic environments, and which are sometimes set aside in a seperate family, Donacidae, for that reason.

Donacia, a genus of nearly 60 species, is renowned for the manner in which the female lays her eggs in concentric rings on the undersides of floating water lily pads or on emergent plants such as *Sparganium, Sagittaria, Potamogeton* or even *Myriophyllum.* When on water lily pads she bites a hole in the leaf and extends her ovipositor down through the hole or else reaches with her ovipositor under the edge of the leaf; occasionally she crawls down the flower peduncle, becoming completely submerged. The larvae feed on submerged parts of the plants and respire by piercing plant tissues with sharp, spiracle-tipped projections of the 8th abdominal segment to obtain the intercellular air. Pupation takes place in silken, watertight cocoons which are filled with air taken from plants in the same way.

Galerucella spends its entire life cycle on the upper surface of floating lily pads. It differs from *Donacia* in having thin lateral margins on the prothorax. Its larvae differ in lacking dorsal spines on abdominal segment 8, and in having abnominal prolegs. *Neohaemonia,* east of the Rockies, usually on *Potamogeton natans,* resembles *Donacia* except that tarsi are not dilated and larvae are green instead of creamy white.

Two-winged Flies—Diptera
Figs. 65–68; Pls. 1, 2, 5

The true flies have only a single pair of wings, the second pair having been replaced by a pair of short, knobbed, balancing organs, the *halteres*; and yet many are numbered among the fastest insect fliers. The mouthparts are modified as sucking, piercing or lapping structures through which only liquid food can be taken; or they are reduced and non-functional. The compound eyes are large and often strikingly colored and patterned. A few are parasitic on man and a few are vectors of common human and animal diseases.

All Diptera have complete metamorphosis. None of the adults are aquatic but many, possibly half, of the larvae and pupae are. They may be of great importance as food for fish and birds. The larvae, often called *maggots,* can usually be recognized by their soft, wormlike appearance and the complete absence of true eyes and jointed legs; many have no recognizable head; some have soft, fleshy prolegs;

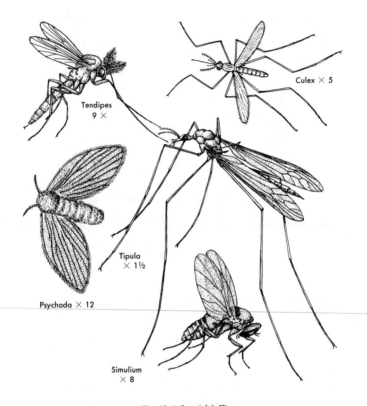

Fig. 65. A Few Adult Flies

but some are remarkably specialized and unlike the typical maggot.

The larval stage may last for a few weeks or for as long as 2 years. The pupae show great variation; some are hard and seedlike, the pupal stage being spent in the last larval skin, or *puparium*; others are soft, with the appendages more or less free from the body; and some remain active. Larvae and pupae often have the number of spiracles reduced to a single pair borne on projections or on a conspicuous, terminal disc.

Grouping of Families of Aquatic Fly Larvae

HEAD WELL DEVELOPED. MOUTHPARTS OPPOSA-
BLE, USUALLY MOVING IN A HORIZONTAL PLANE
  1. With prolegs.
     a. Body flat, with ventral suckers. Lotic (see also Psycho-
        didae).
        Blepharoceratidae. Head, thorax and first abdominal
        segment fused. With six ventral suckers in a median
        row. Fig. 66.
        Deuterophlebiidae. Head, etc., not fused. Ventral
        suckers in two rows at tips of lateral prolegs.
        Western.
     b. Body not flattened.
        Simuliidae. With one pair of prolegs on thorax and
        a sucking disc at end of body. Lotic. Fig. 66.
        Heleidae. With one pair of anterior prolegs but with
        long, lateral processes on abdominal segments.
        Dixidae. With one pair of prolegs on first and second
        abdominal segments; with two pairs of fringed
        processes and a bristly lobe on posterior end.
        Fig. 66.
        Tendipedidae. With one pair of prolegs on prothorax
        and one at posterior end of body (occasionally
        reduced). No spiracles. Fig. 66.
        Liriopedidae. With one pair of prolegs on abdominal
        segments 1 to 3 (occasionally reduced). Abdomen
        ending in long respiratory tube. Fig. 66.
  2. Without prolegs.
        Tipulidae. With a spiracle-bearing, lobed disc at end
        of body (except in *Antocha*). Head capsule incom-
        plete at rear. Fig. 66.
        Psychodidae. Segments divided into annuli, some
        bearing hard dorsal plates. Fig. 66.
        Culicidae. Thoracic segments fused, thicker than rest
        of body. Figs. 66, 68.
        Heleidae. Not as any of the above.
HEAD NOT WELL DEVELOPED, USUALLY
RETRACTED INTO THORAX. MANDIBLES PARAL-
LEL, USUALLY MOVING VERTICALLY, SICKLE-
SHAPED (A few rare families not included)

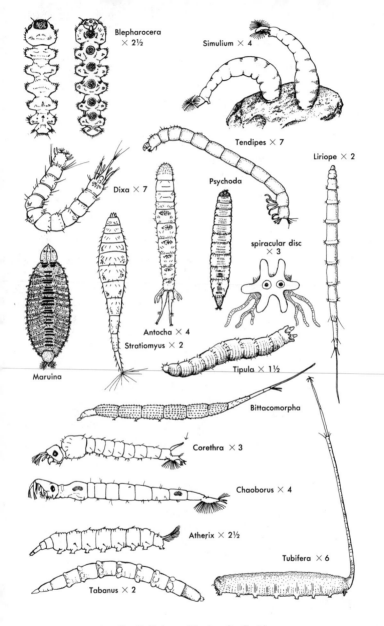

Fig. 66. Fly Larvae (Maruina after Quate)

1. Without prolegs. Body more or less flattened.
   Stratiomyiidae. Body stiff, spindle-shaped. Skin with calcium-carbonate crystals. Circle of bristles around terminal spiracles. Fig. 66.
2. With prolegs, or if without prolegs the body is cylindrical. (Empididae and Dolichopodidae not included.)
   Rhagionidae. Last abdominal segment ending in 1 or 2 pairs of long, fringed processes, longer than prolegs. Eastern. Fig. 66.
   Tabanidae. Most segments bearing a girdle of prolegs (occasionally mere fleshy swellings). Uncommon. Fig. 66.

HEAD VESTIGIAL, MEMBRANOUS OR LACKING. MANDIBLES HOOKLIKE

1. Posterior spiracles at tip of long, telescoped tail.
   Syrphidae. Mouth hooks vestigial. Fig. 66.
2. Spiracles not on tube as above. Mouth hooks present. (Parasitic Tabanidae and leaf-mining Scopeumatidae [= Scatophagidae] of water lilies and pitcher plants, or Sarcophagidae of pitcher plants not included.)
   Sciomysidae (= Tetanoceratidae). Posterior spiracles on a disc surrounded by lobes.
   Muscidae and Anthomyiidae. Without spiracular disc. Mouth hooks sharp and slender.
   Ephydridae. Without disc, or if with disc body ending in needlelike spine. Mouth hooks palmate, digitate, or serrate below.

Blepharoceratidae, net-veined midges (Figs. 66, 67). The wings of these small flies are characterized by a network of folds. The adults of some species are bloodsuckers though not of man. The eggs are laid on wet rocks along the margins of rapid streams.

The larvae, 4–12 mm., gather in numbers, adhering tightly to rocks in the swiftest parts of cold, rushing streams, especially in mountain ravines, and even in the spray of waterfalls. The 6 pairs of laterally placed prolegs make the flattened body appear deeply incised into 6 segments. The first segment is actually the fused head, thorax and first abdominal segment. Each of the 6 apparent segments bears

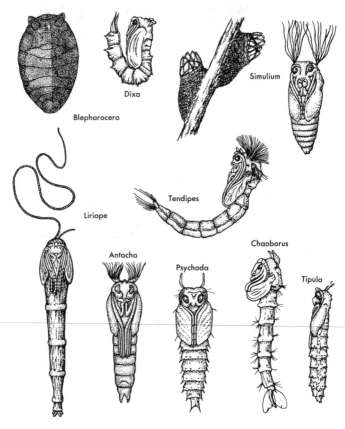

Fig. 67. Fly Pupae

a median ventral sucker, and all but the first have paired, tracheal gill filaments. The larvae feed on algae scraped from stones.

The heavily sclerotized brownish or blackish pupae look like shining black seeds, flattened beneath, rounded above. They adhere tightly to the same rocks as the larvae.

There are at least four North American genera of which *Blepharocera* is the most widespread and common. *Bibio-*

cephala and *Agathon* differ from it in having lateral processes dorsal to the prolegs.

Deuterophlebiidae, mountain midges. *Deuterophlebia* lives around swift, shallow streams in the Rocky Mts. and Calif. The larvae resemble those of the preceding family differing by the characters given in the grouping of families. They have seven pairs of lateral prolegs each surrounded at the tip by a ring of hooklets.

Simuliidae, blackflies or buffalo gnats (Figs. 65–67). The stout, humpbacked blackflies, 3–4 mm. long, are unmitigated pests the world over. They are annoying in the sheer multiplicity of numbers and irritating beyond belief in the unmerciful stinging and itching of the profusely bleeding "bites" they inflict. The females are diligent in their attempt to find an exposed area of human skin, getting between buttons and under shoelaces in their persistent search for blood. One can only take comfort that species in our country do not carry disease, although they have been known to cause the death of animals from emotional shock and loss of blood.

Eggs. Eggs are laid on submerged vegetation or rocks, in lotic water, even in the riffles of swift streams. I have seen them, and the hatching larvae, looking like a thick coat of slime or moss on the board over which water poured as it flowed from a quiet lily pond at high-water time, utilizing the only bit of fast-moving water for miles around. Some species overwinter in the egg stage.

Larvae. The soft-bodied larvae, 3–15 mm., are yellowish white, grayish brown or blackish. Each plump body "sits" upright, swaying downstream when the water is fast but securely fastened by an adhesive salivary secretion as well as by 50 to 140 minute barbs. It is swollen posteriorly, bears a single prothoracic proleg armed with hooklets, and combs the water with two conspicuous head fans which filter out any bits of organic material that may wash by. At times the larvae move slowly over the surface to which they have been attached, holding on with mouthparts and proleg and spinning a salivary thread as a guide or stay. Three retractile blood gills at the posterior end of the body are an aid in respiration.

Pupation takes place, in 2 to 6 weeks, within a silken cocoon attached to the same surface. The cocoons may be slipper-shaped or vaselike, or may be just a tangled mass of threads; but the structure of the mesh is so consistent as to be useful in identification of the species. The pupa protrudes from the open end of the cocoon with two long respiratory filaments extended. These filaments have from 6 to 25 branches in *Simulium* and as many as 48 in *Cnephia*.

Emergence often takes place under water, the adult coming out of the pupa encased in a bubble of air which carries it to the surface. It then takes flight immediately. Several genera.

Heleidae (= **Ceratopogonidae**), **biting midges or punkies** (Fig. 66). These no-see-ums or sand flies, less than 4 mm., can be a frightful nuisance at times, especially when the wind dies down. They work their way through screening and under clothing, or alight unseen on the bare skin, some of them giving "bites" far more irritating than those of a mosquito. *Culicoides, Lashiohelia* and *Leptoconops* are the bloodsuckers. Several other genera suck blood but only that of insects. Some have become quite specialized: *Pterobosca*, for instance, lives only on the wings of dragonflies, clinging with specially modified tarsi; and one notorious species of the Orient sucks vertebrate blood from the abdomen of a mosquito that has just engorged itself upon a human. Biting midges are known to transmit filarial parasites of man.

Larvae. The larvae, 3–12 mm., live in springs, streams, ponds and lakes; in mud and debris along the shore or in floating masses of algae and other vegetation. Some live in brackish water and some in tree holes and the bracts of plants. They may be herbivorous, or carnivorous and cannibalistic; or they may be scavengers in sand, mud and algae. *Atrichopogon* and *Forcimyia* differ from all others in having long filamentous appendages on each segment and a pair of prothoracic prolegs.

The pupae are conical in shape with a spiny abdomen. Near the base of the abdomen is a pair of processes that enable them to make their way to the surface for transformation.

There are about two dozen genera.

Dixidae, dixa midges (Figs. 66, 67). The adults are most frequently found resting, face upward, on vegetation or stones a few inches from the water; or in pre-mating swarms (males) at dusk. The eggs are laid in shallow water in a gelatinous mass. The black and tan larvae resemble mosquito larvae, differing most noticeably in having their thoracic segments separated and in having paired prolegs on the first 2 abdomenal segments. They live in or near the surface film in all kinds of quiet water. *Dixa* and *Paradixa* assume a characteristic U-shape when at rest but *Meringodixa* lies out straight at right angles to the substratum. They feed on small organisms and on detritus, filtered out of the water by their mouth brushes. Pupation takes place above the water's edge. The pupae remain motionless, attached by their side, often in U-shaped or coiled position.

Dixa is widespread; *Meringodixa* is from the Pacific coast only and *Paradixa* from D. C.

Tendipedidae (= **Chironomidae**), **nonbiting midges** (Figs. 65–67). The adults, often encountered in swarms near the water or near lights at night, are sometimes annoying even though they do not suck blood. They look like small, pale mosquitos but lack the piercing mouthparts and the scales on the wings.

Eggs. The eggs are laid singly or in gelatinous masses or strings. They are deposited on the surface, the substratum or on vegetation, in all types of water.

Larvae. The larvae, 2–30 mm., range from white to red, sometimes with bluish or greenish tints. The red ones, called bloodworms, owe their color to erythrocruorin, a respiratory blood pigment that enables some species to live in water of very low oxygen content. Professor B. M. Walshe[*] has shown that in resting larvae this pigment holds enough oxygen for 9 minutes of respiration. Some species of *Tendipes* have

[*] In Roeder.

fingerlike gills on the last abdominal segment in addition to the respiratory pigment. Most tendipedid larvae construct open-ended tubes made of algae, silt or sand cemented together with salivary secretions. Some are solitary but others are found in enormous aggregations of as many as 50,000 individuals on a square meter of substratum.

Food. Larvae feed on algae, other plants and organic detritus. Some mud-dwelling species of *Tendipes* have a filter system of food-getting. They spin a net across the opening of their tube, catching plankton and detritus from the water as it flows through, then eating catch, net, tube and all. Other larvae remain in their tubes but stretch out to scrape up any edible material within reach. Still others live in the stems of rooted plants, maintaining silk-lined tunnels and building food-getting nets across the stem cavity. Certain stream species of *Calopsectra* construct, at the upstream end of their tube, a complex arrangement of projecting and radiating arms across which strong sheets of saliva are strung, for catching food particles brought down in the current.

Pupation takes place within the tube.

Of the many genera and some 30,000 species, *Calopsectra* (= *Tanytarsus*) and *Tendipes* (= *Chironomus*) are probably the most widespread and common. A few of them live in swift water but most are residents of the large lakes where they sometimes live at great depths. *Symbiocladius* and some *Spaniotoma* are symbionts on mayfly and stonefly larvae, living coiled beneath the wing pads. Some *Metriocnemis* live in the water of pitcher plants and some *Xenochironomus* in the tissues of sponges. The family as a whole is of tremendous importance as food for insects and for fish and all other aquatic carnivores.

Liriopedidae (= **Ptychopteridae**), **false crane flies** (Figs. 66, 67). The adults are similar to the true crane flies. The striking *Bittacomorpha clavipes* (Pl. 2) has long, buoyant, black and white banded legs which it holds outspread like the spokes of a wheel as it floats, wraithlike, in shaded areas around vegetation.

The larvae live in decaying vegetation in shallow water at the edges of ponds and marshes, lying with the long, terminal respiratory tube projecting above the surface. They feed on decaying vegetation. The white or yellowish *Liriope* is 30 to 35 mm. long; the brown or reddish, tuberculate *Bittacomorpha* is 50 to 60 mm.; and the blackish *Bittacomorphella* with many long, horny projections, is less than 20 mm.

The pupae resemble those of crane flies, differing in having one short and one long respiratory horn, the latter very much longer than the body.

Tipulidae, crane flies (Figs. 65–67). These long-legged flies, some of them looking like giant mosquitoes, occasionally come into the house. They lose their legs as easily as do the daddy longlegs and they flutter about awkwardly and seemingly aimlessly. They range in size from 2 to 40 mm. in body length; one has a wing expanse of over 75 mm. Several are wingless or have the wings greatly reduced; one of these is *Chionea* that often crawls about on the snow and whose larva lives in leaf mold.

Eggs. The eggs of aquatic species are laid as the female flies over the water, dipping the tip of her abdomen beneath the surface.

Larvae. The white, or brownish, translucent larvae, 10–50 mm., are easily recognized by the lobes at the posterior end of the body. These stretch out to form a terminal disc that bears 2 conspicuous, eyelike spiracles (except in *Antocha*). These spiracular discs are of great variety and *very characteristic*. Small anal gills also expand, sometimes becoming quite long and branched. Most species live in sand, gravel and the soil of wet meadows and pastures. Many live in wet moss and vegetation along the margins. *Hexatomia* and the case-building *Antocha* are completely aquatic.

Food. Some tipulid larvae are herbivorous; those of the common leather jackets, *Tipula*, often doing considerable damage to the roots of meadow and pasture vegetation. Others are carnivorous, like the *Dicranota* that preys on tubifex worms.

Pupation takes place in the last larval skin except in *Antocha*. The pupa has long, straight legs extending beyond the ends of the wing sheaths, and long prothoracic horns.

There are nearly two dozen genera.

Psychodidae, moth flies and sand flies (Figs. 65, 66). The heavy bodied adults, less than 4 mm. in length, can be seen in shady spots near the water or coming to lights at night. A few are biting pests: *Phlebotomus* of the tropics and sub-tropics is of serious economic importance as a vector of disease in many parts of the world.

Eggs. The eggs are laid in shallow water. The *larvae*, 3–10 mm., differ from mosquito wrigglers, which they slightly resemble, in lacking prolegs and in having the body segments divided into annuli. They feed on algae and decaying vegetation. They frequently occur in badly polluted water and sewage beds; *Psychoda* and *Telamatoscopus* occur at times in household drains where they tolerate rather hot water and high soap concentrations. One western genus, the flat *Maruina*, lives clinging to rocks in clear, fast streams or just above the waterline where it will be splashed with spray. It is held in place by ventral sucking discs.

The pupae, except for those of the flat, disclike *Maruina*, are cylindrical. They are found in open water. The leg sheaths are short and straight, and the wing sheaths extend to the middle of the body. There are four aquatic or semiaquatic genera in North America.

Culicidae, mosquitoes and phantom midges (Figs. 65, 66, 68; Pl. 1). This family includes two distinct groups of flies: the Culicinae, or mosquitoes, having scaly wings; and the Chaoborinae, the nonbiting phantom midges, that have hairy wings. Nearly all female mosquitoes suck blood; male mosquitoes feed only on plant juices, if at all; and adult phantom midges probably do not feed at all.

Eggs. Mosquito eggs are laid singly, in irregular masses, or in floating rafts. They may be deposited in tree holes, temporary water of all kinds, such as puddles, footprints, rain barrels, flower vases, cemetery urns, etc., or in permanent quiet waters. A few species prefer brackish water.

Phantom midge eggs are usually laid in water charactertisic of the larvae. At times they have been seen to form a brown scum several miles long across the surface of a lake. They hatch in 12 to 48 hours.

Larvae. Mosquito larvae, 3–15 mm., are easily recognized

by the thickened, fused thorax and by their tendency to lie quietly at the surface and then to suddenly swim downward with a violent wiggling motion. A caudal respiratory tube is present in all except *Anopheles*. This is projected through the surface film for air or, as in *Mansonia*, into plants for the oxygen within the plant tissues. They feed on algae, microorganisms, or bits of organic debris. Some *Psorophora* and some species of the giant tree-hole mosquito *Toxorhynchites*, feed on other mosquito larvae, small crustaceans and rotifers. A few nibble on plants.

Phantom midge larvae are transparent. You can watch *Chaoborus* in deeply shaded water, jerkily swimming a short distance and alternately drifting, jerking, drifting, with only its air sacs visible to the eye. Like many other midges, however, it spends most of the day in deep water of large ponds and lakes, coming to the surface only at night. These larvae are predatory, feeding on small crustaceans and insect larvae, which they catch with prehensile antennae. They lack special respiratory devices, so probably respire through the body surface. *Mochlonyx* lives in pools and bogs and *Eucorethra* in cold springs and spring pools.

Pupae. Culicid pupae are aquatic. They are sometimes quite active, coming to the surface for air which they get by means of 2 trumpet-shaped structures located in the back of the bulging thorax. Two paddles at the end of the abdomen are free and movable in mosquitoes but fused and immovable in phantom midges.

Most culicids hibernate as larvae but some spend the winter in the egg stage and some overwinter as adults, hanging in sheds or similarly sheltered areas. Some species complete a generation in 10 days; others require a year.

In relation to disease. Mention should be made of the great importance of mosquitoes throughout the world as vectors of malaria and yellow fever as well as other diseases. Actually only a few species are responsible for the bad reputation given the entire group. In the U. S. the only disease vectors of any importance are *Anopheles quadrimaculata* of the south and east and *A. maculipennis* of the Pacific coast, as carriers of malaria; *Stegomyia fasciata*, of yellow fever (a few species of *Anopheles, Aedes* and *Culex* are potential carriers); and at least one species of *Culiseta*, of encephalitis (a few species of *Anopheles*, *Aedes* and *Culex* are potential carriers of this also). Some diseases of domestic animals are mosquito-borne; heartworm of dogs, for instance, is carried by *Culex*.

Grouping of Genera of Culicidae Larvae

MOSQUITOES. ANTENNAE NOT PREHENSILE, AND WITHOUT APICAL SPINE. MOUTH BRUSHES PRESENT

1. Abdominal segment 8 without a respiratory tube.

   Anopheles. In all kinds of water. Lies horizontal to the surface.

2. Abdominal segment 8 with a respiratory tube.

   a. Respiratory tube with a row of comblike bristles.

   Culex. Head wider than long. Tube with 3 or more pairs of ventral tufts. Rest at inclined angle to surface. Widespread and common; some found chiefly in water containers.

   Culiseta. Head circular. Tube with 1 pair of ventral tufts close to base. Widespread in permanent pools and marshes.

   Uranotaenia. Head elongate and elliptical. Tube with ventral tuft at base or none at all. Eastern, in permanent pools.

   Psorophora. Head circular. Ventral tuft near middle of tube or beyond, or absent. Entire anal segment with complete sclerotal ring pierced by ventral tuft. Widespread in temporary water.

   Aedes. Ventral tuft as in *Psorophora*. Anal segment with dorsal, saddle-shaped, sclerotized plate, or if completely ringed the median ventral brush is posterior to it. Rests at inclined angle to surface. Widespread in temporary water; some species in salt marshes.

   b. Respiratory tube without comblike bristles.

   Wyeomyia. With 1 pair of ventral hairs instead of anal brush. In water of pitcher plants, bromeliads and other epiphytes, or in bog pools. Eastern and southern.

Toxorhynchites. Mouth brushes prehensile, each made up of 10 stout rods. In tree holes and plants. N. J., Kans. to Texas.

Orthopodomyia. Mouth brushes not prehensile. In tree holes and plants. Widespread.

Mansonia. Respiratory tube curved upward, pointed and toothed for piercing. Widespread.

PHANTOM MIDGES. ANTENNAE PREHENSILE WITH LONG APICAL SPINE. MOUTH BRUSHES ABSENT

1. Abdominal segment 8 with single, dorsal respiratory tube.

Corethella. Antennae inserted close together. Spring pools. Uncommon, N. J.

Mochlonyx. Antennae far apart. Widespread, pools and ponds.

2. Abdominal segment 8 without tube.

Chaoborus. Air sacs visible in thorax and abdominal segment 7. Widespread in large lakes.

Eucorethra. Without air sacs. Northern springs.

Stratiomyiidae, soldier flies (Fig. 66). The bright green-and-yellow-patterned soldier flies are usually found in association with flowers. Only a few have aquatic larvae. Eggs of aquatic species are laid on plants or debris along the shore of ponds or slow streams. The larvae, 10–15 mm., are hard-skinned and stiff; heavy deposits of calcium carbonate produce the characteristic shagreen of the surface. The body is flattened dorsoventrally and often spindle-shaped, its posterior end bearing a circle of hairs or bristles. The larvae may remain submerged for long periods; when they come to the surface they project the posterior end with bristles so outspread as to expose the encircled spiracles. They may be found in quite foul water at times, feeding on algae and decaying vegetation and possibly on small animal organisms. Pupation takes place in the last larval skin. The puparium thus formed is also heavily sclerotized: it is shortened and egg-shaped.

Of the 16 genera, *Stratiomys* and *Eulalia* (= *Odontomyia*) are the most common.

Rhagionidae, snipe flies (Fig. 66). The adults fly around grasses and low shrubbery, feeding mostly on blood. Females of *Atherix* lay their eggs in great clusters on twigs overhanging the water and then die upon the mass, other females adding their eggs and their own dead bodies to the cluster until it reaches a tremendous size. Indians are said to have used these for food, gathering them in bushel baskets.

The hatching larvae, reaching 10–18 mm., fall into the water where they take up a life of predation. They respire by means of two protrusible blood gills placed just below the two long, fringed terminal filaments.

Syrphidae, flower flies or hover flies (Fig. 66). The brightly colored adults are usually associated with flowers, feeding on pollen and nectar. Several genera breed in sewage, tree holes or wet and decaying vegetation, logs, etc. The commonest aquatic genus is *Tubifera* (= *Eristalis*) whose larva, the rat-tailed maggot (Pl. 5; Fig. 66), feeds on organic material in stagnant, sometimes foul, shallow water. It breathes by means of a long, terminal, respiratory tube projected above the surface with terminal hairs outspread. This tube is segmented, telescopic and capable of being extended three or four times the length of the body.

Scatophagidae, dung flies. One species, *Hydromyza confluens*, has a dull, whitish larva living in submerged petioles of the yellow water lily.

Ephydridae, shore flies. These small brown or blackish flies live along the shoreline of many types of water. Some of the larvae mine in aquatic plants but *Ephydra* and *Setacera* are free-swimming, sometimes swimming a meter below the surface, the former in brine pools and lakes of the west and the latter in hot and cold springs. They both have two long, retractile terminal respiratory tubes but they do not seem to project them above the surface. They are sometimes so abundant as to form large floating balls or to crowd along the shoreline in shallow waters.

Other families. A few members of the housefly family, Muscidae, have aquatic larvae, as do their close relatives the Anthomyiidae. Some species of the horsefly family, Tabanidae, lay their eggs on foliage or rocks overhanging pools, swamps and streams where the hatching larvae may fall into the water; those of one species of *Chrysops* feeding on organic debris; of *Tabanus* and *Haematopota* on snails, worms and insects. They crawl out of the water to dig burrows in which to pupate. Several species of Dolichopodidae, the metallic blue or green long-legged flies, live during their predacious larval life in a variety of water, including tree holes. A few predacious larvae of dance flies, Empididae,

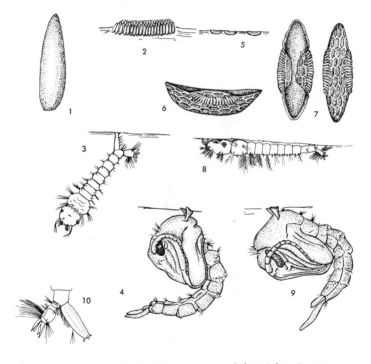

Fig. 68. Comparison of *Culex* and *Anopheles*. Culex: *1*, egg; *2*, egg raft; *3*, larva at surface; *4*, pupa at surface. Anopheles: *5*, eggs at surface; *6, 7*, eggs; *8*, larva at surface; *9*, pupa at surface. *10*. End of abdomen, Aedes.

are aquatic. About 10 genera of marsh flies, Sciomysidae (= Tetanoceratidae), have been reared from snails most of which are aquatic; their puparia are swollen, seedlike and curved at both ends to fit the curvature of the snail shell.

Caddis Flies—Order Trichoptera
Figs. 69–70; Pls. 4, 18

When a cylinder of sand tilts over and slowly moves away, when a frayed bit of vegetation or a minute bundle of fagots creeps across the stream bed, or when a submersed, miniature log cabin rears up endwise, do not be alarmed. Projecting from each will be the sclerotized head and thorax and the forward slanting legs of a caddis.

Caddis flies make up one of the four orders that have become almost wholly aquatic during their immature life. They are the only one of the four that has complete metamorphosis. The mothlike adults are usually brownish and inconspicuous, ranging in size from 1 to 20 mm. in length. A few are bluish black and a few are brightly speckled with yellow or gold. The wings are usually thickly covered with hairs; unlike the scales of a moth's wing, these hairs do not rub off. When at rest the wings are held back over the body slanting down rooflike at the sides. The long, many-segmented antennae are held forward.

The adults are primarily nocturnal, coming in to lights at night in great numbers but hiding during the day in vegetation or under ledges or other shelter. In high altitudes where there is no shelter they may hide beneath stones. The biting mouth parts are greatly reduced, the adults eating but little, if at all, although occasionally sucking sweet liquids.

Eggs. The eggs, encased in a gelatinous covering, are laid in masses or strings attached to submerged vegetation or logs and occasionally to objects above the waterline. When the eggs are laid out of water the gelatinous covering protects them until the next rain dissolves it and permits the hatching larvae to be washed down into the water.

Larvae. The larvae are all aquatic except the European

Enoicyla which manages to live in wet moss. The head and thorax are usually heavily sclerotized and pigmented, but the abdomen is soft and light-colored, although in some free-living species it may be bright green. The legs are characteristically and noticeably directed forward. The abdomen of most case-builders has three tubercles on the 1st abdominal segment, one dorsal and two lateral; these help support the case and hold it out from the body. It also has a pair of strongly hooked prolegs at the posterior end for anchorage within the case.

Very few caddis larvae swim although a few of the Leptoceridae and Phryganeidae may, since they have the last pair of legs modified for swimming.

Food. The larvae are, for the most part, omnivorous. Most case-makers eat diatoms, algae and small bits of plant material but they also eat small crustaceans, insects and worms. The Rhyacophilidae are entirely predacious. The net-spinners consume the plankton organisms that are filtered out in their nets but they also eat bits of plant material. Since caddis larvae are an important item in the diet of trout and other fish they are of significance in the aquatic food chain.

Respiration. Caddis larvae have no spiracles. Most of the case-builders have tracheal gills on the abdomen and sometimes on the thorax also. A few species also have anal blood gills. The species that do not have gills respire through the skin and the chances are that most other species do also, for if the gills are removed they seem to continue to get an adequate oxygen supply. Not only do caddis larvae live in running water but they keep the water surrounding the body in constant motion by means of the undulations of the body and the waving of the abdominal hairs.

Cases. Many of the cases are incredibly beautiful as well as ingeniously constructed. An arched cylinder of crystal-clear sand grains interspersed with bright, translucent pink grains; a slender cone, reflecting light as though made of silver sequins; a rectangular pyramid of alternate layers of dark and light fagots; a helicoidal, simulated snail shell made of sand; all of these, as well as a great variety of short tubes and long tubes, made from a great variety of mineral and

A caddis larva, reaching out of its case.

The larva of a Red-backed Salamander, *Plethodon cinereus*.

PLATE 18

plant materials, are constructed to house the immature caddis, and thereby to delight the collector's eye.

The majority of species build true cases. First they spin a silken tube. In this they embed pieces of leaves, sticks or other vegetation, grains of sand, tiny stones, even tiny shells. Many of the bits of vegetation will have been especially cut to size for the purpose and then laid end to end, or parallel to one another in a geometrically woven pattern or spiral. It is all done with seeming precision and uniformity, for most species always make the same type of case from the same type of material. Occasionally a species will use a variety of materials, and occasionally an individual will start with one substance and then switch to another. Some of the cases appear too heavy and cumbersome for the small larva within. But the heaviest ones are usually built by those living in fast waters where the weight of the case is of value in anchoring it. Furthermore a bubble or two of air inside can give it buoyancy and make it comparatively weightless.

Some species do not build a case during the first few instars. A few remain free-living throughout their entire larval life; they build a silken tube or net so fastened to stones that the current washes down through it, bringing small organisms which the larva, lying in a silken or stone-walled retreat nearby, can garner from the net. This net-feeding is done with consummate skill by species of *Macronema* whose fishing net, spun at the brink of a miniature waterfall, is as delicately contrived as a spider's web and kept in repair with similar diligence, and whose retreat is a firm, stone-walled enclosure. Some of the Psychomiidae build their tubular silken nets in the sand or mud of the substratum with a funnel-shaped opening projecting into the stream's current.

Pupation. The retreat makers construct an elliptical cocoon in which to pupate. Case-makers pupate within their case. At this time the case may be cemented down; it may have a silken screen spun across its opening or a protective door provided by the attachment of a pebble. The pupae remain more or less active within the case, usually undulating the body to keep the water in motion.

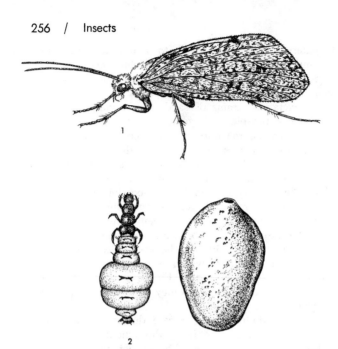

Fig. 69. 1. An adult caddis fly, *Ptilostomis* × 2. 2. An unusual caddis larva, *Ithytricha confusa* and its purse case (after Lloyd).

Emergence. Just before emergence the pupa leaves the case; if in quiet water it climbs out onto projecting objects or onto the shore; if in swift water it swims to the surface, and the emerging adult has the responsibility of leaving the water and taking wing immediately. Caddis flies of some species are emerging all during the late spring and summer; a few take wing on warm winter days.

Collecting. Cases can be picked by hand or with forceps from rocks, especially from the under surface, or from the stream bed. Some must be lifted carefully with a knife blade. Many may be raked from the debris, gathered in a net or Needham scraper, or picked from a hand screen held downstream from some point where rocks and debris have been agitated. Watch carefully for nets of the net-spinners where the water tumbles over a stone or other barrier.

Grouping of Families of Caddis Larvae and Cases

FREE-LIVING LARVAE, WITHOUT CASE. BASE OF
TERMINAL PROLEGS NOT FUSED TO FORM AN
APPARENT TENTH SEGMENT

Rhyacophilidae. Larvae crawl about on stones in cold
riffles and mountain streams; when full grown they
crawl into crevices, construct a case of stones in which
they spin a cocoon and pupate. Anal prolegs with
large hooks; dorsum of abdominal segment 9 with a
chitinous shield; no tubercle on dorsum of 1st abdominal segment; no gills. *Rhyacophila* and the southwestern *Atopsyche.*

Hydroptilidae. These, the smallest of the caddis larvae,
less than 6 mm., are distinctive in having abdomen
much wider than thorax. They build a purselike case
in the 5th instar. (Fig. 69.) Many genera.

NET-SPINNERS, LIVING IN RETREATS. BASE OF
TERMINAL PROLEGS NOT FUSED

Hydropsychidae (Fig. 70.10). Build retreats in front of
which they spin a net crosswise to the current.
Macronema builds a cup-shaped retreat of stones,
open at the upstream end; it may also build on wave-
beaten shores. Larva: abdomen with many branching
gills; base of anal claw with large fan of long hairs;
dorsum of segment 9 membranous; three thoracic
segments each with a single sclerotized shield. Many
genera.

Philopotamidae (Fig. 70.15). Construct long, slender,
fingerlike tubes of silk, usually under stones in rapid
mountainous streams. Several or many nets are found
together. The larvae stay within the nets feeding, but
when ready to pupate build cocoons of stones and
debris. Larvae: Labrum extended distally, membranous; abdomen without gills. Several genera.

Psychomiidae. Build tubular nets, usually open at both
ends, on plants; or they burrow in the bottom of
sandy, rapid streams. Some are communal. *Neuro-
clipsis* builds a long, partially coiled trumpet. Larva:

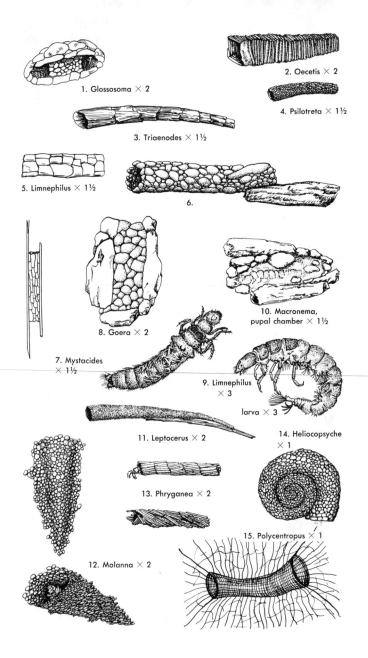

1. Glossosoma × 2

2. Oecetis × 2

4. Psilotreta × 1½

3. Triaenodes × 1½

5. Limnephilus × 1½

6.

8. Goera × 2

10. Macronema, pupal chamber × 1½

7. Mystacides × 1½

9. Limnephilus × 3

larva × 3

11. Leptocerus × 2

13. Phryganea × 2

14. Heliocopsyche × 1

15. Polycentropus × 1

12. Molanna × 2

Fig. 70. Caddis Larvae and Cases (15 after Noyes)

abdomen without gills; labrum short, sclerotized. Many genera.

BURROWERS

Psychomiidae (see above).

SADDLE OR PURSE CASE-MAKERS. BASE OF TERMINAL PROLEGS NOT FUSED

Glossosomatidae (Fig. 70.1). Build turtle-shaped cases of stone with a stone bridge across center of opening. Often congregate in numbers on stones in cold running water. When ready to pupate they cut away the bridge and cement the rims of the case to the stone. Larva: dorsum of segment 9 with a sclerotized shield. Several genera.

Hydroptilidae (Fig. 69). After 5th instar larva builds a purse or spectacle case, open at both ends and usually covered with sand, debris or algae; in both quiet and lotic waters. Larva (see above).

PORTABLE TUBE CASE-MAKERS. BASAL SEGMENT OF TERMINAL PROLEGS FUSED TO FORM AN APPARENT TENTH SEGMENT (Fig. 70.9)

1. Case of pebbles.

Goeridae (Fig. 70.8). Cylindrical with large stones on each side; in cold, fast streams. Larva: curved, with small membranous horn between front legs. Three genera.

2. Case of sand.

a. Discoidal, snaillike.

Helicopsychidae (Fig. 70.14). Larva: gills small; teeth on anal lobes comblike. *Helicopsyche.*

b. Straight, flattish, often with lateral, winglike extensions.

Molannidae (Fig. 70.12). Larva: claws of hind legs much smaller than those of other legs. (*Athripsodes,* a leptocerid, makes the same type of case.) *Molanna* and the Alaskan *Molannodes.*

c. Conical or cylindrical.

Odontoceridae (Fig. 70.4). Cylindrical, curved. In cold mountain streams of east. Larva: mesonotum with wide, transverse, straplike anterior sclerite, a pair of oblong sclerites, and a thin, posterior one. Several genera.

Beraeidae. Conical, curved. Larva: hind tarsal claws as long as others but with basal tooth reduced to a fine hair; pronotum with a deep transverse groove. *Beraea.*

Sericostomatidae. Conical at first, later cylindrical; in cold, rapid, mountain streams; not common. Larva: anal hooks formed of 2 to 3 long, overlapping teeth; mesonotum with small, sclerotized plates. *Sericostoma.*

Brachycentridae. Conical. Larva: hind tarsal claws with a basal tooth; pronotum with a transverse furrow. Several genera.

Lepidostomatidae. Conical, smooth. Larva: 1st abdominal segment with no dorsal tubercle; antennae close to the eyes; mesonotum with a single large sclerite. *Lepidostoma* and *Theliopsyche.*

Leptoceridae (Fig. 70.11). Conical or cylindrical; wide range of habitat. Larva: antennae 7 or 8 times as long as wide, rising at base of mandibles (except *Athripsodes* which has a pair of sclerotized parenthesis marks on the membranous mesonotum). Many genera.

3. Case of vegetable material.

Calamoceratidae. Hollowed-out twig, or bits of leaves and twigs; usually with 3 large pieces plus small bits; in springs and rapid streams of east. Larva: with a transverse row of 20 or more setae across middle of labrum. Three genera.

Phryganeidae (Fig. 70.13). Cylinder of bits of vegetation spirally wound or in rings, with bits placed end to end; in cool or mountainous areas. Larva: mesonotum and metanotum entirely membranous (or with minute sclerites), each with lateral tuft of long setae; lateral gills hairy. Many genera.

Limnephilidae (Fig. 70.5). Triangular, circular or flat in cross section, of bits of vegetation or mineral matter. Larva (Fig. 70.9): antennae midway between eye and margin of head or close to mandible; mesonotum with single large sclerite. Many genera.

Brachycentridae (Fig. 70.2). Round or square in

cross section; in cool, mountainous areas. Larva (see above). Several genera.

Lepidostomatidae. Square in cross section; in cool or mountainous areas. Larva (see above).

Leptoceridae (Fig. 70.3,7). Conical, with bits often arranged spirally. Larva (see above).

Caterpillars—Order Lepidoptera
Fig. 71

The butterflies and moths make up the second largest order of insects, but the larvae of only a few genera of the subfamily Nymphulinae of one family, the Pyralididae, have become truly aquatic. Some ten families, however, contain species that are associated with aquatic plants and are found in or near an aquatic environment.

Lepidoptera have the wings covered with tiny, overlap-

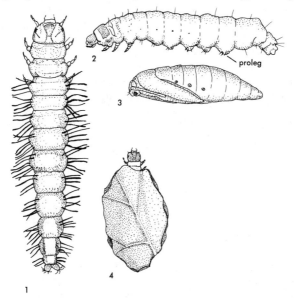

Fig. 71. Lepidoptera. *1.* Larva of *Paragyractis.* *2, 3,* Larva and pupa of *Synclita* (after Lange). *4. Paraponyx* larva in case.

ping scales; their mouthparts, except in the most primitive group, are remarkably modified to form a tubular proboscis that lies coiled like a watchspring beneath the head. The larvae, called caterpillars, have tiny, simple eyes, *ocelli*, of which there are usually 6 on each side of the head; and large, well-developed jaws for grinding the plant tissues which they consume in enormous quantities. They have 3 pairs of short thoracic legs ending in a 1-jointed tarsus bearing a single claw; and a series of *abdominal prolegs* each terminating in a group of small *hooklets*. Aquatic caterpillars look much like terrestrial ones. The adult moths, which have a wing expanse of from 15 to 40 mm., are often abundant in vegetation along shorelines. They have long, slender legs and bodies; and many have boldly and brightly colored patterns.

One group of pyralids, formerly in the single genus *Nymphula* but now separated into 8 genera, make cases from leaves of aquatic plants such as *Nuphar*, *Potamogeton* and *Vallisneria*. The adults of the well-known *Paraponyx maculalis* lay their eggs on the undersides of floating leaves. The larva, upon hatching, sews together two pieces of leaf, making a flat, ovate case (Fig. 71.4); it then lives within the case, crawling about with the anterior part protruding, and feeding on vegetation. The full-grown larva, 20–25 mm. long, is pale yellowish or whitish, with a dark head and with paired, lateral gills which are so branched as to make some 400 gill filaments. The lashing of these filaments drives currents of water through the case. Others of this group may lack gills: *Neocataclysta* makes a round larval case from *Lemna* leaves, and several other genera (Fig. 71.2,3) make oblong cases from a variety of leaves. They lie within their case enveloped in a bubble of air.

Pupation of these case-building species takes place in a silken cocoon inside the case, the case having been attached to vegetation just above or below the waterline.

One little pyralid, *Acentropus niveus*, introduced from Europe and now locally common in the east, lives in a dense silken web on *Chara*, *Cerotophyllum* or *Potamogeton*. The white, unmarked males and winged females fly normally after emergence but some vestigially winged females never leave the water.

Another group of pyralids, once known as *Cataclysta* or *Elophila,* has also been divided into several genera. Their eggs are laid on rocks in rapid streams, sometimes several feet beneath the surface. The larvae live under a silken web cemented to these stones. The larva of *Paragyractis* (Fig. 71.1) has large mandibles and some 120 unbranched filamentous gills. It feeds primarily upon algae and diatoms which it scrapes off the rocks. Before pupating it cuts away the silken canopy and spins a silken cocoon. The adults have a row of scintillant, metallic spots near the edges of the hind wings.

Other caterpillars found in association with aquatic plants are for the most part air-breathing. The legless *Nepticula* mines in the leaves of the sedges *Scirpus* and *Eleocharis.* The noctuids *Nonagria, Bellura* and *Arzama* first mine in the leaves and then later bore in the stems of *Typha, Nuphar, Pontederia* and *Potamogeton.* A few others are similarly semiaquatic.

CHAPTER 13

Snails, Limpets, and Mussels— Phylum Mollusca

Figs. 72–75

ALTHOUGH the vast majority of molluscs are marine, many have invaded fresh waters and a few snails and soft-bodied slugs have become terrestrial.

The marine squids and octopi have a rigid skeletal piece embedded in the soft flesh; but snails, limpets and mussels have a hard exoskeleton. This *shell* is composed primarily of calcium carbonate, covered with a thin, usually pigmented, epidermis, or *periostracum*. The shells of any species may vary in size, shape, surface markings and thickness, the last having a direct relationship to the amount of calcium in the water. They are secreted by the *mantle*, a unique organ composed of a thin layer of tissue covering the viscera and bearing microscopic cilia which, by their constant wavelike activity, pass along to the *mouth* the millions of microscopic particles of food material that are extracted from the water. The mantle also provides the folds which in some species are used as gills.

Collecting. A dip net or strainer (even an ordinary kitchen strainer tied to a 6-foot pole), or a small dragnet or dredge for deep water, should bring up molluscs if it is used diligently in the substratum of streams and rivers, quiet ditches and lakes, on sandy beaches, and in the vegetation of ponds and pools. Sometimes it is necessary to take out a large quantity of material, empty it onto a large piece of heavy cloth, and then pick out the treasures at leisure. Very fragile shells should be transported in small vials or other individual containers. If the soft parts are not wanted they should be removed. After a day in the field a delightful evening can be well spent boiling specimens over the camp stove, with even the junior members of the group assigned the task of extracting snail bodies with a partially unbent paper clip. The identification of many species is dependent upon the body parts, so do not be hasty in discarding them; better preserve a few of each kind in alcohol.

Snails and Limpets—Class Gastropoda
Figs. 72, 73

Gastropods have a single shell and are thus distinct from the clams and mussels which have a bivalve shell. They are to be found creeping about on vegetation and submerged surfaces in all kinds of fresh water.

The *periostracum* is usually drab gray or brownish, but occasionally is brightly colored red, green or yellow. The *aperture* in some species can be closed over by an *operculum*, a chitinous plate attached to the dorsal, posterior part of the large muscular *foot*. The body lies coiled within the shell with back uppermost. The head can be protruded from the aperture; it bears a ventral mouth, one pair of tentacles (land snails have two pairs), and an eye at the base of each tentacle. The tentacles bear receptors of touch. It is hard to believe that the actively exploring tentacles do not also have receptors of smell, but these are in the mantle cavity. The foot also can protrude; it not only serves as an organ of locomotion but also contains portions of the digestive tract (hence the name, gastro-pod = intestine foot), the reproductive system and the nervous system. The *umbilicus* may be a shallow open hole or a hollow tube; or it may be a sealed hole, in which case the shell is described as *imperforate*.

Respiration. Respiration is by gills or by an air-filled "lung," but in either case the animal is able to remain submerged indefinitely. The blood, which contains the oxygen-carrying pigment *haemocyanin*, is pumped by the beating heart (sometimes to be seen through the shell) through arteries

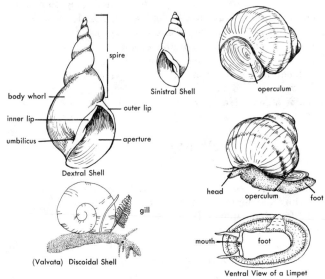

spire

body whorl

inner lip

umbilicus

Sinistral Shell

outer lip

aperture

operculum

Dextral Shell

gill

head   operculum   foot

mouth   foot

(Valvata) Discoidal Shell

Ventral View of a Limpet

Fig. 72. Snails and a Limpet

into open sinuses, thence into a common cavity and back to the heart.

Locomotion. Snails glide over the substratum, submerged objects or the underside of the surface film, by means of a slime track secreted from the ventral surface of the foot. They move along this by muscular contractions of transverse bands on the sole of the foot or by the movement of microscopic cilia. Some snails, mainly *Physa*, *Lymnaea* and *Helisoma*, can also move through the water by "spinning" a mucous thread.

Food. They feed on microscopic algae that coat submerged surfaces, filamentous algae and other green vegetation, as well as on dead plant and animal matter. They may be more nearly omnivorous than is generally realized; *Lymnaea* has been known to feed successively on milk chocolate, peach pulp, apple peel and tiny insect larvae. (I do not recommend the chocolate although our pet apparently suffered no ill effects from an occasional debauch.) Because of their predilection for algae and their importance as scavengers, snails are essential inhabitants of balanced aquaria, cleaning the glass sides of algal scum and cleaning the bottom of organic debris and wastes; but if they are being kept for themselves and not just for their usefulness they should have filamentous green algae and plants such as *Anacharis* as well as lettuce. Calcium carbonate, in some form other than chalk, should be added to the water.

The mouth has a set of from one to three sclerotized jaws behind which lie a strong *buccal cartilage* and a chitinous toothed *radula* which grinds and rasps the food and scrapes the algal scum. The structure of the radula is important in identification.

Reproduction. The pulmonate snails and the Valvatidae are hermaphroditic but all others have the sexes separate. Copulation takes place even between two hermaphroditic individuals although they are also capable of self-fertilization. Eggs are laid from early spring to late fall, sometimes a few at a time, sometimes by the hundreds. Each egg is encased in a gelatinous capsule within a gelatinous mass. A few species are viviparous.

Habitat. Gastropods are seldom in water more than 10 feet deep, or on shores where there is wave action, or in swift streams where the bottom is sandy or gravelly. As a rule they require a high oxygen concentration (limpets even require oxygen-saturated water), so are seldom in polluted water. They cannot withstand extremely cold temperature; in winter the lake species move out into deeper water and the pond and stream species burrow in the mud and debris of the bottom. Those living in temporary water must be able to aestivate; *Lymnaea* does this by secreting a thin sheet of mucus, an *epiphragm*, over the aperture, to prevent desiccation.

Grouping of Families of Freshwater Gastropods
(Fig. 73)

WITHOUT OPERCULUM. RESPIRATION BY INTERNAL LUNG. Order Pulmonata
1. Shell flat or conical, not spiraled.

Ancylidae, limpets. The thick-shelled *Lanx*, 8–18 mm., has apex of cone in the midline (when shell is held dorsal side up and cone nearer one's body); west coast. The thinner-shelled *Ferrissia*, less than 7 mm., has apex inclined to right of midline. *Gundlachia* has apex to right but more posterior and when mature has a flat shelf on anterior part of ventral side; south-central states. *Ancylus* of Colo. has apex inclined to left. Other genera, including the pink-tipped *Rhodacmaea*, Ill. to Ala.

2. Shell discoidal or with low spiral.

Planorbiidae, orb snails. *Planorbula* has lamellae or teeth on internal aperture; eastern. *Helisoma*, more than 12 mm., lacks teeth but has a thick lip; common and widespread in quiet waters. *Gyraulus* has rounded shell and slightly oblique aperture. The northern *Armiger* has a ribbed shell. Two western genera, *Parapholyx* and *Carnifex*, have a shell with a low spiral, the former imperforate, the latter umbilicate. Many other genera.

3. Shell spiral.

Physidae, pouch snails. Shell sinistral. *Physa* has body whorl inflated and inner edge of mantle toothed or lobed, extending over edge of shell; requires moderate, not thick, vegetation and organic debris. *Aplexa* has a more elongate shell with inner edge of mantle not lobed, and not extending over edge of shell; in streams and stagnant pools. Many other genera widespread in north.

Lymnaeidae, pond snails. Shell dextral. Spire of shell elongate, aperture quite large. Many common and widespread species of *Lymnaea* have now been separated into several genera.

SHELL WITH OPERCULUM. RESPIRATION BY GILLS.

Order Prosobranchia

1. Shell globose, thick.

Neritidae. Rare, on Gulf Coast.

2. Not as above.

a. Operculum with concentric markings.

Pilidae, apple snails. *Pomacea*, over 35 mm., greenish,

Physa × 1

Aplexa × 1½

Viviparus

Lymnaea × ⅔

Viviparus × ⅔

Helisoma

Lanx × ⅔

Pleurocera × 1

Campeloma × ¾

Gyraulus

Ferrissia

Valvata

Rhodacmaea

Pomacea × ⅔

Fig. 73. Snails and Limpets

mainly nocturnal; lays eggs above waterline on vegetation; rivers, swamps, ditches, Fla. to Ga. *Marisa*, smaller, with banded, doscoidal shell, recently introduced into Fla.

Viviparidae, mystery snails. 15–35 mm. Greenish or blackish, often top-shaped; on sand of lakes and rivers east of Miss. R. *Viviparus* is often banded, with strongly convex whorl and large aperture; introduced and now becoming very common, replacing the hitherto common *Lymnaea. Campeloma* has turreted shell, thick and moderately convex; light green to olive; often embedded in mud. Several other genera.

b. Operculum with spiral growth lines.

1) Operculum circular.

Valvatidae, round-mouthed snails. Less than 7 mm.; shell turbinate. *Valvata* bears a plumose external gill and projecting male organ; in vegetation along margins or under stones or in empty mussel shells; northern.

2) Operculum ovate.

Pleuroceridae, river snails. More than 15 mm. Shell often ribbed, often tall and with aperture often lengthened. Green to brown, often banded. Mantle border fringed. Many genera.

Bulimidae. Less than 10 mm. Shell narrow or extended, with thin lip. Foot is truncate at each end. With external male organ behind right tentacle. Many genera in shallow water in vegetation. May lay eggs on other snails.

Lepyridae. Shell depressed, imperforate, with broad inner lip. *Lepyrium*, Ala.

Thiaridae. Imperforate, attenuated, yellowish-brown; mantle border not imperforate. *Terebia*, rare in Fla.

Clams and Mussels—Class Pelecypoda
Figs. 74–75

The bivalves occur in all kinds of fresh water but are most common in the muddy bottoms of large rivers or, in the case

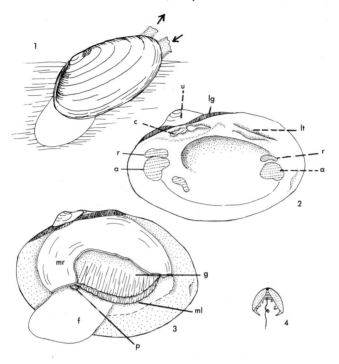

Fig. 74. Mussels. 1. Mussel with foot protruding into the mud and incurrent and excurrent siphons into the water. 2. Diagram of inside of right shell; *a*, adductor muscles; *c*, cardinal hinge teeth; *lg*, ligament; *lt*, lateral hinge teeth; *r*, retractor muscles; *u*, umbo or peak. 3. Diagram of inside with left shell and part of mantle removed; *b*, branchial or incurrent opening; *f*, foot; *g*, gill; *ml*, mantle; *mr*, mantle with edge removed; *p*, labial palp concealing mouth. 4. Glochidium, with bissus. In Figs. 1–3 the anterior end of the shell is toward the left.

of the little fingernail clams, on the bottom of small ponds and brooks. They range in size from 2 to 250 mm. The two valves of the shell are held together at the hinge by an *elastic ligament,* by *hinge teeth* and by two large *adductor muscles* (the scallop of the scallop oyster of commerce). Relaxation of the adductor muscles opens the shell; thus a wide-open shell showing no tendency to close usually indicates a dead animal. In the normal resting position the shell remains partly open with foot extended. A retractor muscle is situated just above each adductor.

Shells range from white to black; many common ones are yellow, green or brown. Concentric lines of growth indicate the additions made to the shell by the mantle; many species also have knobs, tubercles and ridges. The inner surface is sometimes beautifully nacreous.

Unlike the gastropods, clams and mussels have no head. The anterior end is opposite the incurrent and excurrent siphons (the neck of the marine clams).

Locomotion. Bivalves are mainly confined to the bottom but they can move about in much the same manner as snails. The protruding foot is hatchet-shaped (hence the name pelecy-pod). By pumping blood into the foot and subsequently withdrawing it, they are able to alternately expand and contract the foot, an action which pulls the clam forward and downward, leaving a furrow of irregular depth.

Respiration. Two gills, each composed of two flat lobes fastened to each other only on the ventral side, lie on each side of the body. The space between the two layers of each gill is divided by parallel partitions into water tubes which lead into a common suprabranchial chamber.

Food. They feed on microscopic plankton and microscopic organic debris brought into the incurrent siphon with the water. The water passes through the mantle cavity and into tiny openings on the gills; the food particles become caught on the outer mucous surface of the gills and mantle and are then carried by ciliary action to the mouth. The inedible material is separated out possibly by the *labial palp* on each side of the mouth or by the edge of the incurrent siphon, or even by the mouth itself, and then carried away by ciliary action. Mussels are eaten by many fish and by muskrats.

Reproduction. The Sphaeridae are hermaphroditic and are probably self-fertilized. The young develop inside the water tubes of the gills, as many as 20 individuals in various stages of development to be found at a given time. When released, though still immature, they may be one-fourth or one-third as large as the parent. Breeding may continue throughout the year.

In the Unionidae, however, the sexes are separate. The eggs move into the water tubes where they are fertilized by the sperm brought in with the water. The embryos, numbering several thousand or even 3,000,000, are not retained as long as those of the Sphaeridae. In certain species gravid females are to be found only from April to August; in others, from July to the following spring or summer. The emerging larva is called a *glochidium* and is no more than .05 to .5 mm. in length. It drops to the bottom where it is dependent upon chance contact with the body of a fish. It is extremely sensitive to touch, clamping the toothed edges of its shells upon any passing object. If that object proves to be the correct species of fish the glochidium becomes buried in its flesh, living there for several weeks and then dropping to the bottom where, after a period as a *juvenile,* it transforms to an adult. The glochidia of *Elliptio, Anodonta* and *Quadrula* have a long thread, or *bissus,* suspended from between the valves; this is believed to aid them in becoming attached to the host. A few other genera, lacking both the teeth and the bissus, must become attached where they will not easily be rubbed off, usually in the gills. The development of this parasitic glochidian stage is probably an adaptation to life in moving water; not only does it insure distribution of the species but at the same time keeps the tiny clams from being swept out to sea.

The shells of the large Unionidae of the tributaries of the Mississippi River have long been gathered for use in the manufacture of buttons and for their pearls.

Grouping of Families of Freshwater Pelecypods

SHELL NOT NACREOUS. HINGE WITH CARDINAL AND LATERAL TEETH

Sphaeridae, fingernail clams. Shell thin and fragile with concentric lines of growth not prominent; lateral teeth small; 2–25 mm. *Sphaerium,* 7–15, occasionally up to 25 m., has thick, oval shell with two cardinal teeth in left valve, one in right. *Musculium,* 5–12 mm., has thin, polished shell with small or obsolete cardinals and a prominent caplike beak. *Pisidium,* 2–6

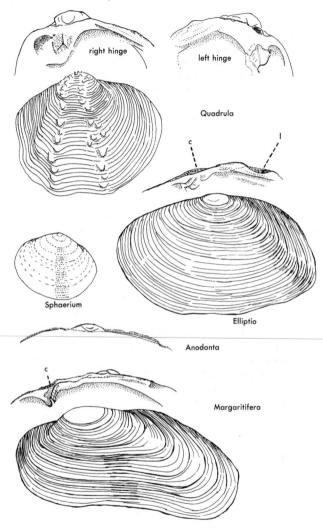

Fig. 75. Mussels, showing outside of left shell and inside of both sides of hinge of *Quadrula;* outside of left shell and inside right hinge of *Elliptio;* right hinge of *Anodonta;* and outside of left shell and inside right hinge of *Margaritifera.* c, cardinal hinge teeth; l, lateral hinge teeth.

mm., rarely to 11, has anterior end of shell large so beak is lopsided. Other genera in Gulf.

Corbiculidae. Shell thick, triangular, with prominent growth rings; lateral teeth serrate; up to 65 mm., often greenish. *Corbicula* introduced to west coast from China. *Polymesoda* in streams of S. C. to Texas.

SHELL NACREOUS. HINGE WITH OR WITHOUT TEETH

Unionidae, pearly mussels or naiads. 25–250 mm. Shells variable in shape. Gills with distinct interlamellar septa parallel with gill filaments. Mantle margins united between siphons. (1) Subfamily Anodontinae have no hinge teeth; eggs are carried in outer gills only. *Anodonta* is widespread; many other genera east of Miss. Valley. (2) Unioninae have cardinal and lateral hinge teeth; eggs are carried in all four gills or in outer gill only. The periostracum is usually dull. *Elliptio,* widespread, carries eggs in outer gills; *Quadrula,* from Mich. and Minn., south to Ark. and Ala., carries eggs in all four gills. Many other widespread and common genera. (3) Lampsilinae has both cardinal and lateral hinge teeth; eggs are carried in posterior part of outer gills. The periostracum is often bright. Many genera east of the Miss. Valley.

Margariteridae. 80–175 mm. *Margaritifera* has an elongate, blackish, laterally compressed shell with cardinal hinge teeth and with or without laterals. Mantle margins not united. Distinct interlamellar septa lacking or, if present, oblique to gill filaments.

CHAPTER 14

Lampreys and Fishes—
Class Pisces

Figs. 76–81

THE fisherman has a lore and language all his own; he will find no mention here of hurl or hackle, or of "grayling rising to the minnow." Here, however, he can make the acquaintance of the fish families that have invaded our fresh waters, some as permanent residents and others as visitors who have come only to spawn or grow to maturity.

In recent years many of our fishes have suffered a serious decline in population chiefly because of predation by man and the works of man. Overfishing and pollution threaten the survival of many species; so also do new roads and dams, deforestation and overgrazing. We must all work to preserve our wilderness areas and to support conservation measures that aid in safeguarding the future of our freshwater fishes.

Fish are cold-blooded vertebrates that breathe by means of gills. With the exception of the lampreys, which are not true fish, they have jaws, paired fins and usually additional unpaired fins. They have a sense of touch, sight, smell, taste and hearing; and some are able to make sounds by vibrating the air bladder or grinding their teeth. The skin is slimy and usually covered with overlapping scales, a combination that waterproofs the body and reduces friction. Lampreys, catfishes and some sticklebacks are "naked," or without scales; paddlefish, the Common Carp and the sculpins are partially so, having scales or prickles in some areas only; eels, the Brook Trout and the Burbot appear to be naked but actually have small, deeply embedded scales.

Red, yellow and black pigment granules are present in the skin in the special nerve-controlled cells, the *chromatophores*. Along the sides of the body is a *lateral line* composed of a row of sense organs, each consisting of a cluster of sense cells embedded in a tiny pit. These are connected with two long hollow tubes running the length of the body and up onto the head.

Locomotion. Fish move through the water by the lateral flexion of body and tail, propulsion from the caudal fin and ejection of water from the gill chambers. Those fishes having a forked tail are the fastest swimmers.

Swimming movements are regulated by the fins, which are projecting folds of skin usually having internal skeletal supports called fin rays. Fins may be soft or rigid. Primitive

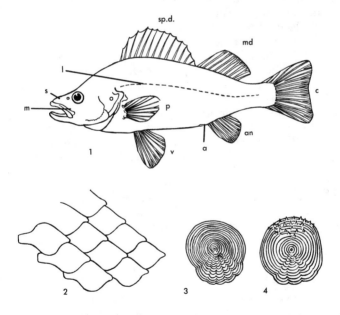

Fig. 76. 1. Diagram of fish; *a*, anus; *c*, caudal fin; *l*, lateral line; *m*, maxillary; *md*, membranous dorsal fin; *o*, opercle; *p*, pectoral fin; *s*, snout; *sp.d.*, spiny dorsal fin; *v*, ventral fin. 2. Ganoid scale. 3. Cycloid scale. 4. Ctenoid scale.

Fig. 77. Caudal fins. *1*, Heterocercal; *2*, modified heterocercal; *3*, homocercal.

fishes, mostly deep-sea forms, and many young fishes, have a keel-like median fin which is continuous along the dorsal ridge, around the tail and along the ventral ridge; among freshwater forms such a fin can be seen in the eels and lampreys. Most species now have this median fin interrupted to form a *dorsal, caudal* (tail) and *anal* fin. The dorsal fin may be long, short or divided into two, the foremost one being spiny and often used in defense. Most fishes also have paired *pectoral* and *ventral* (or pelvic) fins used primarily in balancing and maneuvering, although the pectorals also seem to be used by sculpins and darters in sculling. The pectorals, supported by the pectoral girdle, are located just behind the *opercle,* which makes up part of the cheek; the ventrals are in front of the anus in primitive fishes, but are beneath or even anterior to the pectorals in some specialized forms. An *adipose fin,* lacking skeletal support, is occasionally present on the middorsal line just anterior to the tail; since it is fatty it may be of some value as a float. These fin characters are important in the identification of fishes.

Respiration. Many fishes are confined to waters with a narrow range of oxygen concentration and can tolerate very little variation. Trout, for example, can barely remain alive in waters in which carp will thrive.

Respiration is by means of gills. In the lampreys the pharynx is divided longitudinally by a partition which creates a dorsal food channel and a ventral respiratory one. Seven pairs of pockets lie between this ventral respiratory channel and the outside of the body and have an opening to each; these pockets contain the *gill filaments.* The true bony fishes have only five pairs of these pockets; the thin *gill arches* lying between them bear projecting, close-set *gill rakers* on

Fig. 78. Types of dorsal fin. *1*, Median keel-like dorsal fin continuous with caudal and anal fin; *2*, dorsal, caudal and anal fins separate but dorsal very long; *3*, dorsal fin moderately long; *4*, short; *5*, with anterior spiny portion and posterior membranous portion connected; *6*, with spiny and membranous portions separated.

the inner side and feather *gill filaments* on the external side. The gill rakers strain particles from the water; when long and fine they enable a fish, swimming along with open mouth, to filter out large quantities of microscopic plankton. The gill filaments lie in a common chamber covered by the opercle and opening to rearward through a single aperture, the *gill slit.* Exchange of gases takes place as the water taken in through the mouth is pumped over the filaments.

Many species have an *air bladder* that serves as a depth regulator. At times, especially in those species living in stagnant waters, it also serves as a supplementary respiratory organ.

Food. Most fishes consume a wide variety of food substances; some, however, ingest a limited range of food because of their characteristic feeding habits.

Grouping of Freshwater Fishes Based on Feeding Habits

Parasites. Feed on blood and body fluids of other fish and attach themselves to the body of their host by a sucking mouth.

    Lampreys (some species)

Plankton feeders. Having close-set gill rakers. They often show a migratory pattern, following the fluctuating plankton population.

Golden Shiner	Silversides
Minnows (some species)	Smelt
Paddlefish	Sticklebacks
Perch	Whitefish
Shad	Young bass and trout

Bottom feeders. Obtain food by sucking. Many locate their food by sensitive barbels hanging below the head, and are often seen swimming a short distance above the bottom with barbels dragging. The stoneroller, however, picks up food with its protruding lower jaw.

Catfishes	Sturgeon
Paddlefish	Suckers
Sculpins	Sunfishes (some species)
Stoneroller	Whitefish

Vegetation feeders. Spend much of their time browsing or nibbling on vegetation. They also feed on invertebrates.

Carp	Goldfish
Creek Chub	Killifishes (some species)
Eels	Minnows
Golden Shiner	Sculpins

Invertebrate feeders. Prey on insects and crustaceans primarily. They also feed on molluscs.

    Majority of freshwater fishes

Invertebrate feeders. Also prey upon fish and other vertebrates.

Bass	Sculpins (occasionally)
Bowfins	Sunfishes
Burbot	Trout
Darters	Walleye
Eels	Yellow Perch

Vertebrate feeders. Use their long, sharp teeth for grasping frogs, snakes, and even turtles, as well as many fish

Gars   Pike

Pickerel   Muskellunge

Notorious omnivore.

Catfishes

Reproduction. Most of our freshwater fishes are oviparous, the male spreading the sperm-containing milt over the eggs as they are laid. The Poecillidae and a few of the killifishes are live-bearers, with internal fertilization; the male uses a modified anal fin as the intromittent organ.

Fishes of warm waters usually spawn in the spring or summer; their eggs require only a few days for hatching. Cold-water species usually spawn in the fall or winter; their eggs require a longer period for development, those of the whitefishes needing several months.

At mating time the male is often brilliantly colored and in some species of minnows is profusely covered with nobs and excrescences, especially on the head.

Many fishes show a marked migratory tendency at spawning time. Some move from rivers to streams to farther upstream; or if they live in lakes, from deep water to shallow, weedy shores. Others, present in fresh waters only at spawning time, have made a journey of many, many miles from their haunts in the ocean; such fish are *anadromous*. A few, like the lampreys and eels, go from small streams out to the deep waters of the ocean; they are *catadromous*.

The eggs may be laid singly or in gelatinous masses. They may be attached to some object or scattered loose in the water, some to float, others to sink. Or they may be laid in a nest. Such a nest will be made in advance, usually by the male who then lures the female to it; he sometimes attracts successive females as well, until the complement of eggs is complete. The nest may be deserted as soon as the eggs have been fertilized or it may be guarded, usually by the male, and the eggs aerated, turned and cleaned. Sometimes the parent stays to watch over the newly hatched young. The young fish carries a yolk sac for several days and from it draws nourishment.

Grouping of Freshwater Fishes Based on Egg-laying Habits*

Fishes that scatter their eggs

At random
Darters (most species)
Minnows (most species)
Pike
Pickerel
Suckers (most species)
Walleye

Over plants
Carp
Gars
Golden Shiner
Goldfish
Northern Pike

Over sand, gravel or rocks
Basses
Chub
Ciscoes
Grayling
Lake Trout
Paddlefish
Sturgeon
White Sucker
Whitefishes
Yelloweye

Over mud or vegetation
Buffalo Fish
Carpsucker
Killifishes

Near surface
Alewife
Brook Silverside

In a single rope
Yellow Perch

Fishes that build a nest but desert their eggs

Fallfish
Grayling
Hornyhead Chub
Lamprey
Rainbow Darter

River Chub
Salmon
Trout (except Lake Trout)

Fishes that build a nest and guard their young

Nests a circular depression
In mud, silt, sand or vegetation
Bowfin
Bullheads

* Based partially on Lagler, Bardach and Miller.

    Crappies
    Largemouth Bass
    Rock Bass
    Sunfishes
    Warmouth
  In gravel
    Creek Chub
    Largemouth Bass (occasionally)
    Rock Bass
    Smallmouth Bass
Nests under stones or other objects; eggs suspended from roof
    Bluntnose Minnow
    Fantail Darter
    Fathead Minnow
    Johnny Darter
    Sculpins (some)
Nests of plant material
    Sticklebacks
Nests tunneled in bank or substratum
    Channel Catfish
    Yellow Bullhead

Hints to the Identification of Some Common Fishes

With long projecting snout
    Gars
    Paddlefishes
    Pipefish
    Sturgeon
With barbels
    Catfishes (long, under mouth)
    Burbot (one, under chin)
    Common Carp (two, each side)
    Sturgeon
    Some chubs, some dace
    Spotted Shiner (very small)
With adipose fin
    Catfishes

    Salmon, Trout, Whitefish family
    Trout-perch

With long, unspined dorsal fin
    Eels (continuous with tail)
    Lampreys (continuous with tail)
    Bowfins
    Burbot
    Common Carp (moderately long, fewer than 30 rays)
    Goldfish (moderately long, fewer than 30 rays)
    Some suckers (moderately long, fewer than 30 rays)

With saw-edged spine on front of dorsal fin
    Common Carp
    Goldfish

With initial spine on dorsal fin
    Catfishes
    Pirate Perch
    Trout-perch

With 2 dorsal fins, the first spiny and separate from second
    Basses, White, Striped and Largemouth
    Darters
    Goby
    Mullets
    Perches
    Silversides
    Walleye

With 2 dorsal fins, the first spiny and connected with second
    Basses, Yellow and Rock
    Crappies
    Drums
    Sculpins
    Sunfishes

Tail blunt or convex (not complete list)
    Bowfin
    Bullheads
    Catfishes (a few)
    Darters (most)
    Gars
    Killifishes
    Madtoms
    Mudminnows

Pirate Perch
Sculpins
Sticklebacks
Sunfishes (a few)
Top Minnows
Trout, Brook and Rainbow

Grouping of Orders of Freshwater Fishes*

FISHES WITHOUT JAWS. MOUTH A ROUND SUCK-
ING CAVITY
    Petromyzontiformes, lampreys. P. 286.
FISHES WITH JAWS. CAUDAL FIN HETEROCERCAL
  1. Mouth inferior. Jaws almost or entirely toothless.
    Acipenseriformes, sturgeons and paddlefish. P. 288.
  2. Mouth terminal. Jaws strongly toothed.
    Amiiformes, bowfins. Snout round. P. 289.
    Lepisosteiformes, gars. Snout produced. P. 289.
FISHES WITH JAWS. CAUDAL FIN NOT HETERO-
CERCAL
  1. Eyes on one side of head.
    Pleuronectiformes, flounders and soles.**
  2. Eyes on separate sides of head. Fins continuous.
    Anguilliformes, eels. P. 290.
  3. Eyes on separate sides of head. Fins separated.
    a. Body covered with plates.
    Syngnathiformes, pipefishes** (Gulf).
    b. Body not covered with plates. Head unscaled.
    Cypriniformes, minnows, suckers, catfishes. P. 291.
    Clupeiformes, salmon, etc. Not the pikes and mud-
      minnows in which head is partially scaled. P. 294.
    Percopsiformes, trout-perch only. P. 299.
    c. Body not covered with plates. Head scaled.
      1. With a single, median chin barbel.
      Gadiformes, burbot. P. 299.
      2. Without barbels and without spines in dorsal fin.
      Cyprinodontiformes, top minnows, killifishes. Tail
        blunt, but lower jaw protrudes. P. 299.

* Very young fish are often difficult to identify.
** Enter fresh water to spawn.

Clupeiformes, pike and mudminnows only. Pike have tail forked but mudminnows have tail blunt and lower jaw protruding. P. 294.

Beloniformes, needlefish. *Strongylura marina* ascends Atlantic coastal rivers. Jaws long and slender.

3. Without barbels; with isolated spines anterior to dorsal fin.

Gasterosteiformes, sticklebacks. P. 301.

4. Without barbels; with spines on dorsum connected by membrane.

Mugiliformes, mullets, silversides. Ventral fins abdominal. P. 302.

Percopsiformes, pirate perch only. Ventral fins thoracic. Anus under throat. P. 299.

Perciformes, sea basses, sunfishes, perch, sculpins. Ventral fins thoracic. Anus normal. P. 302.

Order Petromyzontiformes

Petromyzonidae, lampreys (Fig. 79). The eel-like, scaleless lampreys are not true bony fish.* Their mouth is surrounded by a round, tooth-lined, sucking funnel instead of jaws; their skeleton is cartilagenous; and the gill openings along each side of the head are seven in number. They have no paired fins.

The lake lamprey, 2–3 ft., common in the Great Lakes region, is probably a landlocked form of the Sea Lamprey, *Petromyzon marinus*. In the spring these lampreys migrate up the streams, sometimes even surmounting small falls, in order to reach the shallow riffles above. Here a pair clears a small area, picking up stones with their oral discs and piling them up around the periphery of the clearing to make a nest in which they will mate and the female lay her eggs. The eggs are then covered with silt and sand. The small blind, wormlike *ammocoetes* that hatch two weeks later remain in

---

* They have been set apart in a separate class, Petromyzontes, to distinguish them from the true bony fishes, the Teleostomi.

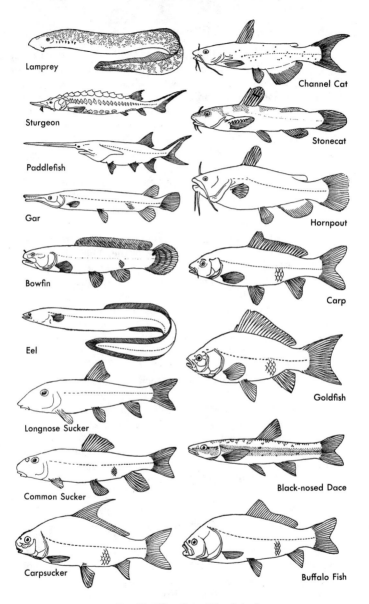

Lamprey

Channel Cat

Sturgeon

Stonecat

Paddlefish

Gar

Hornpout

Bowfin

Carp

Eel

Goldfish

Longnose Sucker

Black-nosed Dace

Common Sucker

Carpsucker

Buffalo Fish

Fig. 79. Fishes (from Schrenkeisen)

or near the nest, feeding on microorganisms and detritus in the sand, and sometimes burrowing in the stream bed or bank. Four to six years later, when about 6 inches long, they transform into adults and move downstream. As adults they feed upon blood and body fluids of other fish, attaching themselves to the body of their host by means of the funnel-like mouth opening. After sucking their fill the lampreys move on to new sites or new hosts, leaving their victims with round, raw sores made by the abrasive action of their tooth-lined, rasping mouths. When sexually mature, which may be in 12 months and possibly not for 20, they go back upstream to spawn, though not necessarily to the stream in which they were hatched.

The Sea Lamprey of the Atlantic Ocean is a marine species that enters rivers to spawn and then to die. Their dead bodies are often carried back downstream in numbers. It has two dorsal fins. In North America there are 12 other species of lampreys, only 6 of which are parasitic. Among the non-parasitic ones are the three Brook Lampreys which spend their entire lives in small streams, feeding on microscopic organisms during larval life but not feeding at all when adult.

Order Acipenseriformes

Acipenseridae, sturgeons (Fig. 79). Sturgeons are the largest of our freshwater fishes. They are sharklike in appearance and are naked except for rows of widely spaced bony plates. The adults are toothless. The Pacific Coast White Sturgeon, *Acipenser transmontanus,* is reputed to attain a weight of 1,800 pounds although it normally weighs about 300. It develops slowly and does not reach maturity for about 20 years, so although a single female may lay from 2 to 5 million eggs the reproductive rate is low. Individuals are said to live for 150 years.

Sturgeons seldom stop to rest. They cruise along slowly, foraging as they go, with the four barbels often scraping the bottom. Their food consists of molluscs, crayfish, insects and some vegetation inhaled from the bottom.

Several species of *Acipenser* live on each coast. They migrate to freshwater streams in the spring to spawn, and occasionally become landlocked in the larger lakes. Two species of *Scaphirhynchus* are isolated in the Miss. Valley.

Polydontidae, paddlefish (Fig. 79). The Paddlefish, 6–8 ft., of the mud-bottomed lakes and large rivers of the Great Lakes region and Miss. Valley, is distinguished in the adult stage by the large, spatulate snout and the small, scattered scales. It feeds on plankton which it filters from the water as it swims along with wide-open mouth. *Polydon spathula* has been widely used for food and its eggs for caviar; it is becoming scarce, probably because of the increasing scarcity of feeding grounds.

Order Amiiformes

Amiidae, bowfins (Fig. 79). The blunt-ended *Amia calva*, nearly 3 ft., is recognized by the long, spineless, dorsal fin which extends to the base of the tail. The tail is characteristically blunt and rounded in the adult but heterocercal in the immature stage. The young fish attach themselves to vegetation by an adhesive disc on the snout.

Bowfins are often seen breaking the surface as they come up for air. They are not considered desirable in any body of water because they feed on other fishes and on crayfish; however, they often live in water too stagnant for most other fish. They are now restricted to sluggish waters of the Miss. basin, eastward to the Great Lakes and Vt.

Order Lepisosteiformes

Lepisosteidae, gars (Fig. 79). These cigar-shaped, long-snouted predators of the Gulf States, Miss. Valley and eastward, live in large streams and rivers and in shallow, weedy lakes. They bask at the surface, breathing atmospheric oxygen; or they lurk in a state of apparent suspension in the weeds and then suddenly shoot out with great rapidity after their prey. They may slash with their long, needlelike teeth at a fish on your line or pick up an unwary vertebrate passing by. Their skin, "so tough it will turn an ax blade," has diagonally arranged ganoid scales (once used by Indians as arrow tips). The Longnose Gar, *Lepisosteus ossus,* 5 ft., from Minn. and Vt. southward, is the most widely distributed; but the 9-foot Alligator Gar, *L. spatula,* of the south, is the largest. Several other species.

Order Anguilliformes

Anguillidae, eels (Fig. 79). The snakelike, seemingly scaleless eels are easily distinguished from the lampreys by the presence of a single gill slit and by paired jaws. They live in shallow, muddy waters of streams, brooks and swamps from Labrador to the Guianas, but travel in late summer and early fall to the deep waters off Bermuda to spawn and die. Their flat, transparent larvae, the *leptocephali,* drift slowly landward for a year when, having attained a length of 4 to 6 inches and called *elvers,* they approach our shores and transform to adults. The males remain in the estuaries or lower parts of the streams. The females continue upstream, resting by day, traveling at night; they feed on molluscs, crustaceans, worms, small fish, frogs, rats and some vegetation, sometimes coming out onto the lowlands of the swamps. They hibernate in the mud. After 6 or 8 years, when they are about 5 feet long, the silvery, large-eyed females join the males in the estuaries. *Anguilla rostrata,* the American Eel, is edible but is not eaten as commonly as the European eel. The blood of eels contains a neurotoxin that infects open cuts, so they should be handled with care.

Order Cypriniformes

This order includes more than half of all living freshwater species.

Grouping of Families of Cypriniformes

WITHOUT AN ADIPOSE FIN. WITHOUT JAW TEETH

 Catastomidae.[*] Dorsal fin usually with more than 10 rays; caudal fin with 16; lips thick, fleshy.

 Cyprinidae.[*] Dorsal fin usually with fewer than 10 rays; caudal fin with 17; lips thin.

WITH ADIPOSE FIN. WITH JAW TEETH

 Ictaluridae. With 8 barbels, 4 of which are under the chin. Body naked.

 Characinidae. Without barbels. Body scaled. Characins have been introduced into coastal streams of Texas.

Catastomidae, suckers (Fig. 79). The suckers make up a large part of the fish fauna of fresh waters. They are often seen swimming in fairly large schools, especially at spawning time when they ascend the streams in enormous "runs." They are easily recognized by the inferior mouth, the fleshy, protrusible lips, and the single comblike row of 10 or more teeth in the throat; and by the manner in which they move quietly over the bottom sucking up the small worms, insects, molluscs and bits of plant material on which they feed. H. T. Walden 2nd describes them as the vacuum cleaners among fishes. The males of many species are adorned with tubercles and bright colors, especially at breeding time. Suckers are edible, but bony.

 The large genus *Catastomus* is widespread. *C. commersoni* (Fig. 79), the Common Sucker, 18–24 in., is in nearly every pond and stream east of the Rockies, where it can be caught easily by any ingenious small boy. It spawns early in the spring, each female usually accompanied by a rosy-finned male. In the western states, in addition to *Catastomus*, there are many species of *Pantosteus* most of which are local in distribution.

---

 [*] It is always difficult to distinguish between suckers and minnows. The Hubbs and Lagler rule is: If the distance from the front of the anal fin to the snout is more than 2½ times the distance from the front of the anal fin to the caudal fin, the fish is a sucker; if less, it is a minnow.

Several species of the big, deep-bodied, golden or reddish-brown Buffalo Fish, *Ictiobus* (Fig. 79), sometimes 3 ft., are common in lakes and rivers of the north central region and Miss. drainage and may even dominate the waters of a lake to the point where they have to be removed. Carpsuckers, *Carpiodes* (Fig. 79), are excellent food fishes in the mid-western lakes and rivers. Redhorses and jumprocks, *Moxostoma*, of more than two dozen species are widespread west to N. D. and south to Texas. Hogsuckers, *Hypentelium*, west to Minn., are characterized by the concavity between the eyes.

Cyprinidae, minnows, chubs and carp. There are probably 200 or more species of minnows in North America. Some are only 1½ inches long but others range up to 18 inches, and the Carp, *Cyprinus carpio* (Fig. 79) may reach 3½ feet. Many are brightly colored, especially at breeding time when the males often become ornamented with nuptial tubercles on the head, body and along the fins. Minnows are the tiny fish so commonly seen schooling. They are of importance as food for larger fish, often being raised for bait as well as for food.

Each streamside visitor, or collector, has his favorite in this group. The Carp and the introduced Goldfish, *Crassius auratus* (Fig. 79), have more than 12 rays in the dorsal fin. Of the several genera of dace, the 3-inch Blacknose Dace, *Rhinicthys atratulus* (Fig. 79), is one of the most common east of the Rockies. It is to be found in gravelly brooks and trout streams and easily recognized by the black lateral band. During the breeding season the male fins are red-tinged and the black band is bordered with golden brown. The Horned Dace, or Creek Chub, *Semotilus atromaculatus* (Fig. 81), related to the Fall Fish, *S. corporalis,* is often found with the Blacknose Dace. It is identified by the dusky blue color and round black spot at the base of the tail. Only the male is horned and he only at breeding time. Chubs of the genus *Hypobsis* are widespread, as are the shiners, *Notropus,* of which there are more than 100 species, including the Common Shiner or Redfin, *N. cornutus* (Fig. 81), one of the commonest east of the Rockies and north of Va., in all types of brooks. It spawns in shallow riffles, one male schooling with several females. The stonerollers, *Campostoma,* east of

the Rockies, have a short lower lip, the protruding lower
jaw being useful in gathering food from the bottom. The
Golden Shiner, *Notemigonus crysoleucas*, up to 10 in. (Fig.
81), has now been introduced west of the Rockies; and the
Hitch, *Lavinia exilicauda*, up to 12 in., is common in Calif.
The long-nosed Squawfishes, *Ptychoceilus* (Fig. 81), up to
2 ft., inhabit western rivers and lakes; *P. lucius* is a good
food fish. Many species of *Gila*, called variously minnows,
chubs or dace, are to be found in western waters.

Ictaluridae, catfishes and bullheads (Fig. 79). These smooth,
scaleless fishes have a broad, flat head; soft adipose fin; and
barbels, or "whiskers." The barbels are located, four under
the chin, two above the upper jaw and one on each side
of the mouth. The dorsal and pectoral fins have a sharp
anterior spine capable of giving a quite sharp jab which,
from the madtoms, may be irritating or toxic. Ictalurids are
extremely tenacious of life and are probably the hardiest
of all freshwater fishes. They survive in waters of greatly
reduced oxygen content, burrowing in the mud when the
waters dry up, and hibernating regularly. They are omnivorous feeders and sometimes destructive to fish eggs and young
fish.

The Common Catfish, *Ictalurus nebulosus* (Fig. 79) up
to 18 in., sometimes called the Brown Bullhead, but in New
England always the Hornpout, is now widely introduced.
It is the traditional catch of the nighttime fisherman in the
cow pond, the ice pond or the back channel. The Channel-
cat, *I. punctatus* (Fig. 79) has also been introduced widely
and successfully; it has a deeply forked tail instead of the
blunt tail of the Common Catfish. There are many other
species including the 50-pound Blue Cat, *I. furcatus*; the
100-pound Flathead Catfish, *Pylodictus olivaris*; and the
2-foot-long White Cat, *I. catus*, of the larger rivers of the
midwest and introduced westward.

The madtoms of the large genus *Noturus*, 2–5 in. all have
the adipose fin more or less fused with the dorsum and
sometimes with the caudal fin also. One of these, the Stonecat, *Noturus flavus* (Fig. 79) is widespread east of the
Rockies.

Order Clupeiformes

Grouping of Families of Clupeiformes

FISHES WITH ADIPOSE FIN
    Salmonidae.
FISHES WITHOUT ADIPOSE FIN
  1. Head at least partially scaled.
      Umbridae. Snout short and rounded; caudal fin rounded.
      Esocidae. Snout elongate; caudal fin forked.
  2. Head naked.
    a. With a lateral line.
      Hiodontidae. Belly with a sharp, but not saw-ridge, margin.
      Elopidae. Belly with rounded margin. *Tarpon* of the Atlantic coast; and *Elops*, the Tenpounder, of both coasts, enter fresh waters to spawn.
    b. Without a lateral line.
      Engraulidae. Mouth large, maxillary extending beyond the middle of the eye. The Anchovy, *Anchoa mitchelli* (Fig. 80) may enter streams on Atlantic and Gulf coasts; belly with a saw-tooth margin. Other species.
      Clupeidae. Mouth not large, maxillary not extending beyond middle of eye. Body compressed; belly with a sharp or saw-tooth margin.

Salmonidae, salmon, trout, whitefish, chars and smelt. These fishes are separated into several families by many authors.

The slender, silvery smelts (formerly Osmeridae) are a fine food fish of coastal waters that enter cool, fresh waters to spawn. *Osmerus mordax* (Fig. 80), up to 14 in., has become landlocked in the Great Lakes region and the northeast. Three other genera are on the west coast; one of the largest, *Thaleichthys pacificus*, 12 in., is so oily that it was dried by the Indians, attached to a stick and burned as a candle. Smelt feed mainly on plankton, insects and some fish. They can be distinguished from other fishes of this large family by the absence of the axillary process in front of the ventral fin.

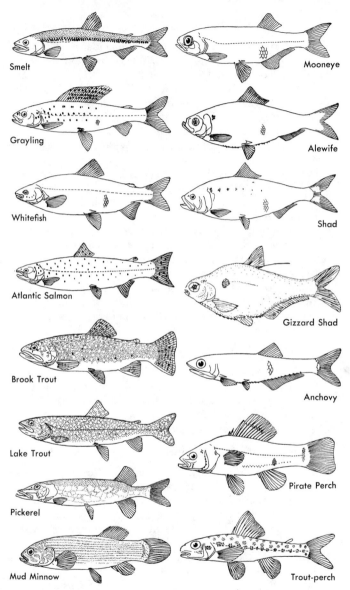

Smelt

Mooneye

Grayling

Alewife

Whitefish

Shad

Atlantic Salmon

Gizzard Shad

Brook Trout

Anchovy

Lake Trout

Pirate Perch

Pickerel

Mud Minnow

Trout-perch

Fig. 80. Fishes (from Schrenkeisen)

The Grayling (formerly the Thymallidae), *Thymallus signifer* (Fig. 80), up to 15 in., differs from others of the family in having a sail-like dorsal fin with 15 or more rays. The body is varicolored silver, gold and violet blue. This prized arctic game fish is restricted to fresh water. It spawns in the spring when the eggs, half the size of those of the trout, can be well aerated. The fish has a faint odor of thyme. It feeds primarily on insects. Widely planted in cold water.

Whitefishes (formerly Coregonidae), of which there are over 20 species in North America, are important food fishes restricted to the Great Lakes and northward, occasionally entering streams. They resemble the salmon and trout in having fewer than 15 rays in the dorsal fin, but they differ in two ways: they have no teeth at all on the jaws and tongue, or else very weak ones; they have a shorter maxillary, not extending beyond the center of the eye. Whitefishes live in cold, clear waters, feeding on bottom organisms. They spawn in the fall. The Lake Whitefish, *Coregonus clupeiformis*, is probably the largest, weighing normally about 4 pounds (one 26-pounder has been reported). The Shallow water Cisco, *C. artedii*, is also widely distributed across the north; so is the Round Whitefish, *Prosopium cylindraceum*. Other species.

Salmon, trout and chars all have strong canine teeth on jaws and tongue; maxillaries extending beyond the middle of the eyes; and more than 100 scales in the lateral line. They prefer well-aerated water below 70°F.

Grouping of Common Species of Salmon and Trout

FISHES HAVING ANAL FIN OF 13 OR MORE RAYS
Onchorhynchus. Five species of these salmon, with unspotted dorsal fin, ascend the streams on the Pacific coast to spawn and die; three have now been introduced in Maine. At breeding time the male's beak is strongly hooked.
FISHES HAVING ANAL FIN WITH 9 to 12 RAYS
1. With dark spots on a light background.
a. Without spots on tail, or only a few dorsal ones.
Salmo trutta, Brown Trout. Up to 2 ft. Breeds in fall. Tail not forked.

b. With spots on tail.

Salmo salar, Atlantic Salmon (Fig. 80). Up to 10 pounds (there are records up to 80). With X-shaped spots on sides. Lives in north Atlantic, entering rivers south to Maine to spawn in the fall, sometimes leaping falls 10 feet or more in height. Landlocked in a few eastern lakes. Tail deeply forked.

Salmo gairdneri, Rainbow Trout. Up to 3 ft. With pink band on side. In swifter water than the Brown Trout. Breeds in spring. The steely blue Steelhead is the sea run of the Rainbow. Tail shallowly forked if at all.

Salmo clarki, Cutthroat Trout. Up to 15 in. With pink or red streak on underside of lower jaw. Breeds in late spring. Tail shallowly forked.

Salmo aquabonita, Golden Trout. Up to 20 in. Sides brilliantly yellow and gold. California. Tail shallowly forked.

2. With light spots on a dark background.

a. Tail barely concave. Eastern.

Salvelinus fontinalis, Brook Trout (Fig. 80). Up to 14 in. Spots red or green, sometimes with blue border. Fins mottled and pale-margined. Breeds in fall. Sometimes anadromous.

b. Tail moderately forked. West of Rockies.

Salvelinus alpinus, Dolly Varden Trout. Up to 20 in. Red spots on sides.

c. Tail deeply forked. Widespread across the north and in Rockies.

Salvelinus namaycush, Lake Trout (Fig. 80). Over 3 ft. Breeds in late fall.

Umbridae, mudminnows. 2–6 in., live in soft-bottomed, sluggish streams or swampy ponds, burrowing when alarmed or during drought or time of cold. They feed on insects, crustaceans and some vegetation. There are two species of *Umbra* (Fig. 80), one in the north-central region and one in the west; and one species of *Novumbra* in Washington.

Esocidae, pike, pickerel and muskellunge. All belong to the genus *Esox*, having a complete lateral line, a duck-billed, shovel-like snout, and forked tail. They are distinguishable from each other mainly by the scalation of cheek and opercle, the pickerel having both of them scaled; the muskellunge, both unscaled or half-scaled; and the pike, cheeks scaled and opercles unscaled or half-scaled. Hybridization frequently occurs. The pike, *E. lucius*, and the muskellunge, *E. masquinongy*, are excellent game fish; the former has a maximum weight of 46 pounds, the latter of 102 pounds. The muskellunge is probably now restricted to the Great Lakes region but the pike and pickerel extend through the Miss. Valley and eastward, though they have been widely introduced. The Common, or Chain Pickerel, *E. niger* (Fig. 80), familiar to even the most casual of limnological collectors as it lurks in the weeds of shallow ponds and sluggish streams, differs from the Redfin Pickerel, *E. americanus*, by the chainlike markings along the sides.

Hiodontidae, mooneyes. These silvery, compressed fishes with small head, large eyes and small mouth, live in the Hudson Bay drainage, Great Lakes and Miss. Valley. The Goldeneye, *Hiodon alosoides*, lives in shallow, muddy lakes but the Mooneye, *H. tergisus* (Fig. 80), prefers large, clear lakes. Both go upstream to spawn.

Engraulidae, anchovies. These small, slender, saltwater fishes come up the streams of the Atlantic coast, from Mass. to the Gulf. Two species; *Anchoa mitchilli* (Fig. 80), up to 4 in., is the more common.

Clupeidae, herrings (Fig. 80). Several species come into fresh waters in the spring to spawn, sometimes in enormous numbers; a few have taken up permanent residence. The Gizzard Shad, *Dorosoma cepedianum*, up to 18 in., is one of those having the last ray of the dorsal fin elongate and filamentous; lives in rivers from Minn. to the St. Lawrence and south to the Gulf. The American Shad, *Alosa sapidissma*, 30 in., of both coasts, and the River Herring, *A. chrysochlorus*, 15 in., which comes up the Miss. R., are both anadromous; the former has a row of spots behind the opercle. The Alewife,

A. pseudoharengus, 15 in., of the Atlantic coast is often landlocked.

Order Percopsiformes

Percopsidae, trout-perch. The Trout-perch, *Percopsis omisco-maycus* (Fig. 80), 6–8 in., lives in large lakes of the far north and on the Atlantic coast south to the Potomac and west to Kansas. The Sandroller, *Columbia transmontanus*, of the northwest also belongs to this family.

Aphredoderidae, pirate perch. *Aphredoderus sayanus* (Fig. 80), 4–6 in., has the anus far forward in the thorax, anterior to the pelvic fin. It ranges from Minn. to the Gulf and along the Atlantic coast south of N. Y., in sluggish streams and bayous.

Order Gadiformes

Gadidae, burbots. *Lota lota* (Fig. 81), the Burbot, 30 in., is the only one of the codlike fishes that regularly lives in fresh water. It is easily recognized by the long, second dorsal fin and the median chin barbel. It lives in deep, cool waters of northern lakes, south to Mo. and N. Y., feeding on insects and other fish, and moving out to deeper water in the summer. The Tomcod, *Microgadus tomcod*, 12 in., often enters fresh water to spawn. Its long dorsal fin is divided into three parts.

Order Cyprinodontiformes

Grouping of Families of Cyprinodontiformes

ANUS FAR FORWARD. SCALES SMALL, EMBEDDED
    Amblyopsidae, swampfish and blindfish. Viviparous. Eyes degenerate.
ANUS IN USUAL POSITION. SCALES LARGE, NOT EMBEDDED
    Cyprinodontidae. Third ray of anal fin branched. Oviparous.

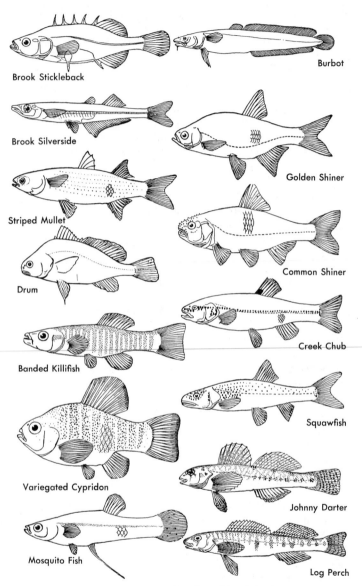

Brook Stickleback

Burbot

Brook Silverside

Golden Shiner

Striped Mullet

Common Shiner

Drum

Creek Chub

Banded Killifish

Squawfish

Variegated Cypridon

Johnny Darter

Mosquito Fish

Log Perch

Fig. 81. Fishes (from Schrenkeisen)

Poeciliidae. Third anal ray unbranched. Viviparous. Anal fin of male elongated.

Cyprinodontidae, top minnows, killifishes and pupfishes. Many live in brackish or salt water and a few in fresh waters but always in the shallows, usually feeding at the surface. They are frequently brightly colored, often with bars and stripes; seldom more than 6 to 7 inches long; and usually with protruding lower jaw. A few live in water far hotter than tolerated by most fish, some having been collected from water over 100°F. Many of the tropical species have been cultivated for aquarium living. Some live in isolated springs in the southwest.

The Banded Killifish, *Fundulus diaphanus* (Fig. 81), is the most widespread and common species east of the Great Plains. Schools of these 4-inch fish shimmer in the sun as they dart in and out of vegetation or swirl close to the surface. Many others of the genus are common, though less widespread. Some are quite deep-bodied, as the Variegated Cyprinodon, *Cyprinodon variegatus* (Fig. 81), of the Atlantic coast states.

Poeciliidae, live-bearers. Except for the surf fishes of the west coast and the blind Amblyopsidae, these tiny fishes, 2 inches or less, are the only viviparous freshwater fishes common in the U. S. They live in ponds, ditches and marshes, feeding on insects, crustaceans and some plant material. *Gambusia affinis* (Fig. 81), the Mosquito Fish, is widespread in the southeast and introduced in the west; other species of *Gambusia* are restricted to the southwest. The Mollies, *Mollienisia* and other genera, are all southern.

Order Gasterosteiformes

Gasterosteidae, sticklebacks. Three species of sticklebacks live in salt as well as fresh water but the Brook Stickleback, *Eucalia inconstans*, 2½ in., lives only in streams east of Kansas. It has from 4 to 6 spines in front of the dorsal fin. The male builds an elaborate nest in the spring, fashioning it of plant stems fastened together with a threadlike secretion from his kidneys. He then entices a female to the nest. She leaves the nest soon after laying her eggs but he remains to care for the eggs, aerating them assiduously and defending them pugnaciously. He may invite other females to add their complement of eggs but he will continue on guard even after the young have hatched. One male may have more than one nest. The Four-spined Stickleback, *Apeltes quadracus*, of the Atlantic coastal region, covers the nest and then aerates the eggs by sucking water from one of the two holes he has made in the top.

Order Mugiliformes

Atherinidae, silversides. None of the freshwater silversides have the unique spawning habits of their marine relative the grunion. They are primarily fish of salt and brackish waters but occasionally come into fresh waters in the east and the Miss. Valley. They are slender, small, 3 inches or less, surface swimmers, often in schools, and often seen jumping and skipping out of the water. The eggs, which are laid in the late spring, each bear an adhesive thread. The Brook Silverside, *Labidesthes sicculus* (Fig. 81), is common in the upper Miss. Valley, Great Lakes region and south to the Gulf.

Mugilidae, mullets. 1–2 ft., are smaller-mouthed and stockier than the silversides and bear the pectoral fins high on the body. They live in the waters of both coasts, occasionally going some distance up the streams and rivers. They feed primarily on vegetation and detritus. The name *mullet* is applied to several species of suckers; it is the White Mullet and Striped Mullet (Fig. 81) that belong to this family.

Order Perciformes

Grouping of Families

BODY SCALED. HEAD NORMAL SIZE
1. Spines of dorsal fin stiff and sharp. Ventral fins separate.
   a. Spines of anal fin 3 or more.

    1) Spines in dorsal fin 6 to 15.
        Centrarchidae. With 2 pairs of nasal openings.
        Serranidae. Opercle spined.
        Centropomidae, snooks (Fla. and Texas).*
        Sparidae, porgies (Fl. and Texas).*
    2) Spines in dorsal fin 16 or more.
        Embiotocidae, surf perches (Calif.)*
        Cichlidae, Rio Grande Perch.*
  b. Spines of anal fin 1 or 2.
        Sciaenidae, drums. Lateral line extending well onto
           caudal fin.
        Percidae. Lateral line not extending on the caudal
           fin.
2. Dorsal spines flexible, not sharp, 6 to 8 in number.
        Eleotridae, sleepers (Calif., N. C., Gulf). Ventral
           fins separate.*
        Gobiidae (Calif., near ocean). Ventral fins joined.*
BODY MOSTLY NAKED. HEAD LARGE
    Cottidae

Centrarchidae, sunfishes, crappies, black bass. These popular little fishes are oblong or nearly circular in outline and compressed of body. The spiny and soft portions of the dorsal fin are joined except in the Largemouth Bass in which the cleft between the two portions is nearly complete. The southern pygmies, *Elassoma*, 1–2 in., lack the lateral line. Of the 6 species of bass, *Micropterus*, 2 are widespread and well-known game fish: the Smallmouth, *M. dolomieui* (Fig. 82), up to 18 in., and the Largemouth, *M. salmoides* (Fig. 82), up to 20 in. The male of the Smallmouth fans out a nest in which as many as five females may lay their eggs. He then guards the eggs and the hatching young. This fish, of the clear, rocky lakes and quiet rivers, is considered by some fishermen the gamiest of all fish. The Largemouth prefers the smaller, turbid lakes or ponds.

    The large sunfish genus *Lepomis* includes many popular species some of which are rather good eating; the ever-popular Pumpkinseed, *L. gibbosus* (Fig. 82), 9–10 in., and

---

* Enter streams to spawn or are in fresh water only occasionally.

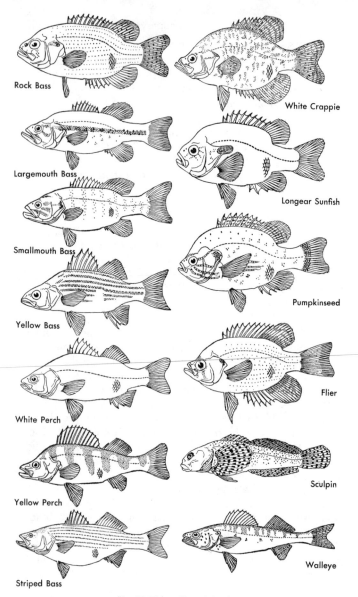

Rock Bass

White Crappie

Largemouth Bass

Longear Sunfish

Smallmouth Bass

Yellow Bass

Pumpkinseed

White Perch

Flier

Yellow Perch

Sculpin

Striped Bass

Walleye

Fig. 82. Fishes (from Schrenkeisen)

the sporty Blue Gill, *L. macrochirus*, 15 in., are but two of these many oft-sought little fishes. Most of them like clear, still, warmish water with some vegetation.

The Flier, *Centrarchus macropterus* (Fig. 82), and the crappies, *Pomoxis* (Fig. 82), have the base of the dorsal fin not much longer than the anal and thus differ from the Rock Bass, *Ambloplites rupestris* (Fig. 82), and the western Sacramento Perch, *Archoplites interruptus*, which have it much longer. Other species.

Serranidae, sea basses. Four species of this large marine genus are found in fresh water. The Striped Bass, *Roccus saxatile* (Fig. 82), 2–4 ft., comes up the rivers on the Atlantic coast to spawn; now introduced on the west coast. The White Bass, *R. chrysops*, 1 ft., is a resident from Wisc. to Minn. and south to the Gulf. The White Perch, *Morone americana* (Fig. 82), 1 ft., and the Yellow Bass *R. interrupta* (Fig. 82), 1 ft., may also be resident, the former on the east coast south to S. C. and the latter from the Miss. Valley to Okla.; they both have the dorsal fins joined. The White Perch seems to be moving into the Great Lakes area, sometimes being landlocked.

Sciaenidae, drums. The freshwater drum, *Aplodinotus grunniens*, may weigh 50 to 60 pounds. It is easily recognized when seen in profile by the highly arched back and straight-lined venter. The scales of the sides are silvery, often iridescent. Each ventral fin has a long filament on its forward edge. The strong throat teeth are valuable in grinding the molluscs and crustaceans on which this fish feeds but are not responsible for the croaking sounds it makes. These characteristic grunts are made by the expulsion of air from the air bladder. Although primarily a warm-water fish, the drum is found from Texas to north of the Great Lakes; in a broad strip east of the plains but west of the Alleghenies and Alabama.

Percidae, perches. The three groups of fishes in this family have the dorsal fin completely divided into two. All are predacious. Of the perches, the Yellow Perch, *Perca flaves-*

cens (Fig. 82), common east of the Rockies, is easily recognized by the 6 to 9 blackish bars on each side. It lives in shallow lakes, ponds and slow streams. The eggs are laid in the spring in a long zigzag string (one of 81 inches has been reported) in vegetation in shallow water. The Walleye, or Pike Perch, *Stizostedion vitreum* (Fig. 82), is an important game and food fish of the north-central and eastern states. The darters, of which there are about 100 species east of the Rockies, are mostly less than 4 inches long though a few reach 9 inches. Some are brightly colored, especially at breeding time. Most species scatter their eggs but the 3-inch Johnny Darter, *Etheostoma nigrum* (Fig. 81), and the Fantail, *E. flabellare*, lay them under rocks where they are aerated, cleaned and guarded by the male.

Cottidae, sculpins. Most of the 25 species of freshwater sculpins belong to the genus *Cottus* (Fig. 82). These big-headed fishes are seldom more than 4 to 5 inches long. They often have spines on the preopercle. They prefer cool, rocky streams, ponds and lakes, hiding under rocks during the daytime.

CHAPTER 15

Salamanders, Frogs, and Toads—Class Amphibia

Figs. 83–85; Pls. 5–7, 19–21

AMPHIBIANS, according to their name, should live both in the water and on land. But, in fact, some never go into the water and others never leave it. The great majority breed in the water; the young usually remain there until maturity and then, as adults, take up their abode on land, returning to the water only when the next breeding season comes around.

Amphibians are cold-blooded vertebrates; they have a bony skeleton and usually two pairs of limbs. The skin, except in the case of some toads, is smooth and moist and is *always without scales.* The coloration of the skin, greatly reduced or lacking in many of the numerous cave and subterranean species, is due to pigments contained in star-shaped *chromatophores* (color-bearing cells) which, by their contraction and expansion, expose varying amounts of the pigment and thus change the intensity of the skin color. A toad remaining in a dark place for several hours becomes pale and washed-out in appearance, or a tree frog that moves onto foliage, from its resting place on the bark of a tree, slowly changes from tan or gray to a dark brownish green.

Amphibians have a keen sense of taste and smell, and most species have good eyesight, tending to be rather farsighted. The ability to hear is more or less linked to the ability to make sounds: the highly vocal frogs and toads hear well; the voiceless salamanders apparently do not, although they sometimes seem to pick up vibrations through the feet or through the lower jaw, and almost certainly through the lateral line organs of the skin. *Lateral line organs*, like those in fishes, are clusters of sense cells located in tiny depressions on the cheeks and sides of most aquatic amphibians; they often show quite clearly as light spots, especially on the pigmented sides of many salamander larvae.

Respiration. Amphibians usually respire by means of gills during their immature or larval life and by lungs in adult life. To this rule there are some exceptions. All species carry on some respiration through the skin and mucous lining of the mouth.

Development. The eggs, each encased in a gelatinous covering, are laid singly or in strings or masses in the water or in damp places under stones and debris. Fertilization is external in all frogs except the Tailed Frog. It is internal in all salamanders except the hellbenders and sirens.

The transformation from larva to adult takes place gradually. The legless larvae that hatch from the egg are equipped with fingerlike gills at the sides of the head and with a tail. In tadpoles (the larvae of frogs and toads) the development of legs and lungs takes place simultaneously with the absorption of the gills and tail and with the accompanying changes in circulation. Changes in mouth and teeth must also take place, and the conversion from the long, coiled intestine of an herbivorous animal to the short intestine of one that is carnivorous. In salamander larvae the tail persists into adult life; so also do the gills of some species.

Collecting. Some people collect amphibians with their hands but it requires patience and speed. A dip net will probably be preferred by most collectors. It can be used to scoop the amphibians out of the water or to swat down over them as they sit resting on the shore or on vegetation, an action that seems simple but is extremely difficult. Many frogs and toads can be located at night, especially when they are singing, by following the sound and then spotting the singer with a flashlight (or better yet, a headlamp). A flashlight directed into the shallow margins of the pond is also productive. The catch may be carried home in jars or cans the lids of which have either been pricked with holes,

Ambystoma tigrinum and freshly laid eggs.

Eggs of *Necturus* on the underside of a stone.

PLATE 19

the points directed outward, or cut out in the center and fitted with screening. Little ventilation is really needed; but specimens must be kept cool.

If amphibians are to be kept as pets they should be in aquaria richly planted with aquatic vegetation, stocked with pond snails to keep the glass sides clean, and with temperature and oxygen conditions close to that of the water from which the particular species has come. It is probably advisable to move the animal to a shallow pan or dish at feeding time so as not to contaminate the aquarium. The best food is live, soft-bodied insects and earthworms. An emergent platform of some sort should be provided for those species who like to come out of the water, sphagnum moss or sand for those who like to burrow, and loose, flat rocks for those who wish to hide.

Comparison of Salamander Stages with Those of Frogs and Toads

	Salamanders	Frogs and Toads
Eggs	Each egg, as well as the entire mass, covered by a gelatinous layer.	Each egg covered by a gelatinous layer. Eggs closer together than those of salamanders.
Larvae	Mouth has jaws and teeth. Body slender, usually with a balancing organ at each corner of mouth when young. Gills plainly visible, often bushy. Legs develop early. Carnivorous, with simple intestine. (Fig. 83.7)	Lips have minute horny rasps, and a beak which gradually evolves into jawbones. Body heavy, short and oval; usually with a pair of suckers beneath chin when young. Gills covered by a fold (operculum). Herbivorous, with long, coiled intestine. (Fig. 83.1,4–6)
Adults	Tailed. Walk and wiggle but do not jump or "sit." Hind legs short, similar to forelegs.	Tailless. Capable of jumping. "Sit" with long hind legs bent back at knees and forward at ankle.

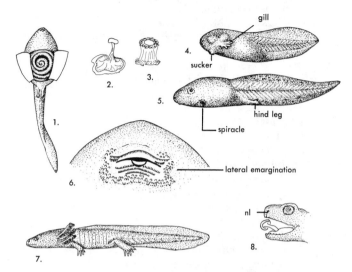

Fig. 83. Amphibians. *1.* Tadpole with abdominal wall cut to show coiled intestine. *2.* Spermatheca of *Eurycea*. *3.* Spermatheca of *Ambystoma*. *4.* Young tadpole with gills. *5.* Older tadpole with gills absorbed and hind legs developing. *6.* Mouth of Bull Frog tadpole, showing rows of teeth and papillary lips. *7.* Larva of *Ambystoma*. Stream species tend to have smaller gills and a shorter tail fin. *8.* Head of *Eurycea* showing tongue and *nl*, naso-labral groove.

A Guide to Aquatic Amphibian Eggs
(Not all species included)

Eggs laid singly

> Under stones or other objects.
>> *Desmognathus fuscous*. In clusters.
>> *Eurycea*.
>> *Gyrinophylus porphyriticus*. Stalked.
>> *Pseudotriton ruber*. Stalked. Laid in fall.
>> *Necturus*. Guarded by female.

> On bottom.
>> *Bufo punctatus*. In desert canyons of southwest.
>> *Hyla* (several species).
>> *Limnaoedus ocularis*. Cypress and pine-barren pools of southeast.

On stems or vegetation.

Acris gryllus. East of Rockies.

Ambystoma gracilis. Northwest.

Eurycea (see above).

Hyla (several species).

Limnaoedus ocularis (see above).

Notophthalmus. East of Rockies.

Taricha. West of Rockies.

Eggs in strings

Under objects or on bottom.

Ascaphus truei. In running water in northwest.

Cryptobranchus. In tangle mass of beadlike strings, in a depression, guarded by male.

Attached to vegetation or floating.

Bufo (many species).

Taricha granulosa.

On land, under logs near water.

Amphiuma means. Guarded by female. Often form balls and often washed down into water.

Eggs in bands

Bufo quercicus. In bars of 2 to 8 eggs, like beads. On bottom or vegetation, often radiating from one point.

Scaphiopus. Along plant stem in temporary pools.

Eggs forming a film on surface, or in small packets

Large film, 12–25 in. across.

Rana catesbeiana. Each egg with a single envelope. Usually around brush or vegetation.

Medium-sized film, about 12 in. in diameter.

Rana clamitans. Usually near edge of pond. Eastern.

Rana grylio. Eggs with 2 envelopes. Usually in mid-pond. Ga. to La.

Small film, less than 28 in. square, or in small packets.

Gastrophryne. Black and white eggs with envelopes forming truncated sphere. Ind. to Va. and Texas.

Hyla (several species). Small film or small packets at or near the surface.

Eggs in submerged masses

Loose, irregular masses.

Hyla regilla.

Pseudacris. Less than 1 mm. in diameter.

Scaphiopus. Cylinders, 1–6 in. long, attached to stems
Globular or plinthlike masses.
Rana (several species).
Cylindrical masses on sticks or vegetation.
Ambystoma jeffersonianum. 1 to 40 eggs in a mass.
Ambystoma tigrinum.
Grapelike cluster on stones.
Rana boylei. Each egg with 3 envelopes. Northwest.
Eggs in masses in excavation on bottom
Siren intermedia.

Salamanders—Order Urodela

There are more salamanders in North America than in all
the rest of the world together. They are the only North
American amphibians that have tails throughout their entire
life (the Tailed Frog actually has no tail, only the tail
muscles) and whose legs, when present, are short and not
developed for jumping. Both larvae and adults have teeth,
and all larvae and some adults have gills. They are distinct
from lizards in that they do not have scales on the skin and
never have more than four fingers on each front limb. They
lack vocal cords or sacs and thus are voiceless although they
may emit a faint squeak when handled.

Salamanders are chiefly nocturnal, spending most of their
daytime hours in damp places under rocks and debris or
in holes. Many species are entirely terrestrial; many are
terrestrial as adults but come to the water to breed; a few
are arboreal, living and breeding in the water in tree holes
or in the leaf bases of bromeliads; and many live in caves
and subterranean waterways (but these often have greatly
reduced eyes or are completely blind). But there are also
many that spend years of their life as larvae in the water
and upon becoming adult remain either in or around the
water. These aquatic species spend much of their time under
stones and other submerged objects, or crawling about on
the bottom; only a few are good swimmers.

Food. A few species are scavengers but the majority feed
on insects and other small invertebrates and their eggs, as
well as on tadpoles and small fish.

Development. Except for the species that are entirely terrestrial, breeding takes place in the early spring or late fall in the shallow water of streams and ponds. The males, except those of *Desmognathus*, are smaller than the females. In some species the males also differ in having a keeled tail, an enlargement of the hind legs, or a thickening and darkening of the skin on the underside of the hind legs; and sometimes, a swelling and prominence of the lips around the vent. In some species mating is preceded by an elaborate courtship consisting of much prodding and tail-waving and usually ending with the male mounting the female, rubbing noses with her, or rubbing his chin across her face. Since he possesses a gland beneath the chin the secretion of which stimulates the female, this action appears to be important in starting her upon the proper pattern of behavior. The male then introduces the sperm into the female cloaca or deposits them in a tiny sac atop a gelatinous cone which he has built on the substratum (Fig. 83). In the latter case the female, sometimes having been guided to this *spermatheca* by the male, picks it up with the lips of her cloaca and places it in the internal cavity in which fertilization takes place. Eggs may be laid immediately after fertilization or not for some time. In the hellbenders and sirens the sperm are discharged by the male as the eggs are extruded by the female.

The larvae of a few species complete their transformation to the adult before emerging from the eggs, but these are rare. The larvae of several other species never transform at all but spend their entire life in the larval stage. This failure to complete metamorphosis (known as *neoteny*) is probably due to incomplete thyroid development linked with calcium and vitamin deficiencies. Although these inadequacies seem to be specific and are therefore probably genetic, there is some evidence that low temperature and high altitude may produce neoteny in some individuals. The Mexican axolotl, long considered a separate species, was found to be the untransformed individual of a local *Ambystoma* which matured normally under other conditions.

As a rule salamanders are somewhat local in distribution. The Great Plains, for instance, has been an effective barrier to east-west dispersal; only *Ambystoma tigrinum* is found from coast to coast.

Grouping of Families of Aquatic Salamanders

SALAMANDERS WITH ONE PAIR OF LEGS

Sirenidae. Hind legs and pelvis completely lacking. With 3 pairs of branching gills throughout life.

SALAMANDERS WITH TWO PAIRS OF LEGS

1. Body elongate, eel-like. 2 or 3 toes on each foot.

    Amphiumidae. Adults with 1 pair of gill slits. Eyes lidless.

2. Body depressed, with lateral folds; large (up to 29 in.). 4 toes on front feet, 5 on hind feet.

    Cryptobranchidae. Adults with 1 pair of gill slits. Eyes lidless.

3. Body not eel-like and not depressed with lateral folds.

    a. With 3 pairs of red feathery gills throughout life. 4 toes on all feet.

      Proteidae. Eyes lidless.

    b. Without red feathery gills. Eyes with lids. 4 toes on front feet, usually 5 on hind feet.

      1) Without parasphenoid teeth (Fig. 84.4). Without naso-labral grooves (Fig. 83.8).

        Ambystomidae. With vertical grooves on sides of body (Fig. 83.7).

        Salamandridae. Without distinct grooves.

      2) With parasphenoid teeth. With naso-labral grooves.

        Plethodontidae. With vertical grooves on sides of body.

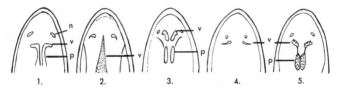

Fig. 84. Diagrams to show teeth in roof of salamander mouth; *n*, nares; *p*, parasphenoid teeth; *v*, vomerine teeth. *1. Gyrinophilus. 2. Notophthalmus. 3. Eurycea. 4. Ambystoma. 5. Desmognathus.* (Partly after Pratt.)

Sirenidae, sirens. Sirens are common in the shallow roadside ditches, muddy swamps, ponds and rice fields of the southeast, hiding under rocks or among weeds, occasionally wiggling out onto the shore or onto a dam; and when the water dries up, encasing themselves in a ball of mud in which they may stay for several months. They feed on crayfish, worms, molluscs and on some plant material. They occasionally make faint whistling noises. Individuals have been known to live for 25 years.

The Great Siren, *Siren lacertina*, 20–30 in., is light gray to olive dorsally with greenish or yellowish markings on the sides. It is slow-moving and mild-tempered. Atlantic coastal plain south of D. C. The Lesser Siren, *S. intermedia*, 11 in., is brown or olive green above with small dark spots, but slate gray beneath. It is commonly found in cypress swamps and in beds of water hyacinth. Coastal plains south of Ga. and up the Miss. Valley. The Dwarf Siren, *Pseudobranchus striatus* (Pl. 6), 5–8 in., differs in having three toes instead of four, and a pattern of longitudinal stripes. It also lives in cypress swamps and hyacinth beds. Southern Ga. and north-central Fla.

Amphiumidae, Amphiumas. These eel-like creatures live in drainage ditches, muddy pools, swamps and streams, hiding under debris or in crayfish holes by day but moving around at night, crawling out on land when the weather is damp but returning to the same burrow or hole. They feed on frogs, fish and other small animals.

The Conger Eel, *Amphiuma means* (Pl. 6), 35 in., is deep brown to grayish black above, with small, useless 2-toed legs, a keeled, compressed tail. It often bites viciously when picked up. The eggs are laid from spring on into winter, the 2-inch larvae usually not hatching for about 5 months. Coastal plain, Va. to the Gulf. *A. tridactylum*, 45 in., is 3-toed and bicolored. Coastal plain, western Fla. to Texas and up the Miss. Valley.

Cryptobranchidae, hellbenders. These big creatures can occasionally be seen crawling about on the bottom of creeks and rivers, especially those with a stony bottom. But since they spend most of the daytime hours hiding under stones, they are more likely to be observed after dusk when they come out to feed. Although general scavengers, they consume many crayfish, worms and insects. Respiration is primarily through the skin, for although they have lungs they seldom, if ever, come out of the water. Our one species *Cryptobranchus alleganiensis* (Pl. 6), 29 in., is easily recognized by its partially depressed, brownish body, sometimes spotted on the dorsum, and by the prominent lateral fold of skin between the fore and hind legs. It is not a good swimmer. It lays between 300 and 450 large eggs which have an incubation period of 68 to 84 days. Although not vicious or aggressive, it will bite, and bite hard, when handled. It is not poisonous, however. It is related to the Giant Salamander of Japan which attains a length of 5 feet and may live for a century. Southern N. Y. to Ala. and Ark., west to Iowa.

Proteidae, mud puppies and waterdogs. These amphibians live in clear streams or in muddy bayous and ditches, as well as in many permanent bodies of water. They are primarily nocturnal. They feed on fish eggs and on small aquatic animals but are not the serious predators of fish that they have been accused of being. Their characteristic red, feathery gills may be small and contracted when the water is cold and fresh, but large and bushy when the water is stagnant. Mating usually takes place in the autumn but the light yellow eggs are not laid until the following spring and then have a long incubation period of 38 to 64 days.

The Mud Puppy, *Necturus maculosus* (Pls. 6, 19), 17 in. or more, is olive or grayish brown or black on the dorsum when mature and is occasionally spotted. When young it has a dark dorsal band narrowly bordered with black. The tail is sometimes tinged with orange or red. It never transforms to an adult. Mud puppies resemble the mole salamanders but differ in having 4 toes on each foot. Eastern, except coastal plain and Fla. The Dwarf Waterdog, *N. punctatus*, 4–5 in. or more, is not spotted beneath and has light dorsal spots. Coastal plain from southern N. C. to Mobile. Other species in the southeast.

Ambystomidae, mole salamanders. This family includes the stout-bodied Pacific Giant Salamander, *Dicamptodon ensatus*, 12 in., which lives in the coastal forests of the Pacific, and west to Idaho and Mont.; the large-eyed Olympic Salamander, *Rhyacotriton olympicus*, 4 in., of the Olympic peninsula and northwestern Calif.; and the genus *Ambystoma* of which there are a dozen species throughout North America.

Most species of *Ambystoma* are terrestrial, spending much of their life underground, even laying their eggs under bark, logs or stones, or in shallow holes. The silvery Marbled salamander, *A. opacum*, for instance, lays her eggs in the autumn in a depression in the ground and remains in contact with them until they hatch when the depression fills with water in the next hard rain. But other species may come by the hundreds in the early spring to ponds and quiet streams. The Spotted Salamander, *A. maculatum* (Pl. 6), 9 in., is said by Dr. Doris Cochran to fill the ponds with a "milling mass of black and yellow bodies" and to leave them full of "balls of tapioca-pudding-like eggs." This handsome, shining, blue-black species, spotted with yellow but uniformly grayish beneath, is common in damp woodlands, shady parts of lawns and in damp cellars, east of the Great Plains. The Tiger Salamander, *A. tigrinum*, 13 in., lays its eggs (Pl. 19) in the deep water of lowland ponds. Its rusty black body is spotted with yellow or olive and has a yellow chin. It is often neoteinic in the south. The midwestern subspecies, the Barred Tiger (Pl. 6), has fewer but larger yellow spots. The dark brown or grayish Jefferson's Salamander, *A. jeffersonianum*, comes to the ponds from Labrador to Virginia in early spring, to lay its small cylindrical egg masses. Other species.

Salamandridae, newts. Newts are slightly rougher and thicker-skinned than other salamanders and not quite as slimy or as shiny. The Red-spotted Newt, *Notophthalmus viridescens* (Pl. 6), 2½–4½ in., is colored yellow and green with red spots when living in water, but in its land phase is orange-red with bright red spots. The eggs, laid in the early spring, hatch in 20 to 35 days. The gilled larvae that emerge are aquatic.

but at transformation lose their gills and move up into the moist woodlands for 2 to 3 years; there they are known as subadults, or *red efts*. They then return to the water for the rest of their adult life, acquiring their distinctive yellow and green colors. Newts feed on insects, leeches, worms, molluscs, crustaceans, tadpoles and frog's eggs. They are not preyed upon by other animals because of the irritating secretions of their skin glands. Common in ponds and streams east of the Rockies.

Several southern varieties are sometimes listed as separate species. The Black-spotted Newt, *N. meridionalis*, 5 in., of the coastal plain from Texas to Mexico, has ventral spots at the base of the tail. The Broken-striped Newt, *N. dorsalis*, 3½ in., is found in southern Ga. and northern Fla.

West of the Rockies three species of *Taricha* have been described. The Red-bellied Newt, *T. rivularis*, 5 in., with a tomato red venter, blackish dorsum and dark brown iris, lives in rapid, rocky streams. The California Newt, *T. torosa*, over 6 in., with yellow or orange venter and yellow-flecked iris, and the Rough-skinned, *T. granulosa*, over 6 in., with tan to black body and pale iris, live in streams and standing water. Eggs are laid in strings of 7 to 29, hatching in 18 to 52 days. When streams and ponds dry out they are able to survive in extremely arid conditions.

Plethodontidae, lungless salamanders. In North America there are more than 18 genera of these salamanders but many of them, including those of the large woodland genus *Plethodon*, are almost entirely terrestrial. A few very handsome ones, however, are often seen near the water's edge and occasionally in the water. *Desmognathus, Leurognathus, Stereochilus* and *Hemidactylium* have the tongue attached at the anterior margin; but *Gyrinophilus, Pseudotriton, Eurycea* and the rare *Hydromantes* from California have it free at the anterior margin and attached by a central pedicel (Fig. 83.8).

Species of *Desmognathus* may be recognized by the light line running from the posterior corner of the eye to the angle of the jaw, and by the large, stout hind legs. They are common in brooks, springs and small fast streams. Their rigid immovable lower jaw is used for pushing or partially lifting the stones under which they wish to hide. The Dusky Salamander, *D. fuscus* (Pl. 6), 5 in., is reddish brown above, grayish beneath, with irregular spots and mottling; it shows considerable color variation. The female lays 15 to 20 eggs in one or two clusters beneath stones or in crevices at the water's edge and remains with them. The larvae live on land for about 2 weeks and then return to the water for 8 or 9 months. Can. and Fla. west to Ill. Other species.

The Shovel-nose Salamander, *Leurognathus marmorata*, 5 in., of the southern Appalachians, resembles *Desmognathus* in having a stiff lower jaw. It differs in having the interior nares concealed (to be seen by examining the roof of the mouth). Its head is small and flat, its tail sharply keeled. The dorsum is brownish, usually with 2 rows of large, light spots; belly mottled.

Brook salamanders of the genus *Eurycea* live, larvae and adults together, near the water's edge of small brooks, springs, seepages and woodland pools, darting in and out of the water to feed. They are chiefly characterized by almost always having some yellow color and by their compressed tail. Several are neoteinic. The Long-tailed Salamander, *E. longicauda* (Pl. 5), 7 in., is quite variable in color but usually has 2 or 3 dark stripes or lines of dots on the dorsum and sometimes vertical dark stripes on the tail; its tail is more than half of its total length. Southern N. Y. and southern Ill. southward, except peninsular Fla. The Two-lined Salamander, *E. bislineata* (Pl. 6), 4½ in., occurs over much the same range but slightly farther northward and into Canada. The two broad dark lines extend from eye to tail and border a middorsal light stripe. Brook salamanders lay their eggs in running water, attached singly to the underside of a stone or twig.

Several species of spring salamanders, *Gyrinophilus*, live in the water. Most are reddish-tinged, patterned with black, and they usually have a dark-bordered light line running from eye to nostril. The Purple, or Spring Salamander, *G. porphyriticus*, to 8 in., is common along the margins of cold brooks and springs from Que. to Ala. The tail is keeled and bears conspicuous vertical grooves. The body is pinkish brown to salmon, with venter flesh-colored and the dorsum and sides mottled. The adults retain the gills.

The Red Salamander, *Pseudotriton ruber* (Pl. 6), 7 in., has the dorsum bright coral red, salmon or purplish brown with many black dots. Its eggs are laid in the fall in small clumps, each egg attached separately by a gelatinous stalk to the underside of a stone that is awash. The larvae hatch in the fall but remain inactive until spring, not transforming into adults for about two and a half years. They are common in and around springs and brooks of the eastern states though not on the coastal plain. The Mud Salamander, *P. montanus,* over 7 in., is similar though darker in color. It is found around springs and small streams, often burrowing in the mud; N. J. to the Gulf.

Two other members of this family should be included here because the adults are so commonly found in the sluggish streams and leafy woodland or swampy pools where their larvae grow up. The Four-toed Salamander, *Hemidactylium scutatum,* 2–3½ in., with 4 toes on the hind feet, a marked constriction at the base of the tail and a black-spotted white belly, is found from N. S. to La., west to Wisc. The Many-lined Salamander, *Stereochilus marginatus,* 2½–4 in., has a small head and short tail. It is marked with yellow and brown lines along the sides. Southern coastal plains, Va. to Ga.

Frogs and Toads—Order Salientia

Frogs and toads differ from salamanders most noticeably in having a squat, tailless body and long, muscular hind legs that fold back at the knee joint and forward at the ankle when in normal sitting position. The names "frog" and "toad" are used loosely and do not denote groups with significant differences.

Voice. Frogs and toads differ from salamanders also in having a voice; at least all males do and most females will croak or scream when angry or frightened. Most males have one or two vocal sacs in the throat (Pl. 20). The true croak is made by pushing air from the lungs into the sac, or sacs,

Acris gryllus calling. Note the single vocal sac.

Rana clamitans, with two vocal sacs.

PLATE 20

through an opening on each side of the tongue or at the corners of the mouth. It is made with the mouth closed and thus can be made when under water. The inflation of each vocal sac causes a swelling of the throat that resembles a bubble made with the expertise of an experienced gum-chewer.

Each species of male has a distinct breeding call, recognized by the herpetologist (and we assume by the female frog), differing in pitch, tempo and periodicity from the call of all other species. Many males have other calls. *Rana pipiens,* for example, has, in addition to the breeding call, a warning call given by a male who has been mistaken for a female and clasped in the breeding position, and a call given by a male when about to mate with a receptive female. A certain amount of sporadic croaking occurs during the summer; this is not associated with breeding or even necessarily with any amphibian stimulus. Just as hundreds of tree frogs start their evening chorus simultaneously when a certain threshold of environmental factors of temperature, humidity, etc., has been reached, so also will some individuals be stimulated by an artificial factor. Over and over again you can initiate a resounding chorus from a group of *Hyla andersonii,* for instance, both when they are in their home in the New Jersey pine barrens or when in a jar on your living-room mantel. But before assuming this to be a reflection on your own good imitation of a pine-barren tree toad, read Dr. Doris Cochran's comment that the passing of a train or the hum of a plane overhead will often start frogs "singing." She once had a green frog in captivity that was regularly aroused to vocal expression by the clanging of the fire engine as it went down the street.

Males start their calling in the ponds before the females arrive in the spring, and in any given area follow a seasonal sequence. The first to make themselves heard in New York and New England are the spring peepers. According to many observers these are followed by the Leopard and Wood Frogs and then in a few days by the American Toad, the Pickerel Frog, Green Frog, Fowler's Toad and the Grass Frog; and then, last of all, the Bull Frog.

Sex differences. Females are usually larger than the males, though in *Bufo* and *Ascaphus* the males have longer legs. The males of *Rana* and *Ascaphus*, especially at breeding time, have enlarged thumbs and forearms; and many other males have horny excrescences on fingers and forearms. The tympanum of the male Bull Frog is much larger than that of the female.

Mating. When the males are in a mood for mating, especially those of *Bufo*, they may clasp any object with which they come in contact; if it does not prove to be another male, who by his warning call will announce that a mistake has been made, the ardent suitor may continue to hang on futilely for hours or even for days. When clasping the female he holds her just behind the front legs, remaining in this position for several hours or for several days, shedding the sperm over the eggs as they are laid.

Eggs. Eggs are laid in the water singly, in long strings, or in masses. Those of *Leptodactylus labialis*, the Mexican White-lipped Frog of the Lower Rio Grande Valley, are laid in a mass of froth on the shore. Eggs may be attached to vegetation or the undersides of stones or may occur in a floating mass or film. They hatch in from 3 days to 2 weeks depending upon the temperature. The size of the egg is no indication of the size of the adult for the eggs of the little chorus frogs are the largest and those of the big Bull Frog among the smallest.

Larvae. Tadpoles are sometimes described as "big-headed fish without fins." Actually their heads are very small and more or less fused with the greatly enlarged body. The long, compressed swimming tail, the long coiled intestine showing through the transparent body wall, and the disclike, ventrally placed mouth are characteristic features. Tadpoles also have a breathing pore, or *spiracle*, eyes, nostrils and an anus. Some are less than an inch long when full grown; others, like those of the Bull Frog, may be nearly 6 inches. Most species complete their transformation to adult in a few days; some require 2 weeks to a month; and some species of *Rana* take 2 years. All, except those of *Scaphiopus*, are essentially herbivorous, scraping algae off rocks and nibbling on vegetation.

Tadpoles are difficult to identify. It is often more satis-

Fowler's Toad, *Bufo fowleri.*

The Queen Snake, *Natrix septemvittata.*

PLATE 21

factory to keep them alive until they transform if one is to be sure of the species. They can be kept in an aquarium with snails and green plants such as *Anacharis* and *Myriophyllum,* with plenty of algae. Give them boiled lettuce and spinach to feed upon, an occasional meat bone to nibble, and a flat projection upon which to climb when transforming.

Grouping of Families of Tadpoles

TADPOLES WITHOUT TEETH AND WITHOUT DISC-LIKE LIP

Microhylidae.

TADPOLES WITH TRANSVERSE ROWS OF TEETH AND WITH DISCLIKE LIP (Fig. 83)

1. Spiracle in center of chest below lip.

Ascaphidae. Lips large. Head with adhesive sucker.

2. Spiracle on left side of body (Fig. 83).

a. Anus median. Eyes small, sometimes close together. Spiracle low on side.

Bufonidae. Lips emarginate laterally. Upper lip without marginal papillae. Nostril often large.

Pelobatidae. Lips not emarginate. Nostrils small. Upper lip bordered with papillae. Often bronzy.

Leptodactylidae. Lips not emarginate. Nostrils small. Upper lip without marginal papillae. Tadpole sometimes completes development within the egg which is laid in a frothy mass on land. Uncommon.

b. Anus on right side of lower tail fin. Eyes medium to large.

Ranidae. Lips emarginate laterally. 1.7–5.5 in. long.

Hylidae. Lips not emarginate laterally. Less than 1.9 in. long.

Grouping of Families of Adult Frogs and Toads

FROGS OR TOADS HAVING PUPIL OF EYE VERTICAL

Pelobatidae. Hind foot with horny digging blade on one side.

Ascaphidae. Hind foot webbed. Male with intromittent organ between hind legs; female with a short anal tube.

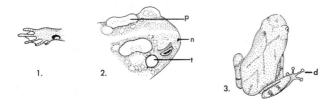

Fig. 85. *1.* Digging blade on forefoot of a spadefoot toad. *2.* Head of Common American Toad to show *p*, parotid gland; *n*, nostril; *t*, tympanum. *3.* Diagram of *Hyla crucifer*, the Spring Peeper, to show color pattern and *d*, toe discs.

FROGS OR TOADS HAVING PUPIL OF EYE HORIZONTAL

1. Tympanum present. Tongue not bicornute at rear.

 Bufonidae. With parotid swelling behind each tympanum.

 Hylidae. Without parotid swelling. Toes with intercalary bone or cartilage and usually with adhesive discs.

 Leptodactylidae. Without parotid swelling and without intercalary bones in toes. Uncommon.

2. Tympanum present. Tongue bicornute at rear.

 Ranidae.

3. Tympanum absent. Tongue not bicornute at rear.

 Microhylidae.

Pelobatidae, spadefoot toads. The slightly popeyed, terrestrial spadefoot toads have a horny projection on the front of each hind foot that is useful in digging and enables them to wiggle down out of sight with incredible speed. In the spring the Eastern Spadefoot, *Scaphiopus holbrooki* (Pl. 7), nearly 3 in., gathers in small or temporary ponds with much clucking and croaking, initiating an uproar that may last for several days. Eggs are laid in a band or mass of 1,000 to 2,500, wrapped about vegetation or along plant stems. Tadpoles may reach a length of 3 inches before transformation is completed. Western species have adapted to the arid conditions of the desert by being ready to breed a few hours after rain has fallen in sufficient quantity to fill depressions and form temporary pools. The males then flock to these pools calling loudly to the females, who soon join them. Mating takes place at once and the eggs are laid in small clusters on the vegetation. The eggs and then the tadpoles develop rapidly. Dr. Cochran says that the eggs of *S. hurteri* may hatch on the third day and the larvae double in size the first day of life, transforming to adults in 12 days. Their development, however, depends upon the amount of nourishment available. As the water evaporates, the larvae may be forced to swallow large quantities of mud for the organic nourishment it contains in order to speed up their development. They may even be driven to cannibalism. They have been known to school together and to fan out a depression in the bottom so that the remaining bit of the rapidly evaporating water will be concentrated; the extra hour of moisture thus obtained is sometimes sufficient to make transformation possible. Those who die without completing their life cycle at least add their organic substance to the mud and supply nourishment for future generations of tadpoles that will hatch and grow in the same spot.

There are four other species in the southwest, one of which, *S. intermontanus,* is found north to Wash. and Mont.

Ascaphidae, tailed frogs. *Ascaphus truei* (Pl. 7), 2 in., lives in cold, rapid mountain streams of the northwest where the temperature of the water may remain as low as 40° C or lower, even in midsummer. It is active and agile, often climbing some distance out of the water. The male is voiceless but since it lives in noisy, rushing water it could probably not be heard by the female if it could call. A special adaptation to aquatic life can be seen in their unique nostrils, the funnels of which are bent downward and are capable of closing. Eggs are laid from May to September, in strings attached to the undersides of stones, 28 to 50 eggs per string. The tadpoles that hatch about a month later have a triangular adhesive organ on the head which holds them to the stones in the fast water.

Bufonidae, toads. The short-legged, plump-bodied hoptoads are rather slow-moving and graceless, but the milky fluid produced by the two large, parotid glands and the secretions of the many glands located in the dry, warty skin, so protect them against predators that they do not suffer from their lack of agility and speed. Toad secretions are irritating in varying degrees to human beings (hence the false belief that they cause warts); they are definitely distasteful and possibly irritating to many animals; and those of the Colorado River Toad, *Bufo alvaris*, 6½ in., are actually poisonous to some animals and are reputedly capable of killing a large dog brazen enough to swallow the toad. Chinese physicians long ago added toad secretions to the potions they prescribed for heart trouble, a custom long considered to have a touch of witchcraft but now known to owe its efficacy to the presence of digitalis.

Toads molt their skin, sometimes as frequently as every 3 to 10 days in warm weather, by splitting it down the back and rubbing it off. Since the skin does not grow in size it must be shed when its limit of elasticity is reached. Frogs molt also but not so noticeably.

Food. The food of toads consists of live insects, mainly beetles, as well as worms and other invertebrates. Prodigious numbers of these small creatures are eaten, proving that a toad in the garden is worth many tins of insecticide. Farmers often report the appearance of large numbers of toads following the onset of a bad insect infestation, and the subsequent cleaning up of the pest.

Reproduction. At breeding time toads gather in ponds and ditches, the males locating the water and then calling loudly to the females. It is believed that they return to the waters in which they grew up. Many are killed as they cross highways and many are suffocated in roadside ditches by the oils washed down from the pavement. Eggs are laid in large numbers, sometimes as many as 35,000 by a single female. (The Cuban *B. marius* lays but a single large egg.) The tiny, black tadpoles often occur in dense schools.

There are 18 species of toads in the U. S. The American Toad, *B. americanus* (Pl. 7), to 4½ in., is the common garden species of the east, with kidney-shaped parotid glands and 1 to 2 warts per spot. Fowler's Toad, *B. fowleri* (Pl. 21), to 3½ in., with oval parotids and 2 warts per spot, is also widespread east of the Great Plains and often very abundant.

A variety of it, *B. woodhousei*, 4½ in. is common in the Great Plains region, westward and south. The Oak Toad, *B. quercicus*, less than 1½ in., is common on the coastal plain south of N. C.; its call is often mistaken for that of a bird. The Giant Toad, *B. marinus*, of southern Texas, may be 7 in. *B. halophilus* of Nev. and Calif. lives in alkaline marshes.

In Canada the commonest toads are: the American Toad, north to James Bay; the Dakota Toad, *B. hemiophrys*, through Alberta; the Great Plains Toad, *B. cognatus*, in the southern, central plains; and *B. boreas* from Alaska southward.

Hylidae, tree frogs. The small, narrow-waisted tree frogs are primarily terrestrial or arboreal. Only two species, *Hyla crucifera* (Fig. 85) and *H. cinerea*, are found in the water except at breeding time. Tree frogs are more often heard than seen, for they climb secretively in the vegetation or remain motionless for long periods of time, clinging by means of the large adhesive discs of the toe tips and fingers.

The large genus *Hyla* is characterized by having toe discs one-half or more the diameter of the tympanum, and in having well-webbed feet. Little *H. ocularis* (now in a separate genus, *Limnaoedus*) is less than an inch in length; it breeds all year in the cypress swamps and grassy ponds of the southeast. The little Green Tree Frog, *H. cinerea* (Pl. 7), up to 2½ in., is considered by some to be our most beautiful tree frog. It is green above, sometimes spotted with yellow, and white or yellow beneath. It often sits on lily pads or along the edges of a pond; but when you approach will leap 8 or 10 feet. Its call is unbelievably loud and carrying.

H. versicolor (Pl. 7), the common Gray Tree Frog, 2¼ in., spends much of the daytime in tree holes or resting on the lichened bark of trees. The irregular star-shaped spot on its back and the oblique stripes on its legs, which are normal characteristics of the species, may be absent; but the bright orange-yellow wash on the underparts will usually distinguish it. The Spring Peeper, *H. crucifer* (Fig. 85), of the eastern and central states and Canada, 1½ in., has an X mark on its back, but aside from that is mostly pale and, at times, nearly translucent. The female lays 800 to 1,000 eggs, each attached singly beneath a stone. When this little peeper first trans- forms and comes out on land it is less than one-half inch long but can jump ten times its own length. Its jingling call has great carrying power, and well it might, for the tiny vocal sacs swell to enormous proportions. The handsome, light green *H. andersonii*, 2 in., of the coastal plain pine barrens, has a light-bordered, plum-colored band along the side of the body and a light orange blush in the groins and on the rear of the thighs. The little Canyon Tree Frog, *H. arenicolor*, 2 in., of the southwest, is unique in its ability to climb the steep rock walls of the canyons. The Pacific Tree Frog, *H. regilla*, less than 2 in., is found at altitudes up to 11,000 feet in the mountains of the northwest; it may be recognized by the dark stripe extending from the snout through the eye and backwards, and by the 2 long dorsal stripes. Other species.

The chorus frogs, 6 species of *Pseudacris* on the Great Plains and eastward, and the cheery Cricket Frog, *Acris gryllus* (Pl. 20), 1¼ in., east of the Rockies, have the toe discs less than half the diameter of the tympanum and thus differ from the tree frogs. *Acris* is extremely agile and dives back into the water when disturbed; its feet are well webbed, whereas those of *Pseudacris* are only partially so.

Ranidae, true frogs (Pls. 5, 7, 20). These are the only frogs having teeth in the upper jaw. They have a streamlined, pointed head with large tympana and protruding eyes; long hind legs with broadly webbed feet; and usually a noticeable ridge running down each side of the back. They are active and agile, good jumpers and persistent travelers, often going some distance from the swamps and lakes in which they live. They feed on insects or, in the case of the big Bull Frog, on young birds, ducklings, turtles and fish.

The eggs are laid in large numbers, 5,000 to 10,000 by a single female, though usually not more than 300 in any one clump.

Since these are the frogs that titillate every small boy's ingenuity and that leap out of the garden pool when the small girl falls in, we include a grouping of the species.

Grouping of Species of Rana

FROGS WITH DARK STRIPE THROUGH EYE AND
TYMPANUM

  R. cascadae, Cascade Range Frog. Groin yellowish
  or pea green.

  R. aurora, Red-legged Frog. Groin reddish, skin
  smooth, with black cheek patch. Pacific states.

  R. pretiosa, Western Spotted Frog. Groin reddish, skin
  warty, back spotted. Northwest.

  R. sylvatica, Wood Frog (Pl. 5). With dark mask
  from snout through eye. Moist woodlands from
  Alaska to S. C.

FROGS WITHOUT STRIPE THROUGH EYE AND
TYMPANUM

1. With distinct dorsolateral folds two-thirds the length of
body.

  R. clamitans, Green Frog (Pls. 7, 20). Color variable, head often bronzy. Brooks and small streams
  east of plains; introduced into Wash.

2. With distinct dorsolateral folds full length of body.

  R. palustris, Pickerel Frog (Pl. 7). Dorsal spots
  rectangular, in 2 rows between folds. Groin bright
  yellow to orange. Prefers cool water as in bogs.
  East of plains.

  R. pipiens, Leopard Frog (Pl. 7). Spotting variable.
  Groin never bright yellow to orange. Light line on
  upper jaw. Wanders far from water.

  R. areolata, Crawfish Frog. Skin warty. Dorsal spots
  with light borders. Ohio to Kans. south to Texas.

  R. capito, Gopher Frog. Spots without light border
  but on a light background. In gopher tortoise holes;
  coastal plain N. C. to Fla.

  R. sevosa, Dark Gopher Frog. Background darker
  than above; belly more spotted. Gulf states.

3. Without distinct dorsolateral folds.

  a. Tympanum smaller than eye. Western.

    R. tarahumarae, Tarahumara Frog. Without tubercle
    on metatarsus. Southwest.

    R. boylei, Common Yellow-leg. With metatarsal tu-

bercle. Skin warty. Light stripe on snout; toe tips
brown. Calif. and Oreg.

    R. muscosa, Mountain Yellow-leg. With metatarsal
tubercle. No stripe on snout; toe tips black. Calif.

b. Tympanum as large as or larger than eye.

    R. virgatipes, Carpenter Frog. 2½ in. Two golden-
brown stripes on each side. Belly spotted; back not
mottled. Sphagnum bogs of coastal plain, N. J. to
Ga.

    R. septentrionalis, Mink Frog. 3 in. Belly not spotted;
back mottled. With minklike odor. Commonly hop-
ping on lily pads. N. E. Can. to Minn.

    R. grylio, Pig Frog (also called Southern Bull Frog
and Joe Brown Frog). 6½ in. Snout pointed, hind
feet fully webbed. Coastal plains S. C. to Texas.

    R. catesbeiana, Bull Frog (Pl. 7). 8 in. Throat light
with dark blotches. Widespread.

    R. heckscheri, River Frog. 6 in. Throat smoky with
white blotches; lower lip with white spots. Coastal
plains, S. C. to Miss.

Microhylidae, narrow-mouthed toads. Five species of this
South American family are found in the U. S.; of these only
two have extended their range much beyond the Mexican
border. *Gastrophryne carolinensis,* 1 in. or less, is found north
to Md. and Ill., and *G. olivacea* from Texas and Neb. The
secretion of their skin glands is not only distasteful to animals
but may be extremely irritating to humans. They are found
in a wide variety of environments, often near swamps and
marshes but also in grassy meadows and partially wooded
hillsides. Their relative, the Sheep Frog of the Texas border,
Hypopachus cuneus, 1.7 in., is narrowly restricted, hiding in
burrows and tree holes, in pack rat nests and under cow
dung; it breeds only when it becomes flooded out by rain
or irrigation.

CHAPTER 16

Turtles, Snakes, and Alligators—Class Reptilia

Figs. 86, 87; Pls. 8, 21, 22

T HE dry-skinned vertebrates grouped in this class are now, for the most part, terrestrial, having accomplished the final steps in development that are necessary if they are to live permanently out of water. They have lungs with which to breathe atmospheric air, and a shell-bearing egg that will protect the growing embryo from desiccation and provide it with nourishment. Relatively few species live entirely in the water and most of those are quite at home on shore. Reptiles are able to pursue the animals upon which they feed and, since the stomach is distensible, they can consume large quantities of food at one time and then survive long periods of deprivation.

Grouping of Orders of Reptiles

REPTILES WITH A BONY OR LEATHERY SHELL
Chelonia, turtles.
REPTILES WITHOUT A SHELL
Squamata, snakes and lizards. Anal opening a transverse slit.
Crocodilia, crocodiles and alligators. Anal opening a longitudinal slit.

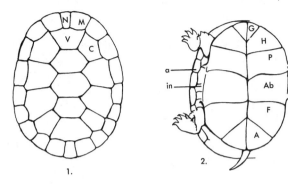

Fig. 86. Diagram of turtle shells with shields named. *1.* Carapace. *2.* Plastron. *A*, anals; *Ab*, abdominals; *ax*, axillaries; *C*,
costals; *F*, femorals; *G*, gula; *in*, inguinals; *M*, marginals; *N*, nuchal;
P, pectorals; *V*, ventrals.

Turtles—Order Chelonia

Many turtles are entirely terrestrial but many others spend
much of their time in fresh water or in the sea. Their shell
is composed of hard plates covered with horny shields; it is
divided into an upper *carapace* which is usually fused with
the bony ribs, and a lower *plastron*. Most species are able
to withdraw into their shell; those that cannot are likely to
be aggressive and bad-tempered when handled. If the shell
becomes broken a slight amount of repair is possible. The
shell is never shed but each shield continues to grow in size
and thickness; in a few species an outer transparent layer
may peel off periodically.

It is difficult to distinguish the sexes. The male usually
has a longer, thicker and slightly more prehensile tail, and
sometimes has longer nails on the forefeet and slightly concave plastron. The male of the musk turtles has patches of
horny scales on the inside of the hind legs.

Respiration. Terrestrial species fill their lungs by gulping
air or by enlarging the body cavity by means of muscular
movements as mammals do. Aquatic species are not dissimilar anatomically so must come to the surface for air or
remain content with the water-borne oxygen that passes into

the mouth or anus. Some species, especially the soft-shell turtles, draw a fairly large amount of water into the anus and then into two thin-walled cloacal sacs. The pumping movements that make this possible are plainly visible. Turtles are difficult to drown and may remain submerged for days at a time.

Food. Turtles vary in their eating habits; some are carnivorous, some herbivorous and some omnivorous.

Senses. Turtles do not have acute hearing but they have a good sense of smell and good vision; individuals kept in our household for many years and addicted to raw hamburg and red cherries would dash across the room to investigate and chomp upon a bright red toenail projecting through an open-toed shoe. Turtles have no voice but they do make respiratory grunts and squeaks.

Reproduction. Mating of aquatic species takes place in the water. Some species, mainly those of *Pseudemys* and *Chrysemys*, have an interesting courtship procedure, the male swimming backward in front of the female and tapping her face with the long nails of his outstretched, vibrating forelegs. The eggs may be hard-shelled or soft-shelled. They are laid in the spring near the water's edge, in a nest excavated in the soil which has been softened, if necessary, by bladder fluid; or they may be laid in a shallow hole or brush pile. They are occasionally covered over by the female. She may also make some attempt to disguise or conceal the location of the nest but she then goes off, leaving it unguarded. Incubation is long, sometimes as much as 80 days; eggs of the Snapping Turtle, normally hatching in about 10 weeks, will overwinter and hatch the following spring if they are laid late or retarded by cold weather. Turtle eggs, alas, are relished by many animals, especially skunks, mink and weasels.

Turtles often live to a ripe old age; individuals of *Clemmys* have reputedly lived to 58; other species, according to unauthenticated claims, have lived to 138 and 150 years. They are more active in warm water than in cold and (with a few exceptions) become inactive when the temperature drops below 50° F, hibernating in the mud and debris of the bottom.

Collecting. Turtles should be sought along the edge of ponds and quiet backwaters, especially in the spring when they are seeking nesting sites, or after a rain; and again in the fall when they are quite active. Most carnivorous species can be caught with a baited hook. Traps of various kinds can be staked to the bottom of suitable waters or left to float. Dr. Roger Conant describes a simple one made of 3 hoops, 30 inches or so in diameter, connected by a stout netting to form a barrel-shaped trap 4 to 5 feet long. One end should be covered with netting but the other with an inward directing throat, the opening of which should be large enough to permit the turtle to enter. A bait can, punched with holes and filled with chopped raw fish, chicken entrails, etc., can be suspended within the trap.

Some turtles make excellent pets but the collector should check with the Conservation Dept. of the Fish and Game Commission for regulations regarding them. When kept as pets they should be provided with both sun and shade, access to water, and soil in which to dig. Some species eat only under water so the water must be sufficiently deep for that purpose and always kept clean of uneaten food. Chopped raw meat, fish, worms or canned dog food can be given the carnivores; various green vegetables and fruit to the others. Live insects are greatly relished; when they are not available a culture of mealworms can be kept in covered containers of bran. Never, never paint their shells.

Grouping of Families of Aquatic Turtles

TURTLES WITH EDGE OF SHELL FLEXIBLE. WITH THREE CLAWS ON FRONT FEET

Trionychidae, softshell turtles.

TURTLES WITH SHELL NOT FLEXIBLE. WITH FIVE CLAWS ON FRONT FEET

1. Plastron with 12 shields (Fig. 87.1).

Testudinidae, land tortoises. Not aquatic but often near water. Toes are short, without webs and with thick claws. Top of head with shields. Margins of carapace usually flared outward.

Emydidae, pond, wood, painted and box turtles. Toes

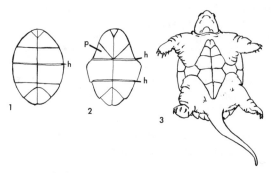

Fig. 87. Diagram of plastrons. *1.* Blanding's Turtle. *2.* Mud Turtle. *3.* Snapping Turtle. *h,* hinge; *p,* pectoral shield.

are long, usually with some webbing and with long claws. Top of head without shields.

2. Plastron with 11 or fewer shields (Fig. 87.2,3).

Chelydridae, snapping turtles. Rear of carapace serrate. Tail very long with horny tubercles.

Kinosternidae, mud and musk turtles. Rear of carapace usually smooth. Tail short with fleshy protuberances.

Trionychidae, softshell turtles. These turtles often bask along the shore, especially along rivers, sliding into the water with lightning speed when alarmed. They are strong swimmers but spend much of the time floating just beneath the surface or half-buried in the mud or sand in shallow waters, with the eyes and the longish, truncate, nostril-bearing snout projecting above the surface. Their soft, leathery shell is quite pliable along the edges and is sometimes almost transparent, exposing the skeletal structures within. They are scavengers as well as carnivores.

Trionyx muticus (Pl. 8), 19 in., is the Smooth Softshell of the south and midwest, eastward to central N. Y. *T. spinifera,* 14 in., with sandpapery shell, is widespread through the east to Colo. and south to Ky. *T. ferox* is southeastern. The two last named differ from *muticus* in having conical tubercles on the anterior edge of the carapace.

Emydidae, pond and wood turtles. This very large family includes the brackish water terrapins and the terrestrial box and gopher turtles, as well as many aquatic species.

Blanding's Turtle, *Emys blandingi* (Pl. 8), 7.5 in., has notched upper jaw and yellow throat and chin. The high-domed carapace is yellow speckled; the plastron is yellow with a black blotch on each shield. Although this little turtle hibernates, it is often seen swimming beneath the ice. It is carnivorous, preferring insects and crustaceans. Of sporadic distribution from N. S. to Neb., rare in N. Y. and New England, often wondering far from water. A good pet.

Turtles of the genus *Clemmys* are in and out of the water, sometimes traveling long distances even though they move slowly. They are more or less omnivorous. *C. insculpta,* the Wood Tortoise (Pl. 5), 8 in., has a rough shell, each shield of the carapace forming an irregular pyramid with concentric grooves and ridges. The neck and legs are often orange or brilliant salmon-red. It makes an excellent household pet, prompt to arrive in the dining room at mealtime and generally interested in the affairs of the household. N. S. to Va., west to Iowa. *C. guttata,* the Spotted Turtle, 5 in., has a smooth, usually blackish carapace with many yellow spots; the head and neck are also spotted. They are normally in or around small bodies of water, basking in groups on floating logs, climbing and tumbling over one another and sliding back into the water with a great splash. They normally feed on insects and crustaceans and occasionally on plant material. Can be kept in captivity if fed under water. *C. muhlenberg,* 3.5 in., of R. I., N. Y. and south to N. C., has a large orange and yellow spot on each side of the head. A good pet.

The map turtles, genus *Graptemys,* take their name from the fine-lined pattern on the keeled carapace. Some species are called sawbacks because of the toothlike projections of the dorsal keel. There are nine species in the Gulf states; but *G. geographica* is the only common species in the north and central states although two others work their way northward along the river valleys. The neck and sides of the head of *geographica* have fine yellow lines; behind the eyes there is a triangular yellow spot; the carapace is flattened and low-spined. This turtle is relatively shy, preferring large bodies of water where it feeds primarily on molluscs. Dr. Archie Carr has written most engagingly about map turtles and their habits.

The Painted Turtle, *Chrysemys picta* (Pl. 8), 6 in., is widespread all across the northern tier of states, southward along the coast, the Miss. Valley and down across N. M. It is the most abundant pond turtle of the east and midwest, basking beside shallow waters where vegetation is rank and the bottom muddy. The smooth, flattish carapace is marked along the margins with red, yellow and orange. The plastron may be all bright yellow, or may be spotted with black or with black and red. The painted turtle is omnivorous and easily kept as a pet providing it has access to water and can be fed under water.

The sliders and cooters of the genus *Pseudemys* are the big basking turtles of the south. The carapace varies in shape, sometimes high, sometimes low, but is usually longitudinally furrowed. It is often marked with whorls of brown or black lines on a lighter background. The side of the face may be marked with patches of red and yellow. *P. rubiventris*, the Red-bellied Turtle (Pl. 8), 12 in., lives along the Atlantic coast from Mass. to N. C. but has a closely related form in Fla. *P. scripta*, the Red-eared Terrapin, or Pond Slider (Pl. 8), 8 in., is the popular little turtle sold widely in pet shops. Its eggs are used for bait and its flesh for food. The young are omnivorous but the adults are primarily herbivorous. This turtle is common in the southwestern states and extends in a wide belt up the Miss. Valley; a yellow-bellied form with a yellow patch behind the eye is coastal from Va. to the Gulf.

The large cooters of several varieties are difficult to distinguish. They and their eggs are eaten locally.

Deirochelys reticularia, the Chicken Turtle, 6 in., is found in quiet waters from N. C. to Texas. It was once widely sold in the markets. The carapace bears a network pattern of yellow but the plastron is all yellow. The neck and legs are striped. This turtle is omnivorous.

Grouping of Genera of Emydidae

PLASTRON HINGED

> *Emys.* Plastron notched at the rear.
>
> *Terrapene.* Plastron not notched at the rear. Terrestrial box turtles.

PLASTRON NOT HINGED, BUT IN ONE RIGID PIECE

1. Axillaries and inguinals absent or small and rudimentary.

   > *Clemmys.* Upper jaw curved downward.
   >
   > *Malaclemys.* Upper jaw curved upward. In brackish water only.

2. Axillaries and inguinals large and well developed.

   a. Rear margin of carapace serrate.

   > *Graptemys.* Carapace keeled, sometimes sawback.
   >
   > *Pseudemys.* Carapace usually wrinkled with longitudinal furrows.

   b. Rear margin of carapace not serrate.

   > *Deirochelys.* Neck long (length from tip of nose to carapace half the length of the carapace). Carapace usually with network of fine lines.
   >
   > *Chrysemys.* Neck normal. Carapace with red markings.

Chelydridae, snapping turtles. Snappers are recognized by the tough, rigid carapace with serrations along the rear margin, and by the long tail (as long as the carapace) bearing two rows of scales beneath and a series of tubercles above. The shell is not sufficiently large to permit concealment of the body and yet snappers are seldom bad-tempered when encountered in the water, although on land they are aggressive and sometimes vicious. Snappers are omnivorous, snapping at any living or dead animal with their strong, beaked jaws, and feeding on vegetation as well. Although they may be of some economic value as scavengers they are a menace to young waterfowl. Their musklike odor is offensive.

Chelydra serpentina, the widespread Common Snapper (Pl. 8), 12 in. or more, and attaining a weight of 60 pounds (or a record 86), is a poor swimmer, spending much of its time lumbering along the bottom or sitting half-buried in the mud. It is to be found in most any kind of water provided it is muddy. The round, leathery eggs, some 10 to 80 in number, are laid in 6-inch holes in the ground along the shore or even back some distance from the water, from June to October. The eggs hatch usually in about 10 weeks but may overwinter. The snapper is common as far west as the Rockies. The Alligator Snapper, *Macroclemys temmincki,* 26 inches and 150 pounds (there is one record of 219 pounds), has a larger head with strongly hooked beak, conspicuous keels along the carapace and a double row of marginal shields along each side. It is less aggressive than the Common Snapper but even more of a menace to fish. Common in the Gulf states and up the Miss. Valley to Ind.

Kinosternidae, mud and musk turtles. There are 5 species of mud turtles of the genus *Kinosternum,* recognized by the 2-hinged plastron, the 3-sided pectoral shields (Fig. 87.2) and the horny, clawlike tip on the tail. The eastern *K. subrubrum,* less then 4 in., has yellow spots on the sides of the head. It is common in meadows, ponds and ditches of the coastal plain from N. Y. south to the Gulf, up the Miss. Valley, and across to Calif., and may even be in brackish water.

The musk turtles are the "stinkpots" that crawl on the bottom of ponds and pools, stealing fishhooks. They rarely leave the water except during a heavy rain or when breeding, preferring to bask in shallow water. They are important scavengers. They secrete a heavy, musky substance when handled. *Sternotherus,* 4–5 in., has 4 species extending west to Okla. Its carapace is smooth and high; the plastron is small with but one inconspicuous hinge, with 4-sided pectoral shields, and with a wide soft median line. The common *S. odoratus* (Pl. 8) is a pugnacious species that lays its eggs under logs and in brush piles or muskrat houses.

Snakes—Order Serpentes
Pls. 21, 22

Since very few snakes are poisonous it is unfortunate to have to begin this paragraph with a warning. *One of our aquatic snakes, the Cottonmouth, or Water Moccasin, is poisonous.* If you are collecting in the region where it may occur, take care, until you are certain of its identification. As a rule, the harmless water snakes move off quickly when disturbed. The Cottonmouth tends to be sluggish, moving off slowly or else standing its ground. In the latter case it may vibrate its tail or throw back its head, opening the mouth and exposing the warning white color within. To one familiar with snakes, the broad head and light lip markings of the Cottonmouth are recognizable features.

No other aquatic snakes are poisonous, so do not allow your caution with the one deter you from enjoying the others; snakes are remarkable creatures. The elongation of the body (it has extra vertebrae), and the absence of external legs, facilitate burrowing and account for the slithering movement of the snake as it progresses through vegetation and water and over the ground. The elastic ligament connecting the upper and lower jaws, and the absence of a breastbone and pectoral girdle, enable the snake to swallow quite large prey intact. The forked tongue, which seems to have an unwarranted and frightening effect upon many people, is entirely harmless; it is a tactile and olfactory organ of great importance to the snake whose vision is acute but whose hearing is nonexistent.

Collecting. When in the water, snakes may be caught by the skillful use of a net; on land they are best captured by being pinned down just back of the head with a forked stick or snake tongs, or by being noosed. Water snakes are often lured at night with a bright light.

Grouping of Families of Aquatic Snakes

SNAKES WITH A PIT BETWEEN EYE AND NOSTRIL
   Crotalidae, pit vipers. Poisonous.
SNAKES WITHOUT A PIT BETWEEN EYE AND NOSTRIL
   Colubridae, colubrids. No aquatic ones are poisonous.

Crotalidae, pit vipers. The rattlesnakes, copperheads and Cottonmouth belong to this family but only the Cottonmouth is aquatic, although the Massasauga Rattlesnake may be in wet, swampy woodlands.

The Cottonmouth, *Agkistrodon piscivorus* (Pl. 22), 4–6

Agkistrodon piscivorus, the Cottonmouth or Water Moccasin.

Natrix sipedon, a black snake from Florida.

PLATE 22

ft., gives birth to living young in the early fall, 5 to 15 in a brood and measuring about 1 foot in length at time of birth. They may be brownish or brilliant red with darker cross bands and with bright yellow tail tip. The broad-headed, short-tailed adults are blackish above, or olive brown with black cross bands, and light beneath. They have a dark line along each side of the light snout. The dorsal scales are weakly keeled.

The Cottonmouth lives in lakes and rivers of the southern lowlands, feeding on fish, amphibians, turtles, baby alligators, birds and mammals. It may sun itself along the banks or may wander some distance from the water in search of food. In the fall it moves to higher ground to hibernate. Individuals have been known to live for 50 years.

Distribution. Great Dismal Swamp of Va. southward through Fla., across the Gulf to central Texas; up the Miss. Valley in a wide band stretching from central Okla. to central Tenn., and up into Mo., Ill. and Kans.

Colubridae. This large family includes about 75 percent of all the snakes in this country, and it includes all our aquatic snakes except the Cottonmouth. Most water snakes belong to the genus *Natrix.* They are widespread in the south, east and midwest, in small, quiet streams and ponds, in ditches, cattle tanks, etc., feeding on cold-blooded animals, chiefly crayfish and frogs. They often sun themselves along the bank, sometimes suspended from bushes overhanging the water. In late summer or fall they give birth to living young, the broods averaging 24 in number although sometimes containing twice that. The common Northern Water Snake, *N. sipedon* (Pl. 22), 3½ ft., of the eastern and mid-central states, is grayish brown with broad, dark cross bands which are thick on the back but narrow at the sides; but the many variations on this pattern are confusing. They are heavy-bodied snakes with strongly keeled scales and abruptly tapered tail. The Brown Water Snake, or Water Pilot, *N. taxispilota,* 5 ft., of the southern coastal plains, is the largest of the genus; it is arboreal as well as aquatic. The more secretive Queen Snake, *N. septemvittata* (Pl. 21) of the southern Great Lakes region south to the Gulf, has a yellow belly with four conspicuous brown stripes. There are 7 other species.

Garter snakes of the genus *Thamnophis* are closely related to the water snakes and, although terrestrial, often go into the water, swimming with lateral undulations of the body while holding the head above the surface, and occasionally diving beneath. They have three characteristic light longitudinal stripes on a darker ground, strongly keeled scales, and a single anal plate instead of the divided one characteristic of the water snakes. They are ovoviviparous.

Three southern snakes with smooth, unkeeled scales are often in the water. The Mud Snake, *Farancia abacura,* 5 ft., is shiny iridescent black with red or pink markings on the sides beneath. Its tail is sharp-tipped. It is a snake of the swamps and ditches, feeding primarily on amphiumas, of the southeastern coastal region and up the Miss. Valley to Ind. Another swamp snake, *Liodytes alleni,* shining brown with a broad yellow band along the lower side and a yellowish tinge to the belly, lives in thick aquatic vegetation, tunneling in the beds of Water Hyacinth and *Utricularia,* feeding on crayfish and frogs. It often travels overland; Ga. and Fla. The Rainbow Snake, *Abastor erythrogrammus,* up to 5 ft., is glossy black above with 3 red stripes, and red below with 2 rows of dark spots. It is a burrower in marshes and springs of the southern coastal plains, but is sometimes aquatic, catching eels and other aquatic animals.

Alligators—Order Crocodilia

The Crocodilia have an elongated body, short neck, short legs, and a long, laterally compressed tail. Their skin contains large, bony plates covered with horny scales. They are all amphibious, their world being that of shoreline and swamp; but only the alligators are in fresh waters. The American Alligator, *Alligator mississipiensis,* 6–12 ft., has a broadly rounded snout and is thus distinguished from the saltwater American Crocodile, *Crocodylus acutus,* which has a sharply pointed snout with a tooth protruding from the lower jaw.

"Don't step there, that log is an alligator," has probably

been said many times around the swamps, lagoons and lakes from N. C. to Fla. and Texas, for our alligators lie for hours at a time submerged except for the eyes and the tip of the tail, immobile and inconspicuous. The young may have cross bands of yellow on the blackish body but adults are mostly uni-colorous. The males can bellow loudly but the females and young just grunt and hiss.

Food. Young alligators feed on insects and crustaceans but as they grow in size they select increasingly larger animals such as snakes, frogs and fish; until by the time they are adult they have developed a predilection for waterfowl and mammals, occasionally relishing a young pig or even a deer or cow.

Reproduction. The female constructs a mound of debris, 4 to 7 feet in diameter and 2 to 3 feet high. In it she buries her hard-shelled, oval eggs and over it she stands guard. At such times, from spring to autumn, she may be quite vicious. The newly hatched young may be 9 inches long but they remain under the mother's care until the following spring.

The alligator sold in pet shops, and which occasionally escapes or is released, is usually the Spectacled Caiman, *Caiman sclerops*, 6 ft., of Mexico and South America. It is greenish to yellowish with dark cross bands and with a bony ridge in front of the eyes. Several of them are said to be living in the labyrinthine passages under the New York subways.

Appendix

Collecting Equipment

Most freshwater forms can be collected with the simplest of homemade equipment. A little ingenuity is the prime requisite. Specialized collecting of the larger animals may call for clam rakes, fish seines, etc., or for more elaborately contrived items to meet particular needs. They will not be discussed here. Rather we will describe a few pieces that have proved useful over the years for general limnological collecting. All of them can be purchased at a biological supply house; many can be made at home.

Keep on hand a small case, such as a discarded pocketbook, tobacco pouch or pencil case, fitted with hand lens, pencil and small notebook for recording observations and locality notes; also a pipette, forceps and lifter (Fig. 88) for picking specimens out of the net. When starting out on a collecting trip, have with you a supply of small jars of assorted sizes with tight-fitting lids, and one or two large jars in which to bring home unsorted material and a supply of natural water. You will also need a few vials of 70 percent alcohol, and some plastic bags. These bags should be heavier than the ones used in the kitchen; they come in a variety of sizes and can be washed and reused. Always carry a deep white enamel or plastic pan for receiving the contents of the net when it is drawn from the water. (I like the straight-sided plastic handbasins that are now so easily obtainable.) This pan will hold the catch while you sort it over and while small creatures are given time to wiggle about and to crawl out of the debris. If large quantities of vegetation or bottom detritus are to be drawn from the water, you will find that a large piece of canvas to spread on the ground is useful. It permits water to slowly drain off the material that is emptied onto it, while you sit comfortably on the ground beside it.

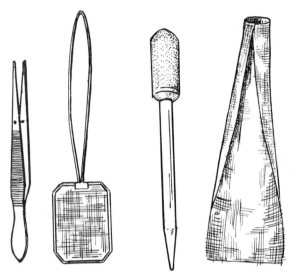

Fig. 88.

Dip nets. An ordinary kitchen sieve tied to a long handle may well be one's first dip net. As time goes on and one's enthusiasm increases, more practicable nets can be made. The frame, made of stiff steel wire, may be circular, semicircular, triangular or diamond-shaped (Fig. 89.1–4), about 8 inches in diameter. There are various ways of attaching the net to the handle. In the method illustrated, the handle has two grooves at one end, one on each side; each is a different length and each ends in an inch-deep hole. The two loose ends of the wire frame also differ in length to match the grooves; they have their terminal inch bent at a right angle. The end of the frame then can be fitted into the grooves and bound in place by stout twine or wire, or held in position by a brass ferule that has previously been slipped over the end of the handle. This type of net has the advantage of being easily disassembled.

The net bag should be made of coarse-meshed, heavy marquisette, bound with heavy muslin around the frame. Before cutting out the two pieces of netting from which

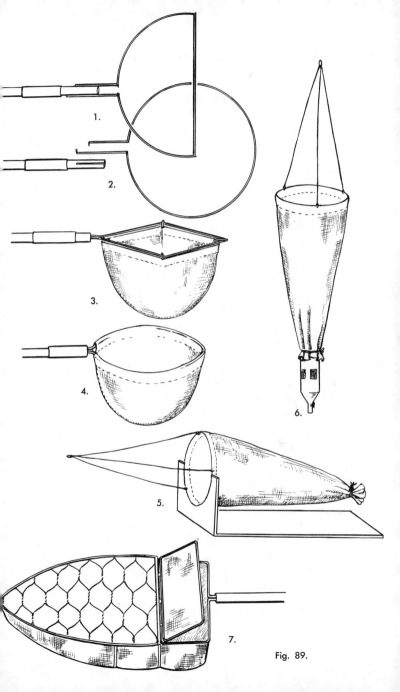

1.

2.

3.

4.

5.

6.

7.

Fig. 89.

the bag will be made, make sure to measure the circumference of the frame and then estimate the width of the cloth needed, after binding, to fit the frame. (Make a paper pattern first.) The pieces should be stitched together with a French seam. The strip of muslin should of course be cut double width then folded lengthwise, the edges turned in and bound to the net bag with the two open ends coming together above one of the seams of the bag and left open for the insertion of the wire frame.

The *Needham apron net* (Fig. 89.7) and the *Needham scraper* (Fig. 90.2). These nets are both made with galvanized iron frame and metal screening, and so are rather heavy. It is hoped that when they are needed a long overland journey on foot will not be required. The former is extremely useful for reaching into dense weed beds and the latter for lifting out masses of bottom detritus and mud or for scraping across a stony bottom.

The hand screen (Fig. 90.1). Easily made at home from window screening and two short handles, this screen supposedly requires the use of two hands. It is designed for being held across the current of a stream while a second person turns over stones or agitates the vegetation, rocks and pebbles of the substratum a foot or two upstream of it. However, one person can quickly develop the agility necessary to hold it steady while stirring around upstream with pole, net handle or the toe of his boot. The hand screen is an extremely valuable bit of equipment and rolls up for easy carrying.

A tow net (Fig. 89.5). Made of fine silk bolting cloth, the tow net has a tape attached at one point about 4 inches from the open distal end. The tape should be the right length to tie around the end, closing it securely. This net can be dragged through the water behind a boat or fastened in position when the current is strong enough to hold it out in horizontal position. If it is to be drawn close to the bottom, galvanized sheet metal should be attached to protect the silk net. When lifted out of the water the net is held upright over a large container, the tape untied and the contents allowed to drop out.

The Birge cone net (Fig. 89.6). This net is similar but

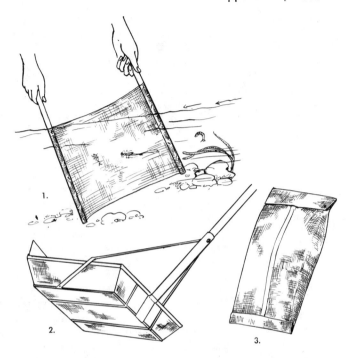

Fig. 90.

has a glass or plastic container tied to the end of the cone; or it may be fitted with a special filtering device consisting of a brass cylinder with fine mesh screening covering the windowlike openings in its sides and a petcock for opening and closing the end of the funnel.

Dragnet. This is on the general plan of the tow net but has a stout, rectangular stiff metal frame, 5″ x 18″, with a metal lip along one of the long sides. The bag should be 24 to 26 inches long and, of course, made to fit the frame. This, with a weight attached, can be dragged along by someone walking or from a slowly propelled boat. Professor Robert L. Usinger and Dr. Paul Needham, of California, have made an improvement on this net by making the frame of flat steel plates, 3 inches wide (like a rectangular bottom-less box), and fastening 17 nine-inch pointed steel tines across the front opening of the box. The ends of the tines are bent forward to rake through the substratum as the net is dragged along. The net bag should, of course, be of very heavy material. The designers of this net have added a protective canvas sleeve and have worked out a device whereby the bag can be zippered onto the frame for easy removal.

Care of Specimens

It is always desirable, when possible, and certainly a lot more fun, to bring specimens home alive, but some fragile species may have to be preserved in the field (hence the vials of alcohol). When this is done each vial should be labeled on the spot, usually by inserting a small rectangular piece of bond paper with the locality and date written in pencil. Animals brought home alive should be separated by locality, and carnivorous ones isolated from anything upon which they might prey. A bit of aquatic vegetation put in with them deters jostling, provides some oxygen and may even give some nourishment. Amphibians not needing to be immersed should also be generously supplied with damp vegetation. Insects from highly oxygenated water, such as stoneflies, should not be carried in water but in damp cotton or moss.

Upon reaching home the animals should be transferred to larger, screen-topped jars or aquaria with rooted plants. Whenever possible, use natural water or tap water that has been conditioned by standing. Use shallow rather than deep containers; and use several small ones rather than one large one. Directions for maintaining a balanced aquarium are easily obtainable but the chief ingredients of success are green aquatic plants to produce oxygen, snails to clean the sides and bottom, and the avoidance of feeding techniques that will contaminate the water. Remember the importance of the limiting factors discussed in Chapter 1 and do not expect all animals to thrive under the same conditions; do not expect, for instance, that insects from highly oxygenated, fast-moving waters will live in the static water of a quart jar.

For insect larvae and nymphs that may soon transform, use a *pillow cage* (Fig. 90.3), made from a square piece of ordinary screening by double-folding it and then pinching the folds. Although the pillow cage can be set in a tub of water it is more satisfactory if placed in a pond or brook, fastened to the shore at a slight incline and so propped that three-fourths of it will be emergent. The conditions natural to the animal concerned should be duplicated as nearly as possible.

Preservation of Specimens

Most small animal specimens in the home collection will be kept in 70 percent alcohol. At best such a collection does not make a particularly attractive display, so more and more collectors have been keeping their specimens with an eye on easy access and safe preservation rather than artistic display. With the great variety of glass containers coming into every household these days, there should be no trouble in acquiring assorted sizes for every purpose. A color scheme might be worked out for painting the lids according to some taxonomic, ecological or geographic sequence. But whatever the plan employed, certain rules should be followed: (1) each jar must contain a label bearing locality and date of collecting; (2) the specimen must be completely immersed in the preservative; (3) the jar must be tightly closed and preferably kept in the dark; (4) all jars must be examined frequently and more preservative added when necessary. The method of keeping small specimens, especially the invertebrates, in cotton-stoppered vials of alcohol which are then immersed upside down in large sealed jars is probably the best of all.

Plants, vertebrates, aerial insects and microscopic forms will call for specialized techniques. Directions for them will be found in books dealing with each group mentioned in the Bibliography.

Keys

Dichotomous keys are here included for a few frequently collected and popular groups of insects. These keys consist of numbered pairs of descriptive statements. (Occasionally the statements are in a trio rather than a pair.) To use the keys: compare the statements of pair number 1; select that which best describes your specimen. The number at the right-hand end of the line of your preference directs you to the numbered pair to which you should then turn. Continue to make your selection of statements, each time proceeding to the numbered pair to which you are directed, until you have arrived at the italicized generic name. Keys are not usually applicable to immature nymphs.

The following abbreviations are used to denote geographic distribution: *e*, eastern North America; *c*, central tier of states; *n*, northern states and across Canada; *ne*, northeastern states and eastern Canada; *nw*, northwestern states and western Canada; *s*, southern states; *se*, southeastern states; *sw*, southwestern states; *w*, western states. Note that *n,w* would mean north and west, not northwest. Other abbreviations: *r*, rare; *unc*, uncommon.

Key to Genera of Stonefly Nymphs
(Figs. 47, 51–53)

1.—With gills on basal abdominal segments 2
  —Without gills on basal abdominal segments 4

2.—With single gills on sides of segments 1–7; w. coast ... *Oroperla*
  —With tufts of gills on segments 1–3; less than
     25 mm.; w. .... *Pteronarcella*
  —With tufts of gills on segments 1–2; 35–50 mm. 3

3.—Abdomen with lateral processes; Que. to Ga. .... *Allonarcys*
  —Abdomen without lateral processes; n. of Ga. ... *Pteronarcys*

357

4.—Body depressed, roachlike; head bent under;
　　 less than 10 mm. ....Peltoperla
　　—Not as above 5

5.—Labium with glossa and paraglossa about same length　6
　　—Labium with paraglossa extending well beyond tips
　　 of glossa 18

6.—Second tarsal segment, seen from the side,
　　 as long as the first 7
　　—Second tarsal segment much shorter than first 8

7.—With gills at base of coxae; Lab. to Gulf,
　　 also Oreg. ....Taeniopteryx
　　—Without gills at base of coxae .... Brachyptera

8.—Hind wing pads strongly divergent; hind legs
　　 surpassing tip of body .... Nemoura
　　—Hind wing pads nearly parallel; hind legs barely
　　 reaching tip of body 9
　　—Hind wing pads absent or rudimentary 17

9.—Abdominal segments 1–9 divided laterally by
　　 membranous fold 10
　　—Segments 1–7, or fewer, divided laterally by
　　 membranous fold 15

10.—Tails fringed with long hairs; 15 mm. or more;
　　 Alaska to Colo. .... Isocapnia
　　—Tails not fringed 11

11.—Body and appendages densely covered with stout
　　 bristles; Newf. to Ozarks .... Paracapnia
　　—Not as above 12

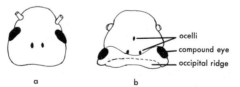

Fig. 91. Top of head of stonefly nymphs. a, with eyes well anterior to hind margin of head; b, with eyes near hind margin of head.

12.—Abdomen with a few slender bristles; nw .... *Eucapnopsis*
—Abdomen not as above 13

13.—Inner margin hind wing pad with median notch 14
—Inner margin notched close to tip if at all;
   e. of Rockies .... *Allocapnia*

14.—Eastern, n. to Ill. and Ind.; r .... *Nemocapnia*
—Western, northern, s. to Mich. and St. Law. R. .... *Capnia*

15.—Segments 1–7 divided by membranous fold; r 16
—Fewer segments divided .... *Leuctra*

16.—Body coarsely pilose; B. C. to Oreg., also Tenn. .. *Megaleuctra*
—Body not as above; B. C. to Colo. .... *Perlomyia*

17.—East of Rockies .... *Allocapnia*
—Western .... *Capnia*

18.—Gills in tufts on thorax 19
—Gills, if present, not tufted 27

19.—Compound eyes near hind margin of head 20
—Compound eyes somewhat anterior to hind margin 26

20.—With two ocelli; up to 13 mm. 21
—With three ocelli 22

21.—With anal gills; n,e .... *Neoperla*
—Without anal gills .... *Anacroneuria*

22.—Dorsum of abdomen freckled; up to 10 mm. .... *Perlesta*
—Dorsum of abdomen not freckled 23

23.—Back of head with a continuous row of spines on a ridge 24
—Back of head with spines not in a continuous row
   and not on a ridge .... *Acroneuria*

24.—With anal gills 25
—Without anal gills; n .... *Paragnetina*

25.—Abdominal segments yellow, banded with black;
   e south of St. Law. R. and Mich. .... *Neophasganophora*
—Abdomen brownish; w,n .... *Claassenia*

26.—With two ocelli; body concolorous;
   s, from Minn., Mass. .... *Atoperla*

—With three ocelli; body boldly patterned;
s, from Minn. to N. S. ....*Perlinella*

27.—Body patterned; hind wing pads divergent 28
—Body concolorous; hind wing pads not divergent 31

28.—With gills on thorax; nw ....*Arcynopteryx*
—Without gills on thorax 29

29.—With small fingerlike gills under labium 30
—Without such gills .... *Isogenus, Diura, Isoperla*

30.—With small labial gills twice as long
as wide .... *Arcynopteryx* and *Isogenus*°
—With labial gills as long as
wide .... *Rickera, Isogenus, Diura, Isoperla*°

31.—Fore wing pads with outer margins straight 32
—Fore wing pads with outer margins rounded 34

32.—Maxillae bulging conspicuously from sides of head 33
—Maxillae not bulging conspicuously; 10–14 mm. ...... *Isoperla*

33.—20 mm. in length; w .... *Diura*
—12–20 mm. in length .... *Isogenus*

34.—East of the Rockies; eyes normal,
near hind margin of head 35
—Western; eyes small, set far forward; up to 18 mm. 36

35.—Inner margin hind wing pads sinuate or notched;
7–13 mm.; n, south to Ozarks .... *Alloperla*
—Inner margin hind wing pad straight;
5–7 mm. ... *Hastaperla* (n), *Chloroperla* (Appalachians, r)

36.—Head as long as wide; w .... *Paraperla*
—Head longer than wide; nw .... *Kathroperla*

Key to Genera of Mayfly Nymphs
(Figs. 55, 56)

1.—Mandibles with tusks projecting forward,
visible from above 2
—Mandibles without tusks 9

° For identification of these genera see Ricker in Ward and
Whipple.

2.—Gills tuningfork-shaped, not fringed; w .... *Paraleptophlebia*
—Gills not tuningfork-shaped, but fringed 3

3.—Gills dorsal, curving up over abdomen, forelegs fossorial .. 4
—Gills lateral, outspread; forelegs not fossorial;
s,e .... *Potamanthus*

4.—Front of head with an elevated process 5
—Front of head without a conspicuous process 8

5.—Frontal process rounded, truncate or conical 6
—Frontal process bifid at tip 7

6.—Mandibular tusks downcurved, laterally serrate ..... *Ephoron*
—Tusks curved upward, laterally smooth .... *Hexagenia*

7.—Tusks toothed on outer margin; c,s .... *Pentagenia*
—Tusks smooth .... *Ephemera*

8.—Tusks with an inner, subapical tooth .... *Tortopus*
—Tusks with several inner teeth .... *Campsurus*

9.—Gills completely concealed under an enormous
thoracic shield; e .... *Baetisca*
—Not as above 10

10.—Sides of head each with conspicuous crown of
setae; gills ventral, fringed .... *Dolania*
—Without crown of setae; gills dorsal or not fringed 11

11.—Gills absent from one or more of segments 1–7 12
—Gills usually present on segments 1–7 (1–5 in *Baetodes*) 17

12. With two pairs of wing buds; se, unc .... *Oreianthus*
—With one pair of wing buds 13

13.—Gills of segment 2 thickened (operculate),
covering other gills 14
—Operculate gills, if present, not on segment 2 .. *Ephemerella*

14.—Operculate gills squarish 15
—Operculate gills triangular .... *Tricorythodes*

15.—Operculate gills fused on midline .... *Neoephemera*
—Operculate gills not fused on midline 16

16.—Head with three prominent tubercles; e .... *Brachycerus*
—Head without three prominent tubercles .... *Caenis*

17.—Head and body strongly depressed; eyes dorsal;
     upper gill of each pair platelike 18
   —Head and body not strongly depressed; eyes
     lateral or anterior; gills variable 28

18.—Upper gill plate with fingerlike projection from
     near middle .... *Pseudiron*
   —Not as above 19

19.—Lower portion of each gill pair a cluster of filaments ... 20
   —Lower cluster of filaments lacking; ne,unc .... *Arthroplea*

20.—With two tails 21
   —With three tails 23

21.—Abdomen with a double row of small dorsal
     spines; w,unc .... *Ironodes*
   —Abdomen without dorsal spines 22

22.—Abdomen with middorsal line of hairs; w,unc .... *Ironopsis*
   —Abdomen without middorsal line of hairs .... *Iron*

23.—Gills inserted ventrally ....(?) *Anepeorus*
   —Gills inserted dorsally or laterally 24

24.—Gills of segments 1 and 7 convergent
     ventrally .... *Rithrogena*
   —Gills not as above 25

25.—Gills of segment 7 each a single filament;
     e. of Rockies .... *Stenonema*
   —Gills of segment 7 similar to others 26

26.—Front of head emarginate; lower gill tufts
     vestigial; w,ne .... *Cynigmula*
   —Front of head entire or hardly emarginate;
     gill filaments normal 27

27.—Gill plates on segment 1 distinctly smaller than those
     on 2; labrum ¼ the width of anterior margin
     of head .... *Cinygma*
   —Gill plates on segment 1 only slightly smaller than
     those on 2; labrum ⅔ to ¾ width of anterior
     margin of head .... *Heptagenia*

28.—Lateral tails fringed on both sides 29
   —Lateral tails with heavy fringes on inner side only 35

29.—Labrum as broad as head; gills fringed; w,r ....*Traverella*
   —Labrum narrower than head; gills not fringed 30

30.—First pair of gills different from all others 31
   —First pair of gills similar to others 33

31.—Gills on segments 2–7 in clusters of
      filaments; e, se .... *Habrophlebia*
   —Gills not as above 32

32.—First pair of gills bifid, others notched and
      tailed ....*Leptophlebia*
   —First pair of gills single and unbranched .... *Choroterpes*

33.—With lateral spines on segments 2–9; sw, r .... *Thraulodes*
   —With lateral spines on segments 8–9 or 9 only 34

34.—Hind margin of segments 1–10 spinulose ... *Paraleptophlebia*
   —Spinules on hind margin of 7–10 only; e, se . *Habrophleboides*

35.—Claws of all legs similar, shorter than tibiae 38
   —Claws of forelegs dissimilar 36

36.—Claws of forelegs bifid 37
   —Claws of forelegs not bifid, with several
      long spines; w, r .... *Ametropus*

37.—Tarsi longer than tibiae .... *Metretopus*
   —Tarsi about as long as tibiae; e .... *Siphloplecton*

38.—Posterior angles of terminal abdominal segments pro-
      longed into thin, flat spines; if spines are weak the
      antennae are less than twice the width of the head 39
   —Posterior angles of terminal abdominal spines not pro-
      longed; if spines are weak the antennae are more
      than twice the width of the head 44

39.—Forelegs with conspicuous double row of long
      hairs .... *Isonychia*
   —Forelegs not so fringed 40

40.—Gill plates on segment 1–7 single 41
   —Gill plates on some segments double 43

41.—Abdominal segments 5–9 very wide; ne, r ....*Siphlonisca*
   —Abdominal segments 5–9 normal 42

42.—Abdominal spines weak; gills with sclerotized band
    along ventral margin .... *Ameletus*
  —Abdominal spines well developed; gills without
    sclerotized band .... *Parameletus*

43.—Claws on middle and hind legs twice as long as
    those on forelegs; Calif. .... *Edmundsius*
  —Claws on all legs similar .... *Siphlonurus*

44.—Gills present on segments 1–5 .... *Baetodes*
  —Gills present on segments 1–7 45

45.—Gill plates on some segments folded double 46
  —Gill plates all single 48

46.—With one pair of wing pads; e, n .... *Cloeon*
  —With two pairs of wing pads 47

47.—Double portion of gill a small flap on
    ventral surface .... *Callibaetis*
  —Double portion of gill a small flap on
    dorsal surface .... *Centroptilum*

48.—With two tails 49
  —With three tails 50

49.—With one pair of wing pads .... *Pseudocloeon*
  —With 2nd pair of wing pads minute; e, r .... *Heterocloeon*
  —With two pairs of wing pads .... *Baetis*

50.—Middle tail shorter and weaker than the others .... *Baetis*
  —Middle tail about the same as others 51

51.—With two pairs of wing pads .... *Centroptilum*
  —With one pair of wing pads 52

52.—Tracheae of gills with well developed lateral
    branches on inner side; e, unc .... *Neocloeon*
  —Tracheae with weak lateral branches 53

53.—Front margin of labrum notched;
    Calif., Puerto Rico .... *Paracloeodes*
  —Front margin of labrum entire; Calif. .... *Apobaetis*

Key to Genera of Dragonfly Nymphs
(Figs. 58–60)

1.—Labium flat 2
—Labium spoon-shaped covering face nearly to eyes 22

2.—Antennae short and thick 3
—Antennae bristlelike 13

3.—Antennae of 4 segments, the third the longest 4
—Antennae of 6 segments; nw .... *Tanypteryx*
—Antennae of 7 segments; e, s .... *Tachopteryx*

4.—Abdominal segment 10 half as long as abdomen; s ... *Aphylla*
—Segment 10 shorter than segments 8 + 9 5

5.—Middle legs closer together at bases than are
   others; U.S. except nw .... *Progomphus*
—Middle legs not closer together 6

6.—Wing pads strongly divergent 7
—Wing pads parallel 8

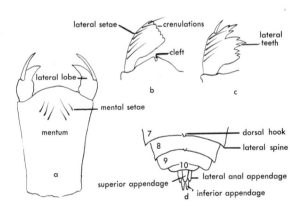

Fig. 92. Odonata nymphs. *a,* mentum of labium showing lateral lobes; *b,* lateral lobe and anterior margin of mentum; *c,* lateral lobe; *d,* segments 7–10 of abdomen with anal appendages.

7.—Lateral anal appendages shorter than inferiors;
    dorsal hooks on 2–9 or 3–9 .... *Octogomphus*
—Lateral appendages as long as inferiors; dorsal
    hooks vestigial beyond segment 4; U.S. ....*Erpetogomphus*

8.—Third antennal segment thin, flat, oval or circular 9
—Third antennal segment linear and cylindrical 11

9.—Body flat; abdomen nearly circular; e, s .... *Hagenius*
—Body and abdomen not as above 10

10.—Short lateral spines on abdominal segments 7–9; third
    antennal segment twice as wide as long; w ... *Octogomphus*
—Short lateral spines on segments 8–9; third antennal
    segment as wide as long; e .... *Lanthus*

11.—Abdominal segment 9 rounded without dorsal spine;
    if spine is present segment is longer than wide and
    spine is elevated ....*Gomphus*
—Abdominal segment 9 with sharp dorsal ridge
    ending in a spine 12

12.—Lateral anal appendages as long as the
    superior; Tex. ....*Gomphoides*
—Lateral appendages not more than ¾ the length of the
    superior; e, s ....*Dromogomphus*

13.—Lateral lobes of labium with strong setae on outer margin 14
—Lateral lobes of labium without such setae 15

14.—Lateral setae of labium nearly uniform in
    length; se ....*Triacanthagyna*
—Lateral setae unequal in length; Fla., Calif. .... *Gynacantha*

15.—Tarsi of forelegs 2-segmented; e .... *Gomphaeschna*
—All tarsi 3-segmented 16

16.—Hind angles of head with two large tubercles 17
—Hind angles of head without tubercles 18

17.—Low dorsal hooks on segments 7–9; e, c .... *Nasiaeschna*
—Without dorsal hooks on abdomen; e, c .... *Epiaeschna*

18.—Hind angles of head angulate (slightly so
    in *Aeschna eremita*) 19
—Hind angles of head broadly rounded 21

19.—Superior anal appendage as long as inferiors; cleft in
    margin of mentum of labium with long spine on
    each side; se .... *Coryphaeschna*
   —Superior anal appendages much shorter than inferiors;
    labial cleft not so armed 20

20.—Lateral lobes of labium squarely truncate at tip; e, c . *Boyeria*
   —Lateral lobes of labium tapering to a point; e, c ..*Basiaeschna*

21.—Lateral spines on abdominal segments 7–9 .... *Anax**
   —Lateral spines on segments 6–9 ....*Aeschna*
   —Lateral spines on segments 5–9; sw ....*Oplonaeschna***

22.—Lateral lobes of labium coarsely and irregularly
    toothed; mentum with median cleft .... *Cordulegaster*
   —Lateral lobes regularly toothed or entire;
    mentum without cleft 23

23.—Head with a prominent horn between the antennae 24
   —Head smooth or with a low rounded process 26

24.—Dorsal hooks on abdomen thick and blunt; e ... *Neurocordulia*
   —Dorsal hooks sharp, flat and cultriform;
    abdomen flat almost circular 25

25.—Lateral spines of abdominal segment 9 reaching less
    than halfway to tips of anal appendages .... *Macromia*
   —Lateral spines of 9 reaching to or beyond tips
    of appendages .... *Didymops*

26.—Abdomen with dorsal hooks (spines or knobs)
    on one or more segments 27
   —Abdomen without hooks 50

27.—Abdominal segment 9 with dorsal hook 28
   —Abdominal segment 9 without hook 40

28.—Lateral spine of segment 9 reaching to end of superior
    anal appendage or beyond inferiors 29

---

* *Aeschna sitchensis* and *A. juncea*, both northern species, also
have spines on 7–9. The former differs from *Anax* in having
mentum less than 1½ times as long as its width at base, instead
of twice as long (Cloyd); the later is a far northern species.

** *Aeschna eremita* may have spines on 5–9. It is a northern
species.

—Lateral spine of 9 not reaching beyond middle of superior   33

29.—Dorsal hooks thick and blunt; with tubercles or
frontal shelf between eye .... *Neurocordulia*
—Dorsal hooks spinelike; without tubercles or frontal shelf   30
—Dorsal hooks vestigial; ne ....*Cordulia*

30.—With dorsal hooks on segments 2–9, 3–9 or 3–10   31
—With dorsal hooks on 6–9 or 7–9; lateral lobes of
labium deeply crenulate; e .... *Helocordulia*

31.—Lateral spines on 9 reaching beyond tips
of inferior appendages   32
—Lateral spines of 9 not surpassing
inferior appendages ....*Tauriphila*

32.—Lateral setae of labium 4–5; e .... *Epicordulia*
—Lateral setae of labium 6–8 .... *Tetragoneuria*

33.—Dorsal hooks on segments 2–9   34
—Dorsal hooks on segments 3–9   35
—Dorsal hooks on segments 3–10   38
—Dorsal hooks on 5–9 vestigial; ne .... *Dorocordulia*

34.—Lateral anal appendages about equal in length to the
superior; mental setae each side 9–15 ....*Somatochlora*
—Lateral appendages much shorter than superior; mental
setae 14–15; dorsal hooks high; sw .... *Brechmorhoga*

35.—Dorsal hooks cultriform like a saw;
lateral setae 5 ....*Perithemis*
—Dorsal hooks not as above (though high-arched
in *Tauriphila*)   36

36.—Abdomen broadly depressed, little longer than wide
(*vide* Needham); lateral setae 8 .... *Tauriphila*
—Abdomen twice as long as wide; lateral setae 6–7   37

37.—Teeth on lateral lobes of labium obsolete; s .... *Dythemis*
—Teeth on lateral lobes of labium large; Tex. ......*Macrothemis*

38.—Lateral anal appendages less than half as long as superior ... 39
—Lateral appendages at least half as long as
superior; s .... *Brachymesia*

39.—Lateral spines on 9 longer than the
segment; Fla. .... *Idiataphe*

—Lateral spines on 9 not as long as the
    segment; s ....*Cannacria*

40.—Eyes small, on front of head; head tending to be
    widest behind the eyes; body usually hairy 41
  —Eyes large, prominent, more lateral than frontal; head
    more or less triangular; body usually not hairy 43

41.—Front margin of mentum of labium smooth ....*Libellula*
  —Front margin of mentum with crenulations 42

42.—Abdomen with dorsal hooks vestigial; s ....*Orthemis*
  —Abdomen with dorsal hooks on 3–6 .... *Plathemis*
  —Abdomen with dorsal hooks on 4–8; n .... *Ladona*

43.—Lateral anal appendages ⅔ of or equal to the superior 44
  —Lateral appendages ½ the length of the superior 46

44.—Lateral spines of 9 longer than middorsal length
    of segment; s ....*Miathyria*
  —Lateral spines of 9 one third or less the length
    of the segment 45

45.—Dorsal hooks on 2–6, decreasing posteriorly;
    lateral setae 9; sw ....*Paltothemis*
  —Dorsal hooks on 4–9 or 5–8; lateral setae 7 ....*Dorocordulia*
  —Dorsal hooks on 7–9; lateral setae 7 ....*Cordulia*

46.—With dorsal hook on segment 8 47
  —Without dorsal hook on segment 8 49

47.—Superior appendage as long or nearly as long as inferiors 48
  —Superior appendage shorter than inferiors .... *Sympetrum*

48.—Lateral spines of 8 as long as middorsal length of
    segment; mental setae 16–21; s, r .... *Macrodiplax*
  —Lateral spines of 8 shorter than length of segment;
    mental setae 10–15; n ....*Leucorrhinia*

49.—Dorsal hooks on 1–7; lateral spine of 9 shorter
    than segment .... *Erythrodiplax*
  —Dorsal hooks on 4–7; lateral spine of 9 much longer
    than segment; e ....*Celithemis*

50.—Anal appendages strongly downcurved at tips 51
  —Anal appendages straight or nearly so 52

51.—Lateral setae 11–12; segment 9 with minute
    lateral spines; s .... *Lepthemis*
    —Lateral setae 7–8; abdomen without lateral
    spines; w .... *Erythemis*

52.—Eyes small, directed forward; head behind eyes
    widened or parallel-sided 53
    —Eyes normal; head behind the eyes narrowed posteriorly 54

53.—Mental setae 3–4; sw .... *Orthemis*
    —Mental setae 9–18; w .... *Bolonia*

54.—Segment 8 with lateral spines 55
    —Segment 8 without lateral spines 62

55.—Lateral spines on 9 greater than length of segment 56
    —Lateral spines on 9 equal to or less than length of segment 57

56.—Teeth of lateral lobes of labium obsolete .... *Tramea*
    —Teeth of lateral lobes of labium large .... *Pantala*

57.—Lateral spines on 9 extending beyond tip of
    superior appendage .... *Pachydiplax*
    —Lateral spines of 9 not surpassing tip of superior 58

58.—Small, 10 mm. or less; abdomen hairy,
    truncated; e .... *Nannothemis*
    —Larger, 12–23 mm.; abdomen not as above 59

59.—Abdomen rounded abruptly at tip; lateral lobes of
    labium without teeth; sw .... *Pseudoleon*
    —Not as above 60

60.—Lateral spines of 8 and 9 subequal in length;
    southern .... *Erythrodiplax*
    —Lateral spines of 9 twice the length of those on 8 61

61.—Northern; superior appendage as long as
    inferior .... *Leucorrhinia*
    —Southern; superior appendage ⅔ or less the
    length of the inferior; Tex. .... *Micrathyria*

62.—Lateral anal appendages about equal to the superior;
    lateral lobe of labium deeply crenulated ...... *Somatochlora*
    —Lateral anal appendages ⅔ the length of the superior;
    lateral lobe of labium scarcely crenulated .... *Tarnetrum*

Key to Genera of Damselfly Nymphs

1.—Basal antennal segment as long as or longer than
   others combined 2
  —Basal antennal segment not longer than other
   single segments 3

2.—Mentum of labium cleft to below level of bases
   of lateral lobes; e ....*Calopteryx*
  —Mentum cleft only to bases of lateral lobes ....*Heteraena*

3.—Labium spoon-shaped, narrowed in middle 4
  —Labium tapered backward regularly 5

4.—Labium with 5 mental setae each side ....*Lestes*
  —Labium with 7 mental setae each side; s, w,
   rarely n, e ....*Archilestes*
5.—Gills half as broad as long; without mental setae 6
  —Gills not more than ⅓ as broad as long;
   with mental setae 7

6.—Lateral setae of labium 0–4 ....*Argia*
  —Lateral setae absent; sw ....*Hyponeura*

7.—Hind angles of head angulate 8
  —Hind angles of head rounded 9

8.—Gills widest in middle, ⅓ as broad as long; n ....*Amphiagrion*
  —Gills widest distally, 1/6 as broad as long; n, e .*Chromagrion*

9.—Mental setae 1–2 10
  —Mental setae 3–7 (occasionally 2) 11

10.—Gills with an oblique line at ⅔ their length; Tex. ...*Neoneura*
  —Gills not so divided; n, e ....*Nehallenia*

11.—Gill tips rounded; sw ....*Hesperagrion*
  —Gill tips tapered or pointed 12

12.—Gills with a dark pigmented pattern 13
  —Gills without pigmentation 18

13.—Each gill with 6 transverse dark bands 14
  —Gills not so marked 15

14.—Antennae 6–segmented .... *Enallagma*
 —Antennae 7–segmented; Calif. .... *Zoniagrion*

15.—Apical sixth of gills forming a terminal angle*
  of 45° or less 16
 —Apical sixth of gill forming an angle of 60° or more 17

16.—Antennae 6–segmented .... *Enallagma*
 —Antennae 7–segmented .... *Ischnura*

17.—Length of gills 3 mm.; body length 11 mm.; s, w ....*Telebasis*
 —Length of gills 8 mm. or more; body length 13 mm.
  or more .... *Enallagma*

18.—Apical sixth of gill with terminal angle of 30° or less 19
 —Apical sixth of gill with terminal angle of 60° or more 20

19.—Lateral setae 4–5; mental setae 2 .... *Anomalagrion*
 —Lateral setae 5–6; mental setae 3 or more .... *Ischnura*

20.—Second segment of each antennae twice as long as first
  (basal); abdominal segment 10 half as long as
  8; e .... *Teleallagma*
 —Not as above 21

21.—Antennae 6–segmented .... *Enallagma*
 —Antennae 7–segmented; n .... *Coenagrion*

 * Angle at tip of gill formed by conjoining of lateral margins.

Bibliography

Chapters 1–2. Our Fresh Waters

Carpenter, K. E., *Life in Inland Waters*. London: Sidgwick & Jackson, 1928.

Coker, Robert E., *Streams, Lakes and Ponds*. Chapel Hill: Univ. of N. C. Press, 1954.

Dowdeswell, W. H., *Animal Ecology*. New York: Harper & Brothers, 1961.

Frey, David C., *ed.*, *Limnology in North America*. Madison: Univ. of Wisc. Press, 1963.

Hutchinson, G. E., *A Treatise on Limnology*. 1957.

Macan, T. T., *Freshwater Ecology*. London: Longmans Green & Co., 1963.

Macan, T. T., and E. B. Worthington, *Life in Lakes and Rivers*. London: Collins, 1951.

Mellanby, Helen, *Animal Life in Fresh Water*. London: Methuen & Co. Ltd., 1938.

Needham, James G., and J. T. Lloyd, *Life of Inland Waters*. Ithaca, N. Y.: Comstock Pub. Co., 1916.

Odum, Eugene P., *Fundamentals of Ecology*. Philadelphia: Saunders, 1953.

Popham, Edward J., *Life in Fresh Water*, rev. ed. Cambridge: Harvard Univ. Press, 1961.

Ruttner, Franz, *Fundamentals of Limnology*, trans. by D. G. and F. E. J. Frey. Toronto: Univ. Toronto Press, 1953.

Welch, Paul S., *Limnology*, 2nd ed. New York: McGraw-Hill Book Co., 1952.

Chapter 3. Microscopic Organisms

Davis, C. C., *The Marine and Freshwater Plankton*. Lansing, Mich.: Mich. State Univ. Press, 1955.

Gallagher, John J., *Generic Classification of the Rotifera*. Proc. Penn. Acad. Sci. (1957), Vol. 31:182–187.

Hall, R. P., *Protozoology*. New York: Prentice-Hall, Inc., 1953.

Jahn, T. L., and F. F., *How to Know the Protozoa*. Dubuque, Iowa: Wm. C. Brown Co., 1949.

Kudo, Richard R., *Protozoology*. Baltimore: C. C. Thomas, 1946.

Needham, James G., and Paul R., *A Guide to the Study of Fresh Water Biology*, 5th ed. San Francisco: Holden-Day, Inc., 1962.

Pennak, Robert W., *Fresh-Water Invertebrates of the United States*. New York: The Ronald Press Co., 1953.

Prescott, G. W., *How to Know the Fresh Water Algae*. Dubuque, Iowa: Wm. C. Brown Co., 1954.

Smith, G. M., *The Fresh-Water Algae of the United States*, 2nd ed. New York: McGraw-Hill Book Co., 1959.

Ward and Whipple, *Fresh Water Biology*, ed. by W. T. Edmondson. New York: John Wiley & Sons, Inc., 1959.

Chapter 4. Mosses and Liverworts

Bodenberg, E. T., *Mosses, a New Approach*. Minneapolis: Burgess Pub. Co., 1954.

Conrad, H. S., *How to Know the Mosses and Liverworts*. Dubuque, Iowa: Wm. C. Brown Co., 1956.

Ward and Whipple (see Ch. 3 above).

Chapter 5. Higher Plants

Fassett, N. C., *Manual of Aquatic Plants*. New York: McGraw-Hill Book Co., 1940.

McGaha, Y. J., *The Limnological Relations of Insects to Certain Flowering Plants*, Trans. Am. Microscop. Soc. (1952), Vol. 71: 355–381.

Muenscher, W. C., *Aquatic Plants of the United States*. Ithaca, N. Y.: Comstock Pub. Co., 1944.

Ward and Whipple (see Ch. 3 above).

Chapters 6–13, 15. Invertebrates (other than Insects)

Buchsbaum, Ralph, and Lorus J. Milne, *The Lower Animals*. New York: Doubleday & Co., 1960.

Hyman, Libbie H., *The Invertebrates*, Vols. I-IV. New York: McGraw-Hill Book Co., 1940–1955.

Jacobson, Morris K., and William K. Emerson, *Shells of the New York City Area*. Larchmont, N. Y.: Argonaut Books, Inc., 1961.

Needham, James G., and Paul R. (see Ch. 3 above).

Pennak, Robert W. (see Ch. 3 above).

Ward and Whipple (see Ch. 3 above).

Chapter 14. Insects

Betten, Cornelius, *The Caddisflies or Trichoptera of New York State*. N. Y. State Mus. Bull. No. 292, 1934.

Boving, A. G., and F. C. Craighead, *An Illustrated Synopsis of the Principal Larval Forms of the Order Cleoptera*. Entomologica Americana, No. 11, 1930.

Claassen, P. W., *Plecoptera Nymphs of North America*. Lafayette, Ind.: Thomas Say Foundation of the Ent. Soc. of America, Pub. No. 3, 1931.

Frison, T. H., *Plecoptera of Illinois*. Bull. Ill. Nat. Hist. Surv. (1935), 18: 345–409, 20: 281–471, 22: 231–235.

Matheson, Robert, *Handbook of Mosquitoes of North America*, 2nd ed. Ithaca, N. Y.: Comstock Press, 1944.

Needham, James G., and P. W. Claassen, *The Plecoptera of North America*. Lafayette, Ind.: Thomas Say Foundation of the Ent. Soc. of America, Pub. No. 2, 1925.

Needham, James G., and Hortense B. Heywood, *A Handbook of Dragonflies of North America*. Baltimore: Charles C. Thomas, 1929.

Needham, James G., and Paul R. (see Ch. 3 above).

Needham, James G., and Minter Westfall, *Dragonflies of North America*. Berkeley: Univ. Calif. Press, 1955.

Pennak, Robert W. (see Ch. 3 above).

Peterson, Alva, *Larvae of Insects*, I, II. Columbus, Ohio, 1948, 1951.

Ricker, W. E., *Systematic Studies in Plecoptera*. Indiana Univ. Pub. Sci. Ser. No. 18, 1952.

Roeder, K. D., ed., *Insect Physiology*. New York: John Wiley & Sons, Inc., 1953.

Ross, H. H., *The Caddisflies or Trichoptera of Illinois*. Ill. Nat. Hist. Sur. Bull., Vol. 23, 1944.

Usinger, R. L., *et al.*, *Aquatic Insects of California*. Berkeley: Univ. of Calif. Press, 1956.

Walker, E. M., *The Odonata of Canada and Alaska*. Vol. I, Pts. I, II. Toronto: Univ. Toronto Press, 1953.

Ward and Whipple (see Ch. 3 above).

Chapter 16. Fishes

Blair, Albert P., and Blair, Brodkorb and Cagle. *Vertebrates of the United States*. New York: McGraw-Hill Book Co., 1957.

Carl, G. C., W. A. Clemens and C. C. Lindsey, *The Fresh Water Fishes of British Columbia*. Brit. Col. Prov. Mus., Dept. Educ. Handbook No. 5, 1959.

Clemens, W. A., and G. V. Wilby, *Fishes of the Pacific Coast of Canada*. Fish. Res. Bd. Can. Bull. No. 68, 1961.

Eddy, Samuel, *How to Know the Freshwater Fishes*. Dubuque, Iowa: Wm. C. Brown Co., 1957.

Herald, Earl, *Living Fishes of the World*. New York: Doubleday & Co., 1961.

Hubbs, Carl L., and Karl F. Lagler, *Fishes of the Great Lakes Region*. Cranbrook Inst. of Sci. Bull. No. 26, 1941.

Lagler, Karl L., J. E. Bardach and R. R. Miller, *Ichthyology*. New York: John Wiley & Sons, Inc., 1962.

Lanham, Urless N., *The Fishes*. New York: Columbia Univ. Press, 1962.

Needham, James G., and Paul R. (see Ch. 3 above).

Schrenkeisen, Ray, *Field Book of Fresh-Water Fishes of North America*. New York: G. P. Putnam's Sons, 1938.

Schultz, L. P., and E. M. Stern, *Ways of Fishes*. New York: Van Nostrand, 1948.

Trautman, Milton B., *The Fishes of Ohio*. Columbus, Ohio: Ohio State Univ. Press, 1957.

Chapters 17–18. Amphibians and Reptiles

Bishop, Sherman C., *Handbook of Salamanders*. Ithaca, N. Y.: Comstock Pub. Co., 1947.

Blair, Albert P., *et al.* (see Ch. 16).

Carr, Archie, *Handbook of Turtles*. Ithaca, N. Y.: Comstock Pub. Co., 1952.

Cochran, Doris, *Living Amphibians of the World*. New York: Doubleday & Co., 1961.

Conant, Roger, *A Field Guide to Reptiles and Amphibians*. Boston: Houghton Mifflin Co., 1958.

Oliver, James G., *The Natural History of North American Amphibians and Reptiles*. Princeton, N. J.: D. Van Nostrand Co., Inc., 1955.

Schmidt, Karl P., and Robert F. Inger, *Living Reptiles of the World*. New York: Doubleday & Co., 1957.

Schmidt, Karl P., and Dwight D. Davis, *Field Book of Snakes of the United States and Canada*. New York: G. P. Putnam's Sons, 1941.

Stebbins, Robert C., *Amphibians of Western North America*. Berkeley: Univ. of Calif. Press, 1951.

Wright, Albert H. and Anna A., *Handbook of Frogs and Toads of the U. S. and Canada*. Ithaca, N. Y.: Comstock Pub. Co., 1949.

Wright, Albert H., *Life Histories of the Frogs and Toads of the Okefinokee Swamp, Georgia*. New York: The Macmillan Co., 1931.

Limnological Methods

Conant, Roger (see Chs. 17–18 above).

Kendeigh, S. Charles, *Animal Ecology*. Englewood Cliffs, N. J.: Prentice-Hall, 1961.

Needham, James G., *et al.*, *Culture Methods for Invertebrate Animals*. Ithaca, N. Y.: Comstock Pub. Co., 1937.

Needham, James G., and Paul R. (see Ch. 3 above).

Pennak, Robert W. (see Ch. 3 above).

Usinger, R. L., et al. (see Ch. 14 above).

Welch, Paul S., *Limnological Methods*, rev. ed. Philadelphia: The Blakiston Co., 1952.

Photo Credits

Plates 1–5, Alexander B. Klots.

      9, William H. Amos; Walter Dawn from National Audubon Society.

    10, William H. Amos; N. E. Beck, Jr., from National Audubon Society.

    11, William H. Amos.

    12, William H. Amos; John H. Gerard from Monkmeyer.

    13, N. E. Beck, Jr., from National Audubon Society; William H. Amos.

    14, Lynwood H. Chase from National Audubon Society; Alexander B. Klots.

    15, Robert C. Hermes from National Audubon Society.

16, Lynwood H. Chase from National Audubon Society; William H. Amos.

17, N. E. Beck, Jr., from National Audubon Society; Hugh Spencer from National Audubon Society.

18, Hugh Spencer from National Audubon Society; William H. Amos.

19, Charles E. Mohr.

20, Charles E. Mohr.

21, William H. Amos.

22, Charles M. Bogert.

Index

Numbers in italics refer to illustrations.